The Politics of Crime and Community

Criminological Perspectives: Essential Readings
(co-edited with E. McLaughlin and J. Muncie), Sage 2003

Crime Control and Community: The new politics of public safety
(co-edited with A. Edwards), Willan Publishing 2002

Crime Prevention and Community Safety: New Directions
(co-edited with E. McLaughlin and J. Muncie), Sage 2002

Youth Justice (co-edited with E. McLaughlin
and J. Muncie), Sage 2002

Imagining Welfare Futures, Routledge 1998

Unsettling Welfare: The Reconstruction of Social Policy
(co-edited with G. Lewis), Routledge 1998

Ordering Lives (co-edited with R. Fergusson), Routledge 2000

Understanding Crime Prevention: Social Control, Risk and Late
Modernity, Open University Press, 1998

The Politics of Crime and Community

Gordon Hughes

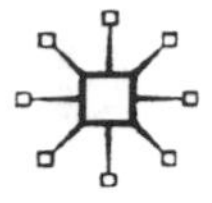

First published in 2007 by
PALGRAVE MACMILLAN
Houndmills, Basingstoke, Hampshire RG21 6XS and
175 Fifth Avenue, New York, N.Y. 10010
Companies and representatives throughout the world.

PALGRAVE MACMILLAN is the global academic imprint of the Palgrave Macmillan division of St. Martin's Press, LLC and of Palgrave Macmillan Ltd. Macmillan® is a registered trademark in the United States, United Kingdom and other countries. Palgrave is a registered trademark in the European Union and other countries.

ISBN-13: 978–0–333–78696–3 hardback
ISBN-10: 0–333–78696–3 hardback
ISBN-13: 978–0–333–78697–0 paperback
ISBN-10: 0–333–78697–1 paperback

This book is printed on paper suitable for recycling and made from fully managed and sustained forest sources. Logging, pulping and manufacturing processes are expected to conform to the environmental regulations of the country of origin.

A catalogue record for this book is available from the British Library.

A catalog record for this book is available from the Library of Congress.

(Library of Congress Card Number: 2006049117)

10 9 8 7 6 5 4 3 2
16 15 14 13 12 11 10 09 08 07

Printed in China

In memory of my sister Sylv and for my grandson Zack

Contents

List of Figures

Acknowledgements

This book has been a long time in gestation. Many thanks to Emily Salz and colleagues at Palgrave for their patience and support. I am indebted to several colleagues for their helpful comments on parts of the manuscript: particular thanks go to John Clarke, Lynn Hancock, Yvonne Jewkes, Tim Newburn, Pat O'Malley, Kevin Stenson and Adam Sutton. I have benefited greatly from collaborative work and debate over recent years with academic colleagues and friends including Kit Carson, John Clarke, Jacques de Maillard, Matt Follett, Ross Fergusson, Dan Gilling, Lynn Hancock, Patrick Hebberecht, Tim Hope, Adrian Little, Eugene McLaughlin, Mike Maguire, Gerry Mooney, John Muncie, Mike Rowe, Rossella Selmini, Kevin Stenson, Rene van Swaaaningen and Sandra Walklate. I have a special debt in this book to Adam Edwards for all his work and inspiration on our collaborative project to try and mould a comparative, critical realist criminology. I have also learnt a great deal from my close involvement and research with practitioners in the field of community safety, and in particular fellow Directors of the National Community Safety Network (NCSN). Like most books it has been a product of a collective enterprise but all the errors and foibles are down to me. There are after all some limits to 'responsibilization'! Finally thanks to Lizzie Dawtrey as ever.

Introduction

Both 'community' and 'crime' are concepts, which many of us take for granted. In the course of my discussion in this book I hope to both 'unsettle' and more ambitiously 're-settle' our thinking on the meaning of these ideas, which have such a strong contemporary resonance for our apparently insecure times. It will be argued in turn that an understanding of the politics of crime and community is a necessary feature of any re-kindling of the criminological imagination above and beyond the criminal justice system. The arguments in this book will aim to combine the following inter-connected conceptual concerns: an introduction to the contemporary theorizing in the comparative criminology of crime control and community safety; a critical review of policies and practices in the field; and the opening up of new normative and political challenges associated with this sphere of governance. In so doing the arguments will draw wherever possible on original research undertaken by the author.

The main empirical focus of the book is Britain and its multiple localities. It is commonplace for the words 'UK' and 'Britain' to be synonymous with research and findings often culled from England rather than Northern Ireland, Scotland or Wales. In mitigation such ethnocentrism is at times difficult to overcome given that the most sustained body of research and evidence still emanates from England as the biggest and most powerful region of the United Kingdom. This book struggles with this bias towards English evidence and examples. However, it is hoped that the debates raised here will stimulate new comparative research projects both across the regions and nations of the United Kingdom and more broadly in localities beyond these shores. Accordingly, throughout the discussion which follows efforts will be made to provide insights from across the United Kingdom, nationally, regionally and locally. Alongside this predominant focus on British developments the discussion which follows also draws on my research and engagement with cognate processes across Europe, Australia and New Zealand and to a lesser extent North America. This focus on the 'West' and the 'North' of the globe means that much of the poor and underdeveloped world of 'the South' and the 'East' and specific geo-historical places and contexts outside most of the affluent zones of the world are not directly examined. This is a gaping omission for which this book like the vast bulk of both European and North American criminology, critical and orthodox, must confess to be guilty. However, it is hoped that the effects of globalization – the 'South' and 'East' within the 'North' and 'West' in the guise of the victims and survivors of globalization – are addressed directly in the analyses in the substantive chapters which follow. It is also methodologically vital to note that the comparative frame adopted in this book is not simply a plea for 'cross-national' research. Equally crucial in these globalizing times is the simultaneous attention to both the local and the global, often fused as the 'glocal'. A comparative criminology worthy of its name for our times must focus on both the sub- and supra-national. Much of the discussion in this book will thus aim to disturb the traditional focus in criminology on the nation as an analytical and empirical frame of reference. Indeed much of the discussion that follows will also seek to prioritize the study of the 'sub-national' and the varied localities encased in but not necessarily determined by the national and the global. In so doing it speaks to the processes of convergence and divergence, similarities and differences between different spaces and scales and also the unevenness of seemingly global trends. That said, it is important to acknowledge that it is still early days in the forging of this comparativist project.

Organization of the Book

The book is structured as follows. Chapter 1 should be read as setting the scene for the substantive chapters that follow. It offers an introductory mapping of the key conceptual themes that underpin the increasingly specific chapters which ensue. Chapter 1 is organized around three questions which each constitute separate organizing sections for the discussion: why community matters? why governance matters? and why comparison and context matter? These three sections hopefully clarify for the reader why it is important for a criminological project on the problem of 'the politics of crime and community' (and we might add as increasingly viewed through the notions of 'safety' and 'security') to encompass these three questions broadly associated with the policy field which I term throughout this book the 'community governance of crime and safety'. In the first section of the chapter the idea of 'governance' is unpacked and its relationship to the older idea of 'government' is explored. Once again it is argued that the criminological study of crime control and public safety is dependent on the recognition of the increasing salience of the more pluralized forms of controlling crime and promoting safety opened up the concept of governance. The second section of Chapter 1 provides an introduction to debates around radical communitarianism and the politics of community. Put briefly it is argued that the notion of community and the normative and political ideas of communitarianism, whilst deeply contentious and capacious, remain key areas of debate in any criminological study of crime and its control. In the third section of Chapter 1 the debate on the importance of comparison and context in criminology, as in the social sciences more generally, is introduced. More specifically, it is argued that a 'critical realist' perspective may be the most productive conceptual 'scaffold' on which to build a comparative criminology, sensitive to both the need for generalization and specification in social scientific inquiry. For the uninitiated, critical realism may be understood as offering a conceptual lens on the human world, which avoids both the simplistic positivist notions of the social sciences as modelled on the detached, general law-like paradigm of the natural sciences and the extreme relativism of post-modernism. The remaining substantive chapters of this book attempt to develop the initial conceptual mapping of Chapter 1 by focussing on more specific areas of institutional form and process in the 'late modern' policy field of control and safety.

In Chapter 2 a broad comparative overview of the emergent 'preventive turn' and its still often inchoate institutional architecture of the community governance of crime and safety is outlined. In particular, the first section of this chapter introduces the work of key theorists of the preventive turn and the new governance of security focussed on David Garland and Les Johnston and Clifford Shearing and to a lesser extent the work of John Lea. Following this exposition of the main components of these grand sociological narratives of change, the chapter then focusses in the second section on the rise of the preventive turn and the emergence of the new community governance of crime and safety as it has unfolded in the national case study of England and Wales. Finally the last section of this chapter draws some comparative lessons from the histories and geographies (or what may be termed 'geo-histories') of localities chosen from across Europe.

Following this institutional overview of the new field of governance, Chapters 3 and 4 focus on the complex unfolding of this broad trend in specific institutional sites and practices. Particular attention is paid to what John Clarke (2004) has termed the 'instabilities' of community governance and the likelihood of 'unpredictable agency' among the carriers, technicians and political actors in this new governmental field. In Chapter 3, attention is turned to the instabilities of the community governance of crime and safety when put in place or implemented locally. In particular it offers a conceptual and empirical evaluation of the work of the 'grand theorists' (particularly Garland, Johnston and Shearing) focussed on the delivery of crime control and community safety by local, multi-agency preventive partnerships. This discussion is again based largely on a case study of recent developments in localities across England and Wales but is also cognisant of examples from outside this national frame. The four parts of this chapter focus on the empirical 'testing' of four inter-related issues opened up by the theses of Garland and Johnston and Shearing. These issues are (i) the nature of the performance management culture and the 'what works' paradigm; (ii) partnerships and fostering of community governance; (iii) partnerships and the seeming de-monopolization of crime prevention; and (iv) the dichotomy of 'rational adaptation' and 'irrational denial' in control and safety strategies. Chapter 4 continues this sympathetic but critical evaluation of the grand theorists outlined in Chapter 2. It focusses specifically on the still relatively under-researched problem of 'who works' rather than 'what works' in the preventive sector. A provisional sociology of 'who works' in this new policy field is provided, focussed on the new (and old) actors brought to the stage and their contested expertise and political agency in this policy field. In the first section of the chapter the focus is on the nature of the changing skills, knowledge and values of local government community safety practitioners and managers. In the second section of the chapter, a broad mapping of the increasingly pluralized division of labour around the implementation of community safety practice and local policing is provided.

Chapters 5–7 build on the earlier discussion in Chapters 2–4 of both the institutional architecture of the community governance of crime and safety and the attendant actors and 'expertises' associated with these developments. However, the focus now shifts more overtly to how new problems are being governed – even 'invented' – by the institutional infrastructure, governmental processes and occupational practices referred to above as well as the broader underlying conditions of their existence. Metaphorically we can characterize Chapters 5–7 as shifting the focus of attention from the 'plumbing' of the system to that of the 'waste' or 'recyclable' products of the system. More specifically, these three chapters focus on three 'new' objects of this governance that have also all been associated with complex tendencies towards both the conditional social exclusions and inclusions of often troublesome, troubling and troubled populations in late modern societies. In each of these chapters or essays I explore the recurrent theme of the contemporary appeal to communities as often simultaneously site, object and agent of governance, drawing both on comparative research evidence from within the United Kingdom but also on cognate work from other countries in the English-speaking world and in western Europe. Much of this theme of community governance also appears to be associated with community-building and protection on the basis of processes of 'othering' of those people viewed as outcasts, whether from the indigenous 'underclass', 'strangers' from abroad or 'degenerated neighbourhoods'. Taken together these essays should be read as detailed explorations of still emerging objects yet increasingly pressing and urgent foci of the new community governance of crime and safety. Specifically Chapter 5 examines the contemporary governmental drive against, and attempted management of, 'anti-social behaviour' in local communities. Following this Chapter 6 explores the governmental problem of asylum seeking and migration in the context of political and policy debates on diversity and community cohesion. The final case study in Chapter 7 examines the theme of urban degeneration and regeneration focussed on the attempted and contested 'purification' of public/private space in many cities across the world and the relationship of urban renewal to crime and disorder reduction as well as more sustainable communities.

Throughout these three chapters, much of my discussion focusses on an engagement with the work of radical scholarship in the social sciences, and particularly that of critical criminology, rather than, for example, that of either moralists of the neo-conservative right ('the criminology of the other') or technicist administrative criminologists ('the new crime sciences') (but see Chapter 8). This focus is borne out of a wish to move the radical debate forward and because there is more to discuss and debate with the various strands of critical scholarship than other intellectual opponents. However, it is not an argument for the sectarian *lack* of open debate such as that which characterized exchanges between 'left realist' and critical 'idealist' or 'interventionist' criminologies in the 1980s and 1990s (Hughes, 1991, 2004c). That said, I argue that much of the critical criminological canon on the three issues under discussion here (anti-social behaviour, asylum-seeking, urban regeneration) has tended to engender conceptual and normative foreclosure on what remain extremely complex and difficult issues for which there are neither easy, pre-given explanations nor simple political and policy solutions. To paraphrase Karl Marx, whilst (much of) the point is to change the world, it is also necessary (following Max Weber) to study and understand it through theoretically informed empirical analysis without pre-given conceptual or political and normative guarantees. I suggest the analysis of the three inter-connected governmental objects foregrounded in Chapters 5–7 lays down a big challenge for all contemporary criminologists. It is perhaps no exaggeration to call them criminological minefields, at the conceptual, empirical, normative and political dimensions.

Finally in Chapter 8 a brief summary of the main claims and findings of the previous chapters is offered in the first section of the chapter. Following this summary, the discussion then focusses on the inter-related 'futures' of both crime control and safety strategies and of criminology itself. In the second section of the chapter the possible future directions of crime control and safety strategies, locally and globally, and following the terrorist attacks of 9/11 in New York and 7/7 in London are examined. In the third section of the chapter the case is made for a reinvigoration of criminology as social scientific inquiry by presenting an argument against those commentators all claiming the need to move 'beyond' criminology. In conclusion the book ends by arguing the case for a 'public criminology' drawing explicitly on the conceptual themes and issues addressed throughout the substantive chapters in this book.

1

Crimes, Communities and Criminology

If values – regarding rights, ethics and more generally the nature of the good – are seen as purely subjective, emotive, a-rational responses, and hence beyond justification through argument, then the critiques which they inform might be dismissed on the same grounds. If they are not to be dismissed in this manner, values need to be scrutinised and justified as carefully as would any explanation. Without such scrutiny, critical social scientists could be accused of basing their critiques on values which are no more than the product of unmonitored peer pressure: 'We're against such-and-such people because people like us generally are'.

(Sayer, 2000: 172)

Introduction

In contemporary Anglophone societies, it is almost impossible to avoid hearing the word 'community' being used in policy and political debates and discourses regarding questions of what is to be done about problems of crime and disorder and concomitant preventive and safety-focussed solutions. Cohen (1985: 116), commenting on the place of 'community' in the mid-1980s crime control discourse, observed wryly that '[i]t would be difficult to exaggerate how this ideology – or more accurately, this single word, has come to dominate western crime control discourse in the last few decades'. It is no exaggeration to observe at the start of the twenty-first century that the influence and pervasiveness of appeals to community in the increasingly inter-meshed domains of crime control and safety/security discourses internationally has developed at a staggering pace. Witness, *inter alia*, the growing appeals to 'community governance', 'social capital', 'collective efficacy', 'social/community cohesion', 'neighbourhood regeneration', 'civil renewal' and by 2005 in Britain, 'safer and stronger communities'. Meanwhile, in non-Anglophone cultures, although the language is unlikely to deploy the close equivalent to the word 'community', cognate words suggesting 'proximity', the 'local', the involvement of 'neighbourhoods' and 'citizens' speak to this admittedly uneven shift in governmental mentalities across much of Europe (Theoretical Criminology, 2005; Stangl and van Swaaningen, 2006). It is difficult to dispute claims that 'communitarian' ideas are now increasingly embedded, at least rhetorically, in most late modern governing strategies for dealing with the range of social ills affecting localities and groups, often sitting (uncomfortably) alongside managerial and technicist discourses (Garland, 2001; Hughes, 2004a).

In the first instance this chapter aims to offer both a broad introduction to these debates as seen through the lens of what has been variously termed the 'local governance of crime' (Crawford, 1997), the 'new preventive sector' (Garland, 2001), the 'governance of security' or 'safety' (Johnston and Shearing, 2003; Crawford, 2002), 'governing through risk' (O'Malley, 2004) and 'community governance and the new politics of public safety' (Hughes and Edwards, 2002).[1] Second, it also aims to offer new insights on these comparative developments by means of an ongoing engagement with what may appear to be the unlikely conceptual bedfellows of 'radical communitarianism' and an emergent 'critical realist criminology'. To help the reader on this journey, this introductory chapter takes up the following themes in its three main sections. In the first section the debate on the extent to which we are witnessing a shift beyond criminal justice as traditionally conceived to that of multi-level and multi-agency governance and the 'preventive turn' is presented. In the second section an introduction to the sociological, political and moral debates on community associated with the major variants of communitarian thought is provided. In this section, I argue for the continuing importance of appeals to communities in any progressive politics and policies of crime control and safety. In the third section the argument is made for the adoption of a critical realist perspective in criminology. In particular, the case is made for both the centrality of 'context' and 'comparison' in criminological research and the need for normative engagement by social scientists in the pressing issues of our time.

Beyond Criminal Justice? Exploring Governance and the Preventive Turn

According to criminological thought in its many hues there appears to be something close to a new 'zeitgeist' (spirit of the age) or 'structure of feeling' (Williams, 1965) which suggests that something close to an epochal shift may be taking place. Such a narrative of a break with the past is not unique to criminology of course. Indeed, it may have its roots in broader developments associated with both the political economies of capitalist societies under neo-liberal, globalizing conditions and associated shifts in the role and importance of the nation-state and its institutions. The shift is captured in a number of different, often dichotomous, metaphors, including the shift from the 'inclusive to the exclusive society' (Hobsbawm, 1995; Young, 1999), from 'social democratic welfarism to neo-liberal consumerism' (Bauman, 1999; Clarke, 2004), from 'collective risk management to privatized prudentialism' (O'Malley, 1997) and more specifically in criminology from 'penal-welfarism to the punitive culture of control' (Garland, 2001), from 'correctionalism to actuarial penology' (Feeley and Simon, 1992) and from 'reactive punishment to proactive prevention' (Johnston and Shearing, 2003). Throughout this book, these grand narratives of change, discontinuity and re-ordering which are to varying degrees dystopian or optimistic will be subjected to critical scrutiny. However, for present purposes, it is sufficient to note that these narratives of change appear to be indicative that at the very least something important is happening in the present historical moment which may be the initial signs of 'new times' and requires criminological thinking in this conjuncture to try and map the emergent contours of the new terrain. Despite important continuities with the past and arguments for, and the recognition of, the uneven complexities of the processes as they unfold in specific geo-historical contexts, a new terrain to which I will refer throughout this book as 'the community governance of crime and safety' is emerging across a growing number of contemporary societies. Let me make a start on this initial mapping of the new terrain and its architecture, design and the objects of the 'building' process before the subsequent substantive chapters interrogate these processes in greater depth.

Governing through Crime and Safety

Questions of crime prevention and control, public and private notions of safety and security, levels of personal and communal victimization and such like are of pressing social and political importance to many citizens across what we may term 'late modern' societies (see Hughes, 1998a). Crime-evoked suffering is a social fact of living today, albeit fed and nurtured by often lurid media coverage. It is also important to note that concerns over the grim realities of criminal victimization chime with the broader desire for security and the absence of fear, conjured up by the terms 'community safety' in countries such as the United Kingdom, Holland, Australia and New Zealand (Hughes *et al.*, 2002) and 'urban security' in countries such as France, Belgium and Italy (Theoretical Criminology, 2005) and by the not so secular crusades against the 'anti-social', 'alien' and 'unproductive' elements in our midst (see Chapters 5, 6 and 7 below). Such concerns may be symptomatic of a deeper sense of insecurity in contemporary culture. The American criminologist Jonathan Simon captures this apparent 'zeitgeist' in the following passage:

> We live in a time of deep social anxiety when questions of what to eat, where to live, and with whom to have sex are all answered with the question of risk. It does not take long , in a society where the largest supermarket chain is named 'Safeways' to recognize that security is something that people demand, not just in general, but in each and everything we do, experience or consume. (1997: 2–3)

The detailed examination of the nature of developments in the governance of crime and safety is the recurrent master theme running throughout the series of inter-locking chapters in this book. In brief the concept of governance may be taken to signify a number of key inter-related developments including what Rhodes defines as 'a change in the meaning of government, referring to a new process of governing; or a *changed* condition of ordered rule; or the *new* method by which society is governed' (Rhodes, 1997: 46, emphasis in original, cited in Edwards, 2006). As Adam Edwards notes with regard to its influence on criminological thought, the concept of governance has been used to signify changes both in the control of crime and to acknowledge other cognate 'objects' of control such as incivility, harm, safety and security. Edwards goes on to specify the principal feature of the concept – for proponents and critics alike – as being its departure from state-centred thinking about the exercise of political and institutional power. Accordingly, power is not something possessed by a sovereign body (e.g. the state/elected government/ruler) but instead is the tenuous, unresolved, outcome of struggles between coalitions of public and private, formal and informal, actors (Edwards, 2006: 189–91). For its proponents, the shift to governance and away from top-down, centralized government implies a new process of governing based on bargaining, negotiation and other types of exchange rather than through coercion and command. Crucially, any would-be 'sovereign' has to appreciate his or her 'power-dependence' on other actors; an example of this in the field of crime control is that of the multi-agency partnerships made up of statutory, commercial and voluntary bodies.

Edwards (2006) observes that some theorists of governance contend that there has been an even more radical departure from state-centred thinking compared to that implied in Rhodes' influential body of work. In particular, social scientists influenced by Foucault's ideas on 'governmentality' such as Johnston and Shearing (2003) and Rose (1999) argue that politics has fragmented and pluralized into a series of competing 'security networks' or 'nodes' in multifarious governable places in which no single actor is able to exercise control over a given territory. This 'more anthropological conception identifies the omnipresent plurality of competing orders or "nodes of governance" rather than any neat correspondence between a single sovereign authority and a national geographical area' (Edwards, 2006: 190). Proponents of this radical governance thesis such as Johnston and Shearing (2003) and Smandych (1999) may exaggerate the 'death' of the sovereign state. Indeed it is more likely that in nation-states across the West sovereignty is being reformulated rather than superseded by nodal governance (Stenson, 2005). The dispersal of what were once state roles and activities is therefore not synonymous with the loss of state power. The state remains a crucial 'power container' and 'steerer' of the governmental functions dispersed to 'responsibilized' actors and agencies. According to Rhodes (1997: 15, in Edwards, 2006), centralization and fragmentation coexist and there is constant tension between the wish for authoritative action (from the state) and the latter's dependence on the compliance and actions of others. As Edwards (2006: 191) concludes, '[e]xploring this tension, how it generates dilemmas and contradictions in the accomplishment of control and drives the politics of law and order beyond the relatively narrow confines of criminal justice, provides a critical challenge for, and to, criminological thought'. It is to this challenge that the substantive chapters in this book will attempt to rise.

The debate on governance has crucial implications for the comparative criminological study of crime control and community safety, which has tended to treat the contexts of crime and control as synonymous with the national cultures and institutions of criminal justice and law enforcement. By way of contrast, such concepts as 'community governance' and 'security networks' also sensitize us to processes of control and safety promotion at sub-national as well as supra-national levels. A fuller interrogation of these concepts and their applicability to contemporary, comparative developments follows in Chapter 2.

Radical Communitarianism, 'Safe Communities' and the Politics of Articulation

In this second section of the Chapter 1 argue for the continuing salience of appeals to communities in any progressive, realist politics of crime control and public safety. It was noted earlier that appeals to community are increasingly clamorous and incessant in contemporary political and policy discourses, locally, nationally and internationally. This political and governmental reality may give intellectuals on the pluralist left serious pause for thought in their deconstructionist efforts to 'wish' community away (Hughes, 2004d). Carson (2004b) contends that in arguing thus, I am guilty of adopting a rather pragmatic and acquiescent position. In defence, this position also speaks to the importance of having conversations with centres and assemblages of power at various institutional levels and thereby being involved in struggles for alternative translations of what it is to govern crime and safety through appeals to community and the local. This politically realist argument appears particularly vital in critical criminological circles given the broad structuring if not determining international context of a culture of 'unvarnished authoritarianism' (Garland, 2001), allied to the state's aim to 'govern through crime' (and disorder) (Simon, 1997) and the seductions of the mass 'penal temptation' (Wacquant, 2001). I would thus challenge the commonly held view that '[w]riters on the left prioritize justice over community, whereas those on the right grant priority to community over justice' (Young, 1999: 153). The bottom-line is that progressive as well as the dominant reactionary voices and positions need to be articulated around 'community' and other elements of the contested 'governmental savoir' (Stenson, 2000) of crime control and public safety.

Radical Communitarianism and Community Safety

The discussion will now focus on arguments for the continuing and crucial importance of a debate with communitarianism in criminology, when articulated in 'critical' (Lacey, 2003) or 'radical' (Hughes, 1996a) forms. In presenting this case, Adrian Little's work *The Politics of Community* (2002) is extensively drawn upon.

Acknowledgement of the dubious seductions and dangers of appeals to community in policy discourses is a common and well-trodden one for any student of the social sciences. It is hardly novel to note that the assumption of communities being akin to 'ye olde idea of community' is both a wrong-headed and dangerous seduction, whether imagined as the bucolic village of a hierarchical but harmonious organic past, or as the homogeneous 'high trust' working class community of industrial society yore. It is a myth to assume that actually existing communities today are commonly characterized by a 'relatively homogeneous group of people, closely bounded, sharing certain values, usually within a defined spatial locality' (Carson, 2004a: 13). Although we do find examples of such 'exclusive clubs' today, such as 'gated communities' (Low, 2003), the late modern realities of living together is that of both more open, mobile social arrangements for consumer-citizens and more closed, immobile relations, especially in the most deprived and least mobile 'communities of fate', left behind by the neo-liberal times of affluence and consumerism. Nonetheless, simple, or 'primitive', notions of community still often have the status of a 'natural category for crime prevention' (O'Malley, quoted in Carson, 2004a). The dangers of such exclusive notions of community today have been graphically captured in the following dystopian observation by Zygmunt Bauman. Writing with regard to many worried citizens' desperate attempts to hang on to the 'primitive' idea of the singular, exclusive and excluding, community today, Bauman (2001: 11) opines:

> What they are after is an equivalent of a personal nuclear shelter; the shelter they are after they call 'community'. The 'community' they seek stands for a burglar-free and stranger-proof 'safe environment'. 'Community' stands for isolation, separation, protective walls and guarded gates.

Such dystopian sociological observations are a necessary starting-point for any informed and progressive debate on 'community' across different policy spheres. However, they have an especially important part to play in the volatile and highly emotive field of crime control and security. That said, such systematic scepticism should not numb social scientists against articulating alternative imaginings of belonging, mutualism and collective solidarities in our contemporary world. It is probable that there is much common ground shared by readers of this book with regard to the dangerous seductions of simplistic takes on 'community'. What is perhaps less certain is how we may take the debate on the 'communal' in community governance of crime and safety forward.

The almost universal response among radical social scientists is to abandon the signifier of community given its capacious, dangerous and inaccurate qualities in the contemporary world of often 'lightly engaged strangers' (Young, 1999). But perhaps this is an elitist response itself, particularly given the at times grim realities for those living together in territorially defined and socially and spatially trapped 'communities of fate', whose members often co-habit 'cheek by jowl' with equally desperate different 'communities of identity'. This stands in sharp contrast to the 'communities of choice' which many of our more affluent citizens – not least intellectuals – are able to inhabit, alongside indulging in the capacity for consumerist, 'de/constructionist' life-style options. More optimistically, some supposed communities of fate may also be a source of new forms of mutualism (see, for example, Pahl, 1995, on friendship networks and 'public spirited work' among single female parents). In turn the work of both Lisa Miller (2001) and Clifford Shearing (2001), for example, illustrates the potential of poor, marginalized communities to produce progressive solidary processes of community capacity-building in their struggles for a voice in decision-making and thus achieving 'bottom-up governance'. Miller's research in Seattle in particular plots the successful counter-struggles of the black community against the criminalizing and racialising 'weed and seed' strategy of the Seattle police against the young black men of that community in the 1990s. Meanwhile, Shearing's involvement in the community capacity-building programme in townships in South Africa highlights the potential for generating 'bottom-up' processes and restorative 'peacemaking' solutions to shared harms and insecurities in the most seemingly marginalized and traumatized communities. Accordingly, appeals to community or preferably *communities* may function as a 'necessary fiction' (Weeks, 1996) for groups struggling against discrimination and marginalization and for the possibility of rights claiming beyond the moral majoritarian norm.

There is then some difficulty with the claim made by such post-modernist critics as Iris Young (1990) and George Pavlich (2001) that the appeal to 'community' is fatally inscribed in a claustrophobic, excluding and conservative moralizing discourse. It is of course vital to recognize in a profoundly non-nostalgic manner that communities often have been generally hard places and conflict-ridden spaces in which disorderly dispute as well as orderly agreement is to the fore. But they remain, even as necessary fictions, especially important in the collective struggles and constructions of poor and stigmatized citizens – and those excluded from citizenship altogether – for both the redistribution of resources and the recognition of identities and alternative ways of existence. Accordingly, the challenge may be to imagine community without recourse to either neo-tribalism or self-immolation (Weeks, 1996). It is also important to recognize that appeals to community literally 'people' the landscape of state and governmental practices (Clarke, 2002) and the new local institutional architecture of crime, justice and safety policy. Put bluntly, community is now a key component of the new sense of the 'national-popular' alongside the figures of the 'consumer' and 'citizen' in many late modern societies (see Hughes, 1998b). No amount of sociological deconstruction of the concept of community is likely to change such material and symbolic relations of power and meaning.

Rather than accept that community is now fatally inscribed in a morally regressive register of meaning which is almost part of the pluralist left's own taken-for-granted 'commonsense', the argument presented in this book is that definitions of community will always be ambiguous and contested and thus always resistant to ideological categorization. In the context of current crime control and safety discourses and community's capture by the conservative intellectual movement of moral authoritarian communitarianism (Hughes, 1996a, 2002a), the onus is on radical communitarians to provide alternative discourses around communities which address the importance of rootedness, collective cohesion and belonging whilst recognizing the extent and consequences of value pluralism, diversity and new inequalities in contemporary societies. The one-dimensional representation of community as exclusionary and backward-looking, based in turn on insular traditions and face-to-face relationships neglects the diverse variety of communities that exist in the late modern world and there is little reason why such out-dated notions of traditional communities should override alternative visions of community (Little, 2002: 17). At the same time this model is not a perfectionist one: we should expect to see vices as well as virtues, whilst the eulogizing of community as a source of consensual governance needs to be avoided. As Little goes on to argue, defending communities is vital today not because of some past or future state of unity and organic harmony but rather because communities are potentially domains where neo-liberal economic rationality need not prevail. The possibilities for communities to develop are also strongly associated with, and often dependent on, a process of 'vertical' political manufacturing with policies directed towards the creation of spaces for them to develop and flourish. In other words, radical communitarianism stresses the importance of political strategies for communities' 'practical enactment' (Little, 2002: 8).

The emphasis given to plural communities in radical communitarianism in late modern nation-states is one which Carson finds unsatisfactory due to the tendency to break the nature of the 'cake' of community down into smaller and smaller pieces until all we are left with are crumbs. To quote Carson (2004b), 'Problems of definition are not resolved by simply proliferating different kinds of community in our analyses.' It is almost a *sine qua non* among social scientists that the notion of *the* community has both a deeply problematic sociological status and its political and moral appeal is dangerously exclusionary and reactionary. However, the debate on the salience of *communities* sociologically, politically and morally, may be less cut and dry. Let me 'unpack' this area of contention in more depth. In late modern societies, many people's membership of communities will necessarily be multi-dimensional and complex. In this light we may thus ask just how lightly engaged and estranged are 'we' late moderns? As Rustin (2004: 144) provocatively notes, authentic relationships and experiences are fashioned within cultures, traditions, institutions, or the interstices between them, in the context of social density. Social relatedness thus entails social constraints. Of course there will be important differences between people in the degrees of both the 'lightness' and 'density' of their social relationships. In late modernity, the simultaneous co-existence of light and dense engagements will also be the norm. The radical communitarian argument presented here is thus not for the single, binding and exclusive community of nostalgic lore but it does place limits on the (unbearable) lightness of our being in the social world. This would seem to be a necessary realistic and sociologically well-founded premise upon which to discuss the complex articulation of 'the communal' in various spheres of action, from health care to crime control and public safety.

The reality of belonging and identity increasingly in western societies is surely that of a 'community of communities, a community of citizens, not a place of oppressive uniformity based on a single and substantive culture' (Parekh, 2000: 56). This position on concurrent membership of communities accords with John Braithwaite's (2000) republican manifesto and should help us rethink how we work with communities in experimental projects 'doing' crime prevention, safety and justice work more generally. In the following extract Braithwaite (2000: 95–6) makes a powerful argument for a progressive political and normative engagement with the communal and the latter's key place in a democratic 'republican' project:

> [r]epublicans can have no truck with a kind of communitarianism that privileges a national society. Nor is a nostalgia for a lost village of previous centuries attractive. Privileging either of these forms of community is in fact a threat to freedom as non-domination. Republican freedom is most likely to be nourished in a world of cross-cutting communities: where one's professional community might act as a check and an alternative to the dominations of one's village, one's church a check on the dominations of one's family, one's network of friends with a common recreational interest a check on the dominations of one's church, and so on. Republicans should not believe in a strong community, but in strong communities.

In this extract Braithwaite offers us a radical communitarian position which foregrounds our membership of a plurality of communities in contemporary society. Such strong communities would also function as part of a shared civic future, predicated not simply on harmony and consensus, but also on opposition and conflict within an 'agonistic' politics. As Richard Sennett (1999: 143) has tellingly observed, 'strong bonding between people means engaging over time their differences'. And here the role of the state as facilitator of the development of communities is crucial to the radical communitarian project. In response to Garland's (2001) valorization of the local knowledge and resources over the national and statist (see Chapter 2), Jock Young (2003a) has asked the important question for radical communitarians, namely can a genuinely transformative politics be realized at the local level? Young suggests not, but without specifying what the alternative is. I suggest Young may be setting up a wrongly conceived problem here. Communities and local processes of solidarity and belonging do need the state to play a crucial, enabling, harnessing, even 'manufacturing' role. Consequently, communities or localities should not be viewed as a replacement for the state. Rather communities can only be empowered as complementary institutions of the state. In other words, a national or regional project of local communal empowerment is required which addresses Carson's (2004b) emphasis on the 'social embeddedness' of communities. This is to envisage 'policy for a complex world' (Little, 2002: 141).

Underpinning this radical communitarian argument is an alternative vision of communities as inherently instable settlements. Jeffrey Weeks has argued for the importance of a dynamic concept of 'sexual community' in the gay and lesbian social movement. More specifically for our purposes here, Weeks argues that:

> communities are not fixed once and for all. They change as the arguments which shape them over time continue, and as other communities exercise their gravitational pull ... .The social relations of a community are repositories of meaning for its members not sets of mechanical linkages between isolated individuals. (Weeks, 1993 in Little, 2002: 46)

For criminology and for the new modes of *governmental savoir*[2] in crime control and community safety, such alternative imaginings of communities open up new, often volatile notions and practices of respect, tolerance and mutuality where expressions of difference may even be a source of solidarity. Such possibilities are missing in both the individualistic rational choice theories of administrative 'criminologies of the self' and the claustrophobic moral closures of the 'criminologists of the other' (Garland, 2001 and see Chapter 8). They also speak more fittingly to the grain of our late modern times.

Towards a Critical Realist Criminology

Much of this section is based on my ongoing work with Adam Edwards (see Edwards and Hughes, 2005 a, b; Hughes and Edwards, 2005). It also engages with one of the *betes noires* of critical criminology of 1980s and 1990s, left realist criminology. Suffice to note for our purposes here, left realist criminology remains an important influence on the current attempt to build a critical realist and public criminology appropriate for the contemporary conditions. To paraphrase Young, we still need to take crime in its many guises seriously but be radical in our analysis and policy (Young, 1994. For overviews of left realist criminology and its project see Downes and Rock, 1997; Hughes, 2004c).

The final conceptual building block of this introductory chapter then is the analytical and normative possibilities opened up by the work of critical realist thinking in the social sciences. It is argued throughout this book that the insights associated with debates in critical realism provide the criminologist with a much needed set of conceptual tools both for studying comparatively the new community governance of crime and safety specifically and ordering more generally and for making normative interventions in 'the politics of crime and community'. Let us now look at how this critical realist perspective helps clarify the contemporary criminological enterprise.

The Realist Square of Crime

It is not difficult to pin down the 'problematic' of contemporary social scientific criminological practice. Clearly it is in part the study of both the causes of crimes and construction of 'the problem of crime'. At the same time it is increasingly focussed on the broader study of crime control, formal and informal, rather than criminal justice writ narrowly. In turn it seeks to relate in a mutually constitutive manner the causes of crimes and the criminalization and victimization of certain actors and actions to the processes of crime control and ordering more generally. As noted by the left realist criminologists, attention to these questions helps us overcome much of orthodox modernist criminology's predilection for studying the causes of offending and possible correction of deviance and its related reluctance to deal in and with the broader political and cultural rationales for its work. The 'square of crime' conceptualized by left realist criminologists of the 1980s and 1990s (Young, 1994; Taylor, 1999) may help us here although, as originally conceived, it is constrained by an analytical preoccupation with the nation state and neglect of informal, non-state mechanisms of control which are now often captured by the concept of governance discussed above. According to its critics, left realism may be interpreted as returning the criminological imagination to the 'citadels of old criminology' and to the discipline's modernist project because of its renewed interest in aetiology and crime causation (for a fuller discussion see Chapter 8). That noted, left realism suggests that the single factor explanations of positivist criminology are to be rejected in favour of a more complex four-fold contextual explanation of the causes ('aetiology') of crime and its control which is termed 'the square of crime' (see Figure 1.1).

The square of crime provides us with a framework of interaction for understanding crime contextually. As a conceptual framework it has four key ingredients: (i) the offender; (ii) the victim; (iii) state and criminal justice agencies (or, I would suggest, more broadly formal crime control and security or safety agencies); and (iv) the various publics and communities. The square alerts us to the need to analyse any criminal element in terms of the co-presence of these elements. This theoretical framework offers the prospect of a sophisticated, non-reductionist and comprehensive contextual explanation that is also sufficiently pragmatic to explore and respond to the

The state and criminal justice agencies	**Offender**
Social control	The criminal act
Publics and communities	**Victim**

Figure 1.1 The square of crime (adapted Lea, 2001).

complex reality of crime as it is experienced in everyday life. Critical realist criminology thus aims to be, in Jock Young's (1987: 337) words, 'true to the actual shape of the phenomenon and the forces which have brought it into being ... it attempts to unpack the phenomenon, display its hidden relationships and pinpoint the dynamics which lie behind the apparent obviousness of a single criminal incident at a particular point in time'. Thus, the definition and subsequent 'treatment' and management of a specific incident as 'crime' or 'disorder' must be analysed as the result of an unfolding of specific processes of action and reaction in particular geo-historical contexts.

In a more recent contribution to left realist criminology, John Lea (2001: 5) notes importantly that the four corners of the square are active participants in the construction and regulation of criminality, in which the state is thereby but one component, albeit a very powerful one. He also argues that the modern stability of such constructions of crime in the nineteenth and twentieth centuries have been eroded in recent decades and that there is a growing decomposition of this historically specific form of crime control which is associated with the rule of law and the specialized realm of criminality and its control by the state. This decomposition in turn points to a sea change in the relationship between key forms of criminality and other aspects of the social and economic system. Put starkly 'crime is less an episodic and rude disruption of normality and increasingly one of its salient features' (Lea, 2001: vii). The distinction between crime and other 'business' as with mechanisms of control, public and private, is thus becoming more blurred in contemporary neo-liberal societies (see Chapter 2 below for a fuller discussion of Lea's thesis). Lea goes on to argue for the necessity of an historical perspective in accounting for these shifts. When viewed chronologically, many of the changes currently taking place 're-present' aspects of modern capitalist societies in their initial stages (for example, gangsterism, private governance etc.).

The square of crime thus represents a geo-historically specific analytical framework:

> Older, pre-modern forms of 'crime control' such as ethnic warfare, feuding, vendetta etc., testify to the essential modernity of criminalisation and its link to the emergence of the notion of the free individual and the abstract legal person. (Lea, 2001: 2)

Lea terms the complex of social relations that make criminalization an objective possibility 'the social relations of crime control': that is an ensemble of actors, roles and interactions that sustains the application of the criminalizing abstraction and the management and control of criminality. Compared to the earlier 'static' use of the realist square of crime, Lea's (2001: 23) more recent conceptualization shifts attention to that of 'the historical constitution, development and crisis of that system of interaction itself'. The future unfolding of this system of interaction and associated geo-historical processes will remain at the heart of a social scientifically infused criminological analysis put forward in this book.

Context and Comparison in Criminology[3]

A casual browsing of the major new publications and conferences in criminology across the world today will confirm the increasing salience of comparative analysis in contemporary criminological thought. Debates in orthodox, positivist criminology over comparative trends in crime control and prevention, and in particular evaluative arguments over 'what works' (Sherman *et al.*, 1998), have been preoccupied with the problem of generalization. Within the Anglophone world, comparative criminology has been dominated by a distinctively American tradition that emphasizes universalizing, quasi-natural scientific 'nomothetic' explanations (Edwards and Hughes, 2005a: 358).[4] Counterpoised to those seeking universal claims about the applicability of crime control strategies and the criteria for their evaluation are those critical, interpretive criminologists who emphasize the unique 'indigenous' qualities of crime and control (De Haan, 1992). This may be termed 'idiographic' explanation. It has been argued by Garland (2001) that this tension between generalization and specificity is unavoidable: the options available are that one either aims at eliciting the broad, comparative structural patterns of crime, safety and control or one conducts detailed local case studies which provide rich descriptions of such experiences but are limited in their broader comparative significance. Whilst individual authors cannot escape this dilemma in their own analyses, the best that can be hoped for, according to Garland, is that the scholarly community as a whole encompasses a division of intellectual labour between 'nomothetic' and 'idiographic' researchers in which, '[s]weeping accounts of the big picture can be adjusted and revised by more focussed case studies' and, '[a]n accretion of small-scale analyses eventually prompts the desire for more general theoretical accounts' (Garland, 2001: vii–viii).

In contrast to this thinking, Adam Edwards and myself (Edwards and Hughes 2005a: 347–51) argue that the trade-off between generalization and specificity and between what may be termed the falsely universal ('nomothetic') and the falsely particular ('idiographic') accounts is an incorrect one, premised on a pre-dominant but misleading conception of explanation in the social sciences. It is argued that social scientists have too often adopted the natural scientific model of causation as a premise for studying social relations. This 'successionist' model of causality, in which generalizations inform and are informed by the observation of regular events, misunderstands the qualitatively different character of the objects of the social sciences as opposed to natural sciences. Whereas the latter are sometimes capable of being observed in controllable (experimental laboratory) conditions, social relations are 'open systems' that are subject to change and alteration precisely because their objects – human beings and their collective interactions – are reflexive and thus capable of altering their behaviour on the basis of monitoring and reflecting on their own actions. This position recognizes the necessity of an interpretive understanding of meaning in social life. Reflexivity implies that we should expect observations of regularity in social relations to be rare and therefore alternative criteria of explanation are needed.

Specific implications for explanation in the social sciences follow from an acknowledgement that social relations, like crime and its control, are open-ended. Whether the real causal mechanisms that social relations necessarily have (by virtue of their structure) are actually activated is a contingent feature of the different conditions these relations inhabit. It can be argued, for example, that any crime event is structured by the necessary presence of certain mechanisms, such as a supply of motivated offenders and suitable targets (whether commodities or vulnerable persons), and the absence of others, such as capable guardians (whether these be police officers, park wardens, parents etc). Nonetheless, the activation of these mechanisms depends on the specific conditions in which they are exercised, these conditions being other mechanisms, such as changes in local labour and housing markets, the manufacture of high value and highly portable consumer durables from the mobile phone to the ipod, the decisions of public authorities to expand or reduce the provision of leisure and educational facilities for young people, changes in the tolerance for and censure of deviant behaviour etc. According to this critical realist position and in opposition to the claims of idiographic post-modernists, it is claimed that there are necessary qualities of social relations that are indifferent to context and which make comparison meaningful. However, their concrete outcomes are conditioned by diverse and contingent social contexts. These contexts and conditions are not simply the backdrop to, but are constitutive of, interactions between crime and deviance and its control. From a critical realist perspective they cannot, therefore, be 'controlled' for in some quasi-natural scientific experiment. Rather, explanation of these interactions proceeds through a focus on concrete processes of crime control and safety in particular places and at certain historical moments, articulating what causal mechanisms were activated in these concrete instances and identifying how, in turn, they were generated by the structure of crime – control interactions. As the leading critical realist commentator Andrew Sayer (2000: 15) notes, 'events arise from the workings of mechanisms which derive from the structures of objects, and they take place within geo-historical contexts'.

Much of the above discussion may appear on the surface somewhat arcane and complex. However, in subsequent chapters of this book the necessary 'concretisation' of these claims will be undertaken. Central to Edwards' and my argument here is the claim that the exploration of the varying contexts (for example, the political, economic, cultural, organizational, spatial) in which policies and practices of community-based safety and crime control are institutionalized and performed, cannot be adequately understood if viewed as mere background and superficial 'wallpaper' covering the real 'stuff' of crime- controlling and safety-promotive measures. Rather context is central to any social scientific understanding of crime control and community safety because it is constitutive of such processes and not merely the peripherally relevant 'vessel' in which such activity takes place. Furthermore, context is not restricted to the determinant effect of macro-social transitions, such as 'globalization', 'risk society', 'neo-liberalism', or 'late modernity' (Hughes, 1998a). Instead it is to acknowledge the spatial and temporal scales of social relations and processes which may include such macro-theoretical concerns but must also accommodate the local conditions of safety and control given that general structures do not float above particular contexts but are always reproduced within them (Sayer, 2000: 133). A related key insight of such geo-historical explanations of social relations is an understanding of their uneven development not only between but within national territories.

It is this insistence on geo-historical accounts that distinguishes the critical realist understanding of crime control and safety from both the broad-sweeping 'nomothetic' theorizing and research into general patterns of crime control and 'idiographic' studies of particular localities that have hitherto polarized debate and argument over crime control and the new politics of safety. Throughout this book an argument is made for the conceptual and policy-oriented gains that can be made through this acuity to the specific geo-histories of control and public safety strategies, and in particular the need for theory and research to be self-conscious about the spatial and temporal scales of its analysis. This research agenda focusses on the production of geo-historical explanations that are sensitive to, and explicit about, the spacing and timing of social relations. It speaks to a preoccupation of current social and political thought with processes of so-called 'glocalization', that is the interplay between global and local political, cultural and economic relations in accentuating the uneven development of social relations across different spatial and temporal scales.

The Normative Turn: Critical Realism Meets Radical Communitarianism

It may appear odd if not contradictory for the discussion in this chapter to encompass both potentially utopian communitarian thought and that of critical realism. Indeed my imaginary reader may claim understandably that 'utopian' and 'realist' thought are surely at odds with each other. However, I wish to argue, following Sayer (2000), that the attempt to formulate normatively utopian claims is compatible with critical realist argument in the social sciences. All too often, the word 'utopia' is used to mean not just an imagined better future state but a demonstrably infeasible one. The latter meaning of utopia may be easily dismissed but a utopianism that attempts to think about the feasibility of desirable alternatives in terms of how the proposed social processes would work, the asking of counterfactual questions, and conducting thought experiments and scrutinizing critical standpoints cannot be so readily discounted in critical social scientific debate (Sayer, 2000: 178). Surely a critical criminology 'worth its salt' presupposes the possibility of a better way of life since 'to expose something as illusionary or contradictory is to imply the possibility and desirability of a life without those illusions and contradictions' (Sayer, 2000: 161). However, Sayer (2000: 157) goes on to note that there is a remarkable imbalance between our ability to think about the social world scientifically, as something to be understood and explained, and our ability to think about it normatively, or even to think how it might be. In debates on morality and the question of how things might or ought to be different, critical realism, like that of radical communitarianism, insists that morality cannot be reduced to a set of principles abstracted from concrete situations but rather involves responses to those situations by actors with specific histories and geographies. Accordingly moral action is precisely about grappling with the diverse demands of different social relations. This argument is especially important in the debate on 'human sameness' and 'difference' that lies at the centre of much contemporary criminological debate on crime, control and the community and which Chapters 5–7 explore in depth through the case studies of anti-social behaviour, asylum seeking and urban regeneration.

Let us briefly look at an example of the normative turn in social sciences with regard to the issue of utopias built around the notion of community. It may be noted that both moral authoritarian communitarians and post-modernists invoke the utopia of 'community' but with little specification of what form it may take. For these conservative communitarians, community is the stuff of traditional (families) or territorial (neighbourhoods); for post-modernnists, it is an identity-based group. Implicitly both perpetuate the honorific status of community in popular ideology as a warm and secure alternative to the anomie of contemporary society (Hughes and Mooney, 1998). This is unsatisfactory and the slippage between descriptive and normative uses of community both conceals the divisions of the former and the harmony of the latter. Sayer (2000: 179) correctly recognizes that communities often define themselves over and against their 'others' and purely in terms of their interests, whether this be the anti-social youth, repeat offender or racialized stranger. This is problematic not only because of its exclusivising tendencies and its potential to suppress internal dispute, but also because it has little to offer 'wider humanity'. Sayer's (2000: 179) alternative normative position on the 'community' question takes us back to the earlier radical communitarian debate in the second section of this chapter in suggesting that:

> It could be argued that communities should mobilise participants in such a way that they are compatible with other communities, and more than this, they should have something positive to offer wider humanity. On this latter view, communities are not defined purely in defensive terms – through mere 'boundary wish' – but must propose something which is universal, out of their situated particularities. ... it needs to be remembered that communities are not discrete but are invariably embedded in wider social systems, participating in wider divisions of labour and exchange, sharing infrastructure, often language and a host of wider economic and cultural phenomena.

This normative position may provide us with a crucial acid test for judging the progressive or regressive potentialities of the many guises of appeals to community in the governance of crime and safety, which we encounter in the following chapters. It suggests that we may be advised to put aside group classifications, especially binary ones ('us and them') and try to work out how to act in relation to hybrid identities given that respectful relations with others has become 'far more intricate and fraught than any insider-outsider, us-and-them formulations can ever grasp, and this is in part a consequence of the fact that our social geographies are overlapping and interdependent too' (Sayer, 2000: 185). Critical realism also avoids any facile form of utopianism given its emphasis on studying the flows and sedimented forms of the micro- and macro-geographies of power in specific contexts. Subsequent chapters return to these debates with regard to concrete and pressing issues in 'the politics of crime and community'.

Conclusion

This chapter has focussed on three thematic issues, which help structure the arguments in this book as a whole. In the first section of the chapter the concept of governance was unpacked and its centrality to contemporary debates on the new preventive sector in late modern societies explained. The argument here was not that the state had been 'air-brushed' out of the picture of control and safety. Rather this discussion alerts us to the complex processes of fragmentation and pluralization of processes, which are better captured by the phrase 'the community governance of crime and safety'. In the next section the radical communitarian debate on the progressive as well as regressive potentialities of appeals to community were explored. The argument of this section suggested that social scientists need to acknowledge the capacious nature of the term community and thereby move beyond the purely negative register of community as, for example, solidarity through exclusion and 'othering' or reactionary nostalgia. This discussion is suggestive that connecting 'community' to 'governance' need not have any necessary ideological direction. Rather definitions of community will always be ambiguous and contentious and thus always resistant to ideological categorization in any one direction. Finally in the third section of this chapter the perspective of critical realism was presented as a useful conceptual lens with which to explore the world criminologically. In particular it was argued that the critical realist perspective helps to centre the questions of context and comparison – particularly via the concept of 'geo-histories' – and engagement with normative theory in contemporary criminological debates.

These three conceptual themes provide the overarching spine for understanding the specific and substantive issues as well as the broader field of the community governance of crime and safety, which this book both surveys and interrogates. In the next chapter a broad mapping of the new preventive field and its institutional architecture is provided.

2

Mapping the Preventive Turn

The new infrastructure is strongly oriented towards a set of objectives and priorities – prevention, security, harm-reduction, loss-reduction, fear-reduction – that are quite different from the traditional goals of prosecution, punishment and 'criminal justice' ... Today's most visible crime control strategies may work by expulsion and exclusion, but they are accompanied by patient, ongoing, low-key efforts to build up the internal controls of neighbourhoods and to encourage communities to police themselves.

(Garland, 2001: 17)

Where the old paradigm seeks to mobilise specialist, often force-based, expertise, the new one seeks to mobilise and integrate a spectrum of resources, placing particular emphasis on local knowledge and capacity as a key ingredient in any governance programme.

(Johnston and Shearing, 2003: 16)

Introduction

This chapter takes up the debate opened up in Chapter 1 on governance and the preventive turn alongside an exploration of the politics of community in the new policy field when understood with due attention to comparative geo-historical contexts. In so doing the chapter addresses such questions as how are such broad processes of change and ordering to be understood social scientifically?; and what are the main convergent and divergent trends at work in contemporary western societies? The main aims of this chapter are as follows. In the first section some of the most influential criminological interpretations of the links between what may be termed the 'preventive turn' and its connections with broader historical, economic, political and cultural transformations associated variously with 'late modernity', 'neo-liberalism' and 'post-fordism' are introduced. The focus here is on providing an accessible exposition of what may be termed the grand sociological narratives of transformation as represented by the influential work of David Garland (2001), Les

Johnston and Clifford Shearing (2003), and John Lea (2001). In doing so the question what is the nature of the new 'preventive paradigm' and its institutional forms is addressed. In the second section of the chapter a case study is presented which outlines the defining moments in the recent history of the fast changing field of local community safety and crime control in the national context of England and Wales. In so doing the key features of the new legislative and institutional architecture around safety and prevention in the last three decades are mapped out. In the third section the simultaneous comparative processes of convergence and divergence and uneven development of these processes across different western, 'late modern' societies are discussed. The chapter concludes by asking what 'lessons' – analytical and normative – as much as technical – may be learnt from the contextually sensitive, comparative geo-historical understanding of prevention and safety politics and policies across Europe. By the end of this chapter the reader should have both a sound grasp of the 'big picture' around the new community governance of crime and safety but also one that is sensitive to the complex and uneven development and realization of this governmental project, nationally, locally, trans-nationally and internationally, which subsequent chapters then examine in depth.

Grand Narratives of Transformation and the Preventive Turn in Criminology

It was noted in Chapter 1 that the concept of governance may open up a space that allows us to think of a 'process' rather than an 'institution' and to focus on the many dimensions of the experiences and consequences of being governed (Hunt, 1992: 305). This emphasis on moving away from a narrowly defined analysis of the national institutions of 'criminal justice' and towards the new predicates of 'crime control', 'community safety', 'harm reduction', 'risk management' and such like is one of the most important developments in criminological analysis over the last three decades. The idea of prevention as a discrete and *sui generis* focus of crime control policy and practice points to a shift in focus away from control as the special reserve of the criminal justice system and its allied professionals. The enrolment of new actors from a wide range of organizations, statutory, voluntary, commercial, into local multi-agency partnerships has been interpreted in contemporary criminological theory as representing a shift from state-centred government to governance (Crawford, 1997, Johnston and Shearing, 2003). It may be suggested that such transformations, whilst seemingly epitomized in the Anglophone 'community-based' partnerships and the 'community policing movement' are also reflected increasingly in the new institutional architecture across western Europe and to be found, for example, in the establishment of local 'security contracts' in France and Belgium and 'integral' safety policies in Holland and some regions in Italy (Theoretical Criminology, 2005).

Two of the most influential and controversial 'diagnoses' of, and simultaneous 'prognoses' about, the preventive turn and the new modes of governance in contemporary criminology are associated with the texts produced by Garland (2001) and Johnston and Shearing (2003). It is on their work and some of the key criticisms, which these analyses have generated that I now focus in order to clarify the broad brush character of the systemic transformation in control and safety strategies in which 'we' in the affluent West appear to find ourselves.

Garland and the Promise of the Adaptive Preventive Strategy

The discussion that follows presents a largely uncritical overview of Garland's path-breaking work of synthesis on the new culture and politics of crime control in late modern societies. However, in Chapter 3 a sustained empirical evaluation of Garland's work will be developed.

By way of a beginning let me briefly clarify the methodological assumptions underpinning Garland's grand and sweeping analysis. Garland's starting-point is that there is an unavoidable tension between broad generalisation and the specification of empirical particulars (Garland, 2001: vii). He notes that his aim is to plot the emergence of structural properties of a 'field', identifying the recurring social and political dynamics that produce them. 'Structural patterns of this kind simply do not become visible in localized case studies focused upon a single policy area or a particular institution' (Garland, 2001: viii). That said, Garland recognizes that subsequent case studies should be in a better position to confirm, disconfirm or otherwise refine these findings. Garland's position relies on drawing up broad 'ideal typifications' of the general trends and features of the transformation which he accepts may be 'qualified' by the more detailed attention to difference and contingencies in local case studies. The potential danger of this approach is that it prioritizes the general and ideal typical over the local and specific.

At the centre of Garland's comparison of the United States of America and the United Kingdom and what he terms, following Foucault, 'a history of the present' is the claim that the common patterns exemplified in the two societies are not simply a product of policy transfer but instead are explicable in terms of both broader and deeper processes of economic, social and cultural change affecting both. In particular, it is claimed that late modernity brings about a cluster of risks, insecurities and control problems which play a crucial role in shaping the changing response to crime, not just among the agencies of the state but among sections of the wider society. Alongside the broad cluster of cultural changes associated with late modern conditions, Garland also points to the crucial influence across both sides of the Atlantic of free market, socially conservative politics. Taken together it is argued that a similar culture of control involving the coupling of increasingly marked socio-economic inequalities alongside heightened levels of 'crime consciousness' has emerged over the past few decades across many western societies but most graphically epitomized in the UK and USA national cases.

Garland argues that two adaptations, standing in profound contradiction to each other, emerge in the new crime control complex. These are respectively an irrational punitive law and order politics based on a process of 'acting out and denial' and an 'entirely different strategy' of preventative partnerships, community policing and generalized crime prevention (Garland, 2001: xi). Overall, Garland is deeply pessimistic about the dominant and politically reactionary current of culture and politics that characterizes the present in terms, *inter alia*, of moral breakdown, incivility and the decline of the family. This zeitgeist is characterized by a nostalgia for a past order when viewed through the lens of fear and insecurity about both the present and the future. Public opinion is viewed as having become more punitive and exclusionary in the last two decades of the twenty-first century, in part because of political and media manipulation but more especially due the new experience of crime, particularly among the formerly 'liberal' middle classes. In particular, echoing the views of Bauman and Young, Garland opines that the 'open, porous mobile society of strangers that is late modernity has given rise to crime control practices that seek to make society less open and less mobile: to fix identities, immobilize individuals, quarantine whole sections of the population, erect boundaries, close off access' (Garland, 2001: 165).

According to Garland, there is then a two-fold and contradictory response to the collapse of the rehabilitative ideal and of penal-welfarism in crime control systems of late modernity at the end of the twentieth century. The first and dominant response is that of a non-adaptive 'denial and acting out' which invokes neo-conservative principles and is concerned with denying the crisis of record crime rates and the 'failure' of prison. This response is underpinned by a demonizing 'criminology of the other' and conditions criminal justice institutions to act in an exclusionary manner, exemplified by the incapacitative potential of prisons. Let me at this point describe in brief the main features of the expressive, punitive strategy before I focus in greater depth on Garland's claims for its opposite, namely the adaptive, preventive strategy. First, it is characterized primarily by an emotive register rather than a rational, 'evidence-based' one. Second, and relatedly, it is both populist and politicized. Third, and more broadly, this repressive strategy is based on the exclusionary logic of security and segregation as epitomized in mass incarceration, exclusion orders, zero tolerance policing, gated communities and such like. Fourth and finally it privileges victims 'though in fact that place is occupied by a projected, politicized, image of the "victim", rather than by the interests and opinions of victims themselves. The sanctified persona of the suffering victim has become a valued commodity in the circuits of political and media exchange' (Garland, 2001: 143). The crime victim is no longer the unfortunate citizen on the end of a criminal harm, whose concerns are no longer subsumed within 'public interest' that guides prosecution and penal decision. 'Instead, the crime victim is now, in a certain sense, a representative character whose experience is assumed to be common and collective, rather than individual and atypical' (Garland, 2001: 144). This new figure helps shift the debate on crime and punishment to the visceral emotions of identification and righteous indignation. 'Punishment – in the sense of expressive punishment, conveying public sentiment – is once again a respectable , openly embraced, penal purpose and has come to affect not just high-end sentences for the most heinous offences but even juvenile justice and community sentences' (Garland, 2001: 9). Overall the victim and his/her feelings – and increasingly the community as collective victim with rights to protection – are now at the centre of contemporary penal discourse. As a strategy, the expressive, punitive logic rests ideologically on a moralizing and atavistic 'criminology of the other' in which criminals are 'othered' as 'demons', 'beasts' etc (for a fuller discussion of this criminology of the other, see Chapter 8).

In seemingly dramatic contrast the second response is that of an adaptive preventive strategy based on neo-liberal principles. This involves greater rationalization and commercialization of criminal justice functions and specifically a stress on multi-agency crime prevention partnerships, which involve the agencies and actors of 'civil society' as well as statutory agencies. As a strategy, adaptation rests on a 'criminology of the self' derived from what Garland terms the new criminologies of everyday life. Such forms of knowledge see the criminal as a rational actor and crime as a normal social fact of living in contemporary society. It will be argued in Chapter 3 that Garland's neat juxtaposition of these two strategies as 'contradictory' implies too dichotomous a relationship between these two tendencies despite the occasional disclaimer from Garland. That noted, his juxtaposition does enable us to map conceptually the field in a provisional manner. Given the focus on the preventive turn and its institutional embodiment in multi-agency partnerships throughout this book it is important at this point to outline the key features of the 'third sector' of *prevention* as against the two traditional logics of *policing* and *penality* in some depth.

Garland makes ambitious and politically and normatively supportive claims for the new preventive adaptive strategy of crime control in late modern societies. Here are some illustrative statements:

> '(T)his network of partnership arrangements and inter-agency working agreements is designed to foster crime prevention and to enhance community safety, primarily through *the cultivation of community involvement* and *the dissemination of crime prevention ideas and practices'*. (Garland, 2001: 16, emphasis added)
>
> '(H)owever many problems they raise these strategies are characterised by a high level of administrative rationality and creativity' (Garland, 2001: 131).
>
> 'Community safety becomes the chief consideration and law enforcement becomes merely a means to this end, rather than an end in itself'. (Garland, 2001: 17)

According to Garland, it is evident that this new preventive logic and its institutional infrastructure is not to be understood merely as an annex or extension of the traditional criminal justice system. In turn it is possible to discern three key themes to Garland's thesis on the new preventive sector. Let us examine each in turn.

On the elective affinity between the new criminologies of everyday life and the preventive sector

It is important to note the emphasis given by Garland to the emergence of new ways of behaving and thinking in crime prevention. In Garland's view this is clearly an unfinished project that is still unfolding. In terms of the new actors and their institutional practices, they remain a 'rather inchoate and ill-defined set of arrangements' (Garland, 2001: 171). But it is also suggested that there is a 'new crime control establishment that draws upon the new criminologies of everyday life to guide its actions and mould its techniques' (Garland, 2001: 17). The new specialists in the preventive sector are thus viewed as getting much of their ideas – and their emerging 'habitus' – from the new criminologies of everyday life associated with situational crime prevention, routine activities theory, opportunity theory and the new 'crime sciences' (for a fuller discussion see Chapter 8). It is claimed that officials in the new preventive sector recognize the elective affinity between their own practical concerns and the new type of criminological discourse associated with the new criminologies of everyday life. These new 'administrative' criminologies thus express some of the key ways in which crime control is being recast across the field. Whereas previously, official criminology saw crime retrospectively and individually, these new criminologies view it prospectively and in aggregate terms. Criminogenic situations, 'hot products' and 'hot spots', are the new objects of control: this then is a 'supply side' criminology focussed on shifting risks, redistributing costs, and creating disincentives (Garland, 2001: 127–9).

Demonopolizing crime prevention? The balance of state and private sector mobilization and leadership

A closely related element of Garland's thesis is the emphasis given to the increasing importance of the private sector and its actors and institutions in this new preventive sector. The growth of the private security industry, nationally and globally, is impossible to deny. Indeed, Garland claims that the preventive infrastructure is largely 'beyond the state'. In particular, it is argued that

> the present day world of private-sector crime prevention exists in a reflexive relationship to the theories and prescriptions of situational crime prevention. It is in this interchange – between the practical recipes of the commercial sector managers and the worked-out rationales of criminologists and government policy-makers – that one must locate the strategy of preventive partnership and the habits of thought and action upon which it depends. (Garland, 2001: 161)

Garland does go on to argue that the commercial and private leadership of the preventive strategy is more pronounced in the USA than Britain. In Britain the Home Office's, and thus the state's, leadership is evident in current statutory, local reductive partnerships. Furthermore, 'the centralized administrative powers of the British Home Office have allowed it to develop policies with greater speed and coherence than has been possible in the USA' (Garland, 2001: 212). In this sense, the 'British' partnership approach is viewed implicitly by Garland as a world leader in the new preventive model of crime control.

Community governance and the responsibilization project

Most importantly for the arguments of this book Garland sees preventive partnerships as both reflecting the new salience of community governance and offering the potential 'solution' to the loss of sovereign state power and its precarious monopoly over crime control in late modern conditions. Moreover, Garland appears to be normatively and politically supportive of this preventive development given its potential to unleash and harness the forces of 'civil society' to deliver crime prevention in a genuinely 'communitarian' fashion. Much of this new preventive approach is thus predicated on a commitment to relocating and redefining responsibilities in the wake of the widely recognized crisis and limitations of the institutions of the state in their crime control capacities. 'The effort to address these limitations, first reforming the state institutions and subsequently by mobilizing and harnessing non-state mechanisms, has been the basis of the most innovative policies of the recent past' (Garland, 2001: 123). As a consequence, 'The "community" has become the all-purpose solution to every criminal justice problem' (Garland, 2001: 123). Garland notes the long tradition of appeals to community in crime control practices since the 1960s. However, these appeals traditionally consisted of state agents carrying out state policies, under the auspices of state organisations. 'Community' here meant the 'non-custodial' since these practices were actually state sanctions with little involvement of non-state actors. At the same time Garland argues that there have been other experiments in community governance which are 'more innovative and radical', seeking to respond to and enlist the help of local groups and organizations. In effect Garland is distinguishing what may be termed 'thick' versus 'thin' versions of community-based policy developments. In the 1980s and 1990s in Britain this out-reach policy grows into the prominent governmental 'responsibilization strategy ' resulting in:

> an enhanced network of more or less directed, more or less informal crime control, complementing and extending the formal controls of the criminal justice state ... The primary objective is to spread responsibility for crime control onto agencies, organisations and individuals that operate outside the criminal justice state and to persuade them to act appropriately. (Garland, 2001: 124–5)

According to Garland, this shift of emphasis is nothing short of a historical watershed in modern crime control (and more implicitly one to be applauded by criminologists and sociologists alike):

> For the first time since the formation of the modern criminal justice state, governments have begun to acknowledge a basic sociological truth: that the most important processes producing order and conformity are mainstream social processes , located within the institutions of civil society, not the uncertain threat of legal sanctions'. (Garland, 2001: 126)

Thus, instead of holding on to the myth of a sovereign state monopoly of crime control, there is a new vision of the 'dispersed, pluralistic nature of effective social control'. Here Garland lends support to the valorisation of the 'local' in complex societies in a manner close to the neo-liberal 'Hayekian vision' of self-governing communities reliant on local knowledge and resources (Young, 2003a: 240).

Although Garland avoids overtly 'signing up' to a communitarian position for perhaps understandable reasons, the implications of his interpretation of the nature and importance of community-based social control practices are clearly supportive of potentially 'progressive' local communitarian tendencies (for a similar position, see Hope, 2001, Hughes, 2004a and d). The nature of communitarian social control, its relationship to late modernity and its central importance to the new crime prevention sector is captured in the following statement:

> the development of late modernity reduced the extent and effectiveness of 'spontaneous' social control – which is to say, the learned, unreflexive, habitual practices of mutual supervision, scolding, sanctioning, and shaming carried out, as a matter of course, by community members. The current wave of crime prevention behaviour tries to revive these dying habits, and more importantly, to supplement them with new crime control practices that are more deliberate, more focused, and more reflexive. (Garland, 2001: 159)

Garland's venture into the realm of the normative and his retreat from an out and out pessimism over the reactionary turn in the culture of control and law and order politics offers an important corrective to the tendencies of both those on the left to restrict analysis to critique and those in clientalist 'administrative' criminology to avoid the 'contamination' of addressing overtly political and normative issues (for a fuller discussion see Chapter 8). It is worth noting that this position and twist to Garland's otherwise dystopian thesis is largely ignored or down-played in most critical reviews of his work (see, for example, Zedner, 2002). In doing so, Garland's work offers clear points of comparison with the more explicitly normatively driven work of Johnston and Shearing and their claims for the inventiveness of 'nodal governance' and preventive, security-oriented mentalities under neo-liberal conditions. Johnston and Shearing's contribution to this debate will now be considered.

Johnston and Shearing on Governing Security

Both Les Johnston and Clifford Shearing have been leading exponents of an intellectual movement in criminology aiming to reconceptualize what is meant by 'policing' beyond that of the mandate and work of the public police. In common with other theorists of neo-liberal governmentality (Rose, 1999), Johnston and Shearing argue that policing and the governance of security more generally cannot be restricted to the study of the public police and allied specialist institutions of the state. Furthermore, they argue in contrast to such commentators as Loader and Walker (2001) that the state is not necessarily best equipped to act as a meta-authority over the diverse range of actors involved in policing and the governance of security. Indeed, their work may be viewed as a fuller development of and normative argument for the valorisation of community governance, which Garland's analysis more tentatively promotes. Let us examine in some detail where their normatively driven argument for the community governance of security and justice takes us.

According to Johnston and Shearing (2003), the new 'archipelago' of security programmes dispersed throughout the fragmented and decentred neo-liberal societies are dependent on access to local knowledge and capacity and are future-oriented in their efforts to guarantee security. They also note that the 'experiential' is crucial to the work of the emergent 'programmes' and 'nodes' of governance associated with communities. Five crucial elements to security governance programmes are specified, namely (i) a view of what society entails and a (negotiated) definition of order; (ii) some form of authority but not just that of the state; (iii) specific methods or technologies that programmes rely on; (iv) the existence of institutions or structures which provide a means of organizing and relating people and things; and (v) finally the result of the combination of these different elements is the production of a determinate security practice (Johnston and Shearing, 2003: 7–8). Compared to some critics of the 'privatisation' and 'dispersal of social control', Johnston and Shearing (2000: 112) argue that 'the "goodness" or "badness" of programmes for governing security is a function of complex conditions and calculuses which cannot be prejudged'.

In common with much contemporary debate on the new governance and the 'preventive turn' introduced in Chapter 1 above, Johnston and Shearing construct two ideal types of the governing mentality, past ('punishment') and present ('risk management'):

> security governance based on punishment tends to entail a principal focus on past events, an emphasis on physical coercion, a direct mode of governance through discrete, collectively-sponsored institutions and an imposed rather than negotiated process prescribed through generally applicable rules intended to promote some collective interests. A punishment regime that does not display these characteristics may run the risk of losing legitimacy and being charged with vigilantism. By contrast, the risk management mentality favours an emphasis on embedded modes of 'governance at a distance', focused on the future, and achieved through processes of situationally-specific negotiation which privilege the use of less overtly coercive tools of governance and often involve non-expert, 'lay' persons in their implementation. (Johnston and Shearing, 2003: 30)

In practice the authors recognize that there are messier configurations in the present-day governance of security than may be captured in these two dichotomous ideal types. However, this is not to diminish the historical importance of the rise of 'networked' and 'nodal' governance. In a similar vein to Garland, the authors argue that community safety practice and crime and disorder reduction partnerships conform to the model of 'community networked governance' rather than a 'professional police hegemony' (Johnston and Shearing, 2003: 11). It is contended, again in common with Garland, that the functional distinction between partner agencies is becoming increasingly untenable and it is the demise of such distinctions that differentiates the concept of community safety and similar forms of 'future-oriented' community governance from the traditional and narrower concept of crime prevention. Drawing largely on an analysis of both local and central governmental texts on crime and disorder reduction from England in the post-1998 period, Johnston and Shearing appear to accept that crime and disorder reduction partnerships (henceforth CDRPs) are exemplars of such trends and in particular of local networked community governance. Commenting, for example, on the Home Office Guidance to CDRPs in 1999, Johnston and Shearing (2003: 120) note 'Local people, the Guidance insists, are best equipped to deal with these issues' and the content of local strategies must be, to quote the Guidance, 'what matters to local people and not constrained by artificial definitions imposed by central government'. Whilst recognizing that these claims need to be viewed with some scepticism, Johnston and Shearing (2003: 121) conclude – again in common with Garland – that these developments highlight 'the emergence of a new morphology of government in which state rule is no longer exclusive or definitive'. At other points in their argument, Johnston and Shearing (2003: 73–4) note that the rise of a problem-solving approach dovetails with the neo-liberal shift which has sought to promote the 'responsibilisation' of citizens and which regards state-centred governance as both ineffective and wasteful. Such developments in turn have been epitomized in the movement within the public police to promote community policing:

> Community policing is an umbrella term describing a broad 'family' of initiatives through which the police have sought to re-invent themselves and, by so doing, keep control of the steering of security governance while broadening the range of capacities, agents and knowledges engaged in its rowing. (Johnston and Shearing, 2003: 74)

In Chapter 3 these important claims with regard to both CDRPs and the public police's involvement in problem-solving, partnership work will be evaluated and qualified on the basis of an examination of research evidence with regard to the local implementation of crime and disorder reduction in the case of England and Wales. In essence my aim in the next chapter is to examine the complex, contingent and contradictory conditions which mediate between what Johnston and Shearing term 'governing rationalities' and their 'outcomes'.

Johnston and Shearing's important contribution to the debate on how to capture the broad contours of the new community governance of security concludes by making an overtly normative and political argument for the progressive potential for nodal, community governance of security. Their argument shares many of the assumptions associated with the discussion of radical communitarianism and critical realism in Chapter 1. In doing so, they also help move the conceptualization of the trends in community governance beyond the limitations associated with the grand overview of Garland. As Johnston and Shearing (2003: 139) argue, any assessment and promotion of the new 'human inventions' in the field of the governance of security should ask both political and normative questions regarding which political alliances, local conditions and agency configurations are most likely to facilitate the achievement of desired security objectives under any given set of conditions? Whilst acknowledging that it is crucial to be realistic about both the possibilities and limitations of change, Johnston and Shearing (2003: 140) remain committed to the claim that the 'mobilisation of local knowledge is fundamental to the construction of just and democratic forms of security governance'. In turn, they suggest that a risk mentality can be integrated with local capacity governance and may promote outcomes that are experienced as 'just'. The implications of this position will be returned to specifically in Chapter 7 below with regard to the poorest and most marginalized neighbourhoods in the discussion of urban regeneration and community capacity building.

The work of Johnston and Shearing and others influenced by Foucauldian governmentality theory on the preventive turn (Stenson, 2000, 2005) helps open up the study of the new governable places and the new spatial foci for comparison which the inter-related chapters in this book explore in depth. As Stenson and Edwards (2004) note, while it made sense for comparative criminology to take nation-states as its focus when seeking contrasts in criminal justice (given that criminal legal codes are almost always administered on a national scale), the preventive turn disturbs this logic of comparison and instead recognizes a wide range of localities as the origins of innovations in safety, security and control. Following on from this important insight, it may be argued that we are likely to find an unevenness in the development of preventive-safety strategies reflecting the variegated balance of social and political forces within different localities which in turn have their own geo-histories. It will be contended later in this chapter that arguments over the seeming 'globalisation', or failing that the purported 'Europeanisation' of safety and control run the risk of obscuring the complexity of how policies and practices 'travel', and at what pace and to what effect in different localities and contexts.

A Marxist Realist Counterpoint on the New Community Governance of Crime and Safety

An alternative and more pessimistic analysis of the rise of community governance under neo-liberal conditions to that of both Garland and Johnston and Shearing is found in John Lea's Marxist account of the disintegration of crime control in the last decades of the twentieth century. According to Lea (2001), community governance needs to be understood as one variant of the rise of 'private' modes of governing more generally. The new governance arises out of the partial removal of the state by capital with increasing forms of direct rule by private property, individuals and local communities (Lea, 2001: 121). In turn, the future of 'community governance' is viewed as being associated with authoritarian and exclusionary 'solutions' to problems of crime and insecurity. In common with other dystopian social critics such as Bauman (2000), Lea notes that the salience of community has increased in inverse proportion to its material decomposition and fragmentation as a local structure of networks and support mechanisms:

> Much of the assertion of the new viability of community, drawing on a communitarian nostalgia for Victorian ideas of self-help hides the reality of decomposition into, on the one hand, the wasteland areas effectively abandoned to criminal governance and, on the other, largely middle-class and residual Fordist working class areas held together increasingly by fear of crime rather than by cultural or economic cohesion. (Lea, 2001: 178)

Lea also argues that proponents of the private/community governance thesis such as Johnston and Shearing ignore power and in particular the key changes in power relations associated firstly with the ever widening inequalities between the rich and affluent and the poor 'underclass', and secondly with the growing absence of welfare-oriented state support and provision and the residual presence of the state continually appropriating more repressive powers directed at the management of the poor and the combating of organized criminality. In an important critique of any hasty optimism about the prospects of community governance for the poor and marginalized, Lea (2001: 188) argues that:

> Under present circumstances a shift to private governance accentuates inequalities, both between rich and poor communities and within them. Forms of interpersonal violence such as domestic violence and child-abuse could face reduced surveillance in forms of private governance aimed at keeping risks at bay. Meanwhile the decentralised and fragmented communities of the poor could merge even more with forms of criminal governance and become, like the smuggling communities of 18th century England, entirely dependent on social crime.

These sombre warnings are an important qualification to both Garland's and Johnston and Shearing's more positive speculations on the new community governance of crime and safety. However, it may be that Lea and other leftist 'prophets of Catastrophe' over-play the societal disintegration 'card' and the loss of old certainties and down-play the potentially progressive spaces opened up by the 'new localism'. Whichever interpretation is correct, there remains the need for more grounded localized and context-sensitive empirical research into these 'lost', fragmented, and often mis-represented communities (see Chapter 7).

Mapping the Historical and Institutional Context: a National Case Study[5]

From the Crisis of Criminal Justice to the Preventive Solution?

Let us examine the case of England and Wales here as a possible exemplar of broader international developments. For much of the twentieth century the criminal justice system was largely insulated from overt political criticism and public scrutiny, being celebrated for its 'difference', being 'above politics', 'unique' in character, and best left to 'the experts'. Much of this was related to the hegemony and symbolic presence of the legal discourse surrounding criminal justice. Historically the discourse of criminal justice 'difference' (from other areas of public policy and state agencies) and the cluster of storylines about the 'uniqueness' of the criminal justice system in the United Kingdom, constituted the overarching ideological settlement on criminal justice (McLaughlin (1998: 162–4). It meant that all governments had to tread very warily because the criminal justice system deals with fundamental, symbolic issues of principle – rights, duties, order, equity, justice and punishment – that lie at the heart of a social order that is governed by the rule of law.

However, alongside this privileged presence for criminal justice, the post-war social democratic state was also committed to state-sponsored social reform, and thus the eradication of the causes of criminality, by means of both social and individualized programmes of rehabilitation, inside and beyond the correctional system. Such preventive programmes in turn were experiments devised by social scientific experts. There was much optimism about the potential capacity and desirability of the state to 'engineer' social change and to usher in an end to poverty, deprivation and discrimination by direct state intervention. Looking back, the mid-twentieth century regimes of prevention via treatment and rehabilitation and community development now appear as part of an age of criminological optimism. By the post-Second World War period and the rise of the social democratic welfare state, positivist thinking, both psychological and sociological, on crime and its prevention was an integral part of the institutions of government and of the state's programme of national reconstruction and collective risk management. There was a widespread belief that the political will and scientific means existed to remould and improve virtually all aspects of society. The new professionals and bureaucrats of the social democratic welfare state were given the responsibility to intervene proactively in society's whole range of social ills, not least in treating crime 'scientifically'. Positivist crime control and prevention strategies, particularly those targeted at juvenile delinquency and the 'problem family', were thus a small but important element in the post-war welfare settlement in England and Wales and across many Western societies (Hughes, 1998a).

The last decades of the twentieth century witnessed a growing strain on the criminal justice system, and the allied correctional and rehabilitative regimes of the 'welfare-penal complex' (Garland, 2001) in part as a consequence of the broader crisis tendencies affecting capitalist societies and their states. The crisis of criminal justice system and welfare state responses was manifested by, *inter alia:*

- the increasing rate of recorded crime and the numbers of people passing through the different parts of the system;
- overload combined with a crisis of efficiency (e.g. the declining clear-up rates of the police, overloaded courts and the overcrowding of prisons);
- growing awareness of extensive social and economic costs of crime;
- increasing recognition that formal processes of criminal justice (i.e. detection, apprehension, prosecution, sentencing and punishment of offenders) have only a limited effect on controlling crime. (Hughes and McLaughlin, 2002)

This dissatisfaction and pessimism has also been connected with a crisis of confidence, most notably across the USA and UK, in the effectiveness of the social democratic 'rehabilitative ideal', captured in Martinson's phrase, 'nothing works'. Criminologists, of both the right (Wilson, 1974) and the left (Young, 1991), were amongst the most forthright voices criticizing the 'old' social democratic criminal justice settlement.

In response to the widespread acknowledgement of this crisis of the criminal justice system, two preventive logics have come to the fore internationally since the 1980s. Namely:

- primary situational crime prevention
- social crime prevention and community safety

These logics capture 'the essential problematic which remains at the heart of crime prevention theory today: namely the tension between reducing opportunities through situational measures and social modes of intervention' (Crawford, 1998: 140). Situational or 'environmental' crime prevention chiefly concerns 'designing out' crime and opportunity reduction, such as the installation of preventive technologies in both private and public spaces. Social crime prevention, on the other hand, is focused chiefly on changing social environments and the motivations of offenders, and 'community' development initiatives. Social crime prevention measures thus tend to focus on the development of schemes, such as youth clubs and activity-based projects, to deter potential or actual offenders from future offending. Both situational and social crime prevention approaches tend to be what is termed 'multi-agency' in orientation, rather than being driven by one agency alone, such as the police. Common to both elements of situational and social crime prevention is their claim to be both less damaging and more effective than traditional, reactive and 'law and order' approaches.

Both approaches have long 'submerged' histories in crime control (Hughes, 1998a) but the last three decades have witnessed the key shift in terms of their combined policy and political prominence in field of crime control and community safety. As Adam Crawford (1998: 35) notes, 'the "nothing works" pessimism has precipitated a criminological shift away from the offender as the object of knowledge towards the offence – its situational and spatial characteristics – as well as the place and role of the victim ... As a consequence, a new prominence began to be accorded to crime prevention and community safety, with appeals to informal control and wider responsibility'.

Appeals to the combined techniques of situational and social crime prevention are now commonplace in governmental discourses and policies, both public and private, across the world. They represent the often taken-for-granted starting-point of crime prevention as policy and governmental technology. We may note, for example, the following policy statement on the principles of crime prevention from the State of Victoria, Australia in its document *Safer Streets and Homes: A Crime and Violence Prevention Strategy for Victoria 2002–2005:*

> The practical implementation of specific crime and violence prevention approaches varies greatly, but two broad approaches inform the overall Safer Streets and Homes strategy:
>
> - Situational crime prevention – involves reducing the opportunities for crime through the systematic management, design and manipulation of the immediate physical environment in which crime occurs or is likely to occur. This approach aims primarily to reduce the risk of, and opportunities for, crime to occur in particular contexts.

- Social crime and violence prevention – deals with the complex, underlying motivational causes of criminal and anti-social behaviour and focuses on promoting social inclusion through the measures designed to reduce social marginalization and, at the same time, enhance opportunities for law abiding behaviour. Social crime prevention models promote multi-agency collaboration between government and non-governmental agencies and 'community-building' to generate inclusive and supportive community environments. (Crime Prevention Victoria, 2002)

This type of criminologically-infused thinking is increasingly typical of contemporary state discourses on fostering crime prevention initiatives. It may be read as a vindication that criminological theory and research 'matter'. It is also indicative of what has been termed the 'governmental project' that lies at the heart of 'modernist' criminology (Garland, 2001 and see Chapter 8). Viewed optimistically, the penetration of crime prevention theory and practice in governmental discourses highlights the possibility of criminologists offering alternative policy agendas to the still dominant reactive and punitive, 'law and order' framing of problems and solutions. Such developments also imply an official recognition of the limits to the state's capacity and resources for reducing crime via the formal criminal justice and by implication the requirement to enlist resources and expertise from non-state actors. At the same time, it is of course crucial to note that the state continues to draw massively on its punitive and repressive powers to deal with the problem of crime and disorder. Indeed the complex interweaving of both punitive and preventive logics in contemporary systems of crime control and safety remains a major conundrum for ongoing criminological debate as subsequent chapters in this book will highlight.

Central Government and the Manufacture of the New Local Governance of Community Safety in England and Wales

To return to our national case study the local governance of crime and disorder reduction and community safety has been on a statutory footing since the Crime and Disorder Act (CDA) 1998 in England and Wales. However, its roots can be traced to developments emanating from the Home Office and Conservative administrations since the 1980s and to the report of the Morgan Committee of 1991, set up by the Home Office to review the local delivery of crime prevention (Home Office, 1991). Two of the latter's recommendations have emerged as the foundation for the central government approach: namely, the introduction of the concept of community safety to signify a comprehensive and targeted local approach to crime control (as against crime prevention more narrowly defined); and a statutory responsibility for local authorities, working in conjunction with the police, for delivering the multi-agency partnership approach. Two further features of the approach instituted in the CDA 1998 illustrate a general concern to try and avoid overt 'political' considerations in the framing of local prevention strategies and which resulted in the virtual exclusion of elected representatives from effective involvement in reducing crime and disorder in the community. First, there has been a 'neo-corporatist' concern to develop an executive administration for local crime prevention within the multi-agency framework, through the promotion of the office of local authority Chief Executive who along with the Chief Officer of Police act as the responsible authorities for crime reduction. According to Tim Hope (2005), the CDA was thus a 'politically satisficing' solution to a long term dilemma, namely how to incorporate (and thus 'responsibilise') local authorities into crime reduction without antagonizing the police and threatening their near sacrosanct operational autonomy. Second, the official guidance since the CDA emphasized the primacy of objective data analysis and the model of rational, 'what works', 'evidence-based' policy making, as the cognitive basis for partnership strategies, disseminated from central government by new expert criminologists of everyday life in the Home Office (Hope, 2005). In particular, the much vaunted £250 million Crime Reduction Programme (1999–2002) appeared to usher in a new era of rational experimentation with regard to what could be proven by rigorous research and evidence-based evaluation to 'work' in reducing crime. It was envisaged that this ambitious, and originally 10 year long experiment would contribute to reversing the long-term growth rate in crime and ensure that the greatest impact for the money spent could be achieved[6]. As a consequence, there has been an emphasis on the administrative-managerial rather than the political nature of crime reduction and community safety activity. However, changes in the 2000s associated with central government's 'modernizing agenda' on local government, particularly with regard to local political leadership may well be increasingly disturbing this administrative and managerial partnership settlement of the local governance of crime, disorder and safety (see Chapters 3 and 4).

What is difficult to deny in any overview of the English and Welsh context is that there has been a highly prescriptive and directive central government shaping of the contemporary preventive infrastructure. This is indicative of a sovereign state strategy which stresses greater central control ('steering'), that is also strategic and allocative in form, alongside the diffusion of responsibility for the delivery of crime control ('rowing'). The key elements of the post-1998 framework include legislation requiring and enabling local government to address issues of crime and disorder, and the establishment of local CDRPs, resting upon the new statutory duties imposed upon local government. Between 1998 and 2006 all 376 statutory partnerships in England and Wales have had to:

- carry out audits of local crime and disorder problems;
- consult with all sections of the local community;
- publish three year crime and disorder reduction strategies based on the findings of the audits and the consultative approach;
- identify targets and performance indicators for each part of the strategy, with specified time scales;
- publish the audit, strategy and the targets;
- report regularly on progress against the targets.

This framework has also been associated with a new regime for public auditing of local government performance and service-delivery ('Best Value') arising out of the Local Government Acts 1999 and 2000. Furthermore, it may be that this auditing element will have the most significant impact on the future governance of crime and disorder in the long term given that the regime of incentives and penalties constitutes a powerful disciplinary tool to bring about compliance (Hope, 2005).

Changing Discourses of Prevention, Safety and Reduction

It is evident from the above points that there are well-established legislative and institutional arrangements for bringing about the compliance of local government to deliver services concerning crime and disorder reduction in England and Wales. However, Tim Hope (2005) argues that uncertainty remains about the question of towards what purposes, standards and values of community safety is such compliance being directed. The dominant 'official' definition of the primacy purpose of the new local governance of crime is that of crime and, increasingly disorder, reduction. Meanwhile, there is another response to the insecurity of the citizen that has also characterized the recent history of local government in Britain – that of community safety. The implementation of these arguably different policy objectives may be producing an underlying tension in the resulting local practices which have not been acknowledged sufficiently by either legislators or researchers to date. As Hope (2005) again observes, whilst the goal of crime and disorder reduction is associated with concerns about the performance and delivery of services that would attain the aim of reducing the incidence of crime (including anti-social behaviour that has 'crime-like' consequences), in contrast, the goal of community safety reflects an aspiration to construct a new public good of safety in response to a range of actual and perceived risks and harms. The attainment of such a 'public good' aspires to contribute to the 'quality of life' of citizens and consequently is associated with identifying and addressing community needs for safety rather than a narrower concern with targeted crime reduction. Commenting on the goal of community safety, Hope (2005: 375) suggests:

> Here, the overall order of society is seen as a composite of local, specific social orders and informal (non-statutory) modes of regulation – in schools, communities, and other settings of everyday life ... The ultimate goal, in which the prevention of crime and disorder is a means rather than an end in itself, is to raise citizens' 'quality of life', which derives from their personal safety and their sense of security in everyday life.

It would appear that the scrutiny and disciplinary logic arising from the introduction of the new public management into central-local government relations is uncovering a struggle to conceptualize and develop values, criteria and standards for the goods of safety and security to be delivered to citizens, which remain contested and profoundly unfinished (see Chapters 3 and 4). These struggles too can be seen as a consequence of the contradictions and ambiguities between the contrasting notions of 'crime (and disorder) reduction' and 'community safety'. According to Pease (Wiles and Pease, 2000; Byrne and Pease, 2003), community safety is a misnomer as the function circumscribed within the CDA for it deals only with the sources of danger occasioned by human agents acting criminally or in disorderly ways. This 'distorts the recognition and prioritisation of all the threats to safety which a community may encounter, and neglects the distributive justice which is appropriately achieved by the equitable sharing of unavoidable risks ... Rather than start with crime per se we believe it would be more useful to start with the broader issue of hazard and hazard management, of which crime and disorder are then sub-sets' (Byrne and Pease, 2003: 287–8). Despite this important clarification of the distinction between the two terms, the dominant discourse promoted by the central government agenda has been one where community safety is a sub-set of crime and disorder reduction rather than the reverse. At the time of writing (2006) this conclusion remains true. However, there are some emerging tendencies associated with 'civil renewal' and 'community cohesion' which may unsettle the currently dominant discourse in as yet uncertain directions (see Chapter 4).

Further legislative and institutional developments from the 'dirigiste' central government have occurred since the watershed legislation of the CDA 1998. For example, the Police Reform Act, 2002 included amendments to the CDA with the review of the levels and patterns of drug misuse established as a new statutory responsibility for CDRPs. The Anti-Social

Behaviour Act 2003 has seen a further reformulation and extension of the tasks and legal responsibilities of partnerships with regard to anti-social behaviour (see Chapter 5). In turn, there is now a Home Office national Public Service Agreement (PSA) target for reducing crime and the fear of crime. National targets to be met by 2006 with regard to reducing vehicle crime, domestic burglary and robbery have also been set by the first National Community Safety Plan (2005) and local partnerships are required to prioritize these alongside local crime and disorder targets. It would appear we are living, to paraphrase Mao Tse-tung, under conditions of 'permanent revolution' in the public services with an agenda driven largely by central government!

Local partnerships continue to be seen as being at the forefront of work associated with the central government's stated commitment to delivering a reduction in crime, the fear of crime, anti-social behaviour and in reducing the harm that drugs cause to communities, individuals and their families. More broadly, the use of the technique of multi-agency partnership may reflect a broader challenge associated with governing today: namely the recognition that decision-making has multiple locations, both spatial and sectoral, and is driven by the complex interplay of forces across these multiple locations. It is hard to argue with the claim that complex challenges such as tackling crime and disorder, require input from a variety of institutional sources and in turn people have 'joined-up' problems which do not follow the bureaucratic demarcations of traditional public services. Partnerships are also meant to make a significant contribution to a number of other central PSA targets associated with the communitarian-inspired civil renewal agenda, such as increasing voluntary and community sector activity and making sure that the views of local people are taken into account. As Stoker (2004: 125) notes, it is too early to be certain of the consequences of such officially sponsored initiatives around 'democratic renewal' but it is possible that they could, if sustained, help create a 'civic infrastructure supportive of community organisations and stimulate individual political participation'.

Finally, recent years have witnessed the growing importance of regional government structures across England and Wales and the United Kingdom more broadly. There are now nine regional offices in England each with a Home Office team dedicated to supporting crime reduction. The National Assembly for Wales is responsible for comparable monitoring and advice in Wales. The main tasks of these teams in formal terms are liaison between local CDRPs and the Home Office; co-ordinating bids from the region and identifying regional priorities; and acting as the first point of contact for partnerships within the region. The regional government office crime reduction teams have been given a mandate to monitor work of CDRPs in meeting the evolving national targets and modernization agenda. According to some commentators (Byrne and Pease, 2003: 295), the regional government offices should be viewed primarily as the agencies, which act as conduits for central government funds and thus enable central government oversight of CDRPs to an extent hitherto impossible. The historical analogy with the deployment of regional governors to keep the regions passive and compliant in the Imperial Chinese bureaucratic system (Wittfogel, 1957) is a very tempting comparison to make. It is perhaps too early to be certain of the consequences of this piece of the jigsaw although the centralizing thrust of a national 'steering' government is difficult to ignore. Further research on the emergent regional infrastructure around crime and disorder reduction and community safety is required and the possibility of divergent regional political cultures and thus different 'translations' of the problems of crime control and public safety remain as yet unanswered issues for the criminological community in the United Kingdom (see, for example, McAra, 2006, on recent Scottish developments and McEvoy, Gormally and Mika, 2002, Gormally, 2005, on Northern Ireland).

Taking Stock of the National Experiment

What does this hive of legislative and institutional activity add up to? It is categorically not the end of the central state's mission to direct and modernize public services and local government, including community safety partnerships. This is not an era of 'governance without government' (Stoker, 2004: 193). Rather it is suggestive of a *dirigiste* nation-state project of self-conscious modernization and transformation of institutional practices involving a growing battery of centralizing powers and concomitant reduction of the discretionary scope for the local tailoring of policy (Stenson and Edwards, 2004: 222). Accordingly, the new preventive sector of governmental practice is both the object of national policy making and the object to be created 'at a distance' from central government, given that each locality is required to construct its own strategy and put it into practice. It is also the focus of evaluative, auditing agencies acting on behalf of the central state such as the Audit Commission and the Criminal Justice and Community Safety Inspectorate created in 2006 . Indeed, such evaluative inspection and scrutiny is an essential part of relativizing the autonomy of partnerships across the public sector (Clarke *et al.*, 2000).

The centrally propelled and Home Office-directed development of creating CDRPs is strikingly apparent across every local government authority in England and Wales and increasingly across both Scotland and Northern Ireland under the respective auspices of the Scottish Executive and the Northern Ireland Office in the first decade of the twenty-first century. In any overview of the changing national context of local crime control in the United Kingdom, more generally it is difficult to ignore the growing salience of the developing local and, increasingly, the regional institutional architecture and the allied institution-building associated with the new governance of crime and disorder and the promotion of safer communities through the partnership approach. Partnership has become both a key technique of the new local and regional governance and more specifically a vital rhetorical principle of 'prevention' and 'safety' policies. This has involved, on the surface, the re-arrangement of responsibilities between central government, public services and local government as well as the 'sharing' of responsibilities between the police and local government, alongside a dispersal of responsibilities between public and voluntary agencies and private interests in local communities. Are such developments peculiar to Britain or are they instead indicative of broader transnational shifts as implied by Garland and Johnston and Shearing? These issues are addressed in the next section of the chapter.

The Return of the Convergence Thesis? Comparative Geo-histories of Safety and Control in Europe[7]

The appeal of discovering general trends and common comparative futures across different societies has a long and at times tarnished tradition in the social sciences, stretching back to the 'founding fathers' of classical sociology (Kumar, 1978). The concept of 'convergence' is one such idea associated in the 1960s with American theorists such as Clark Kerr (Kerr *et al.*, 1973) and the claim that all modern societies and their varying political, cultural and economic forms, including 'totalitarian-communist' ones, would necessarily converge over time due to certain technological imperatives into a common 'industrial society'-type broadly reflective of the United States exemplar. Such functionalist and technocratic prediction-cum-speculation has arguably re-surfaced in much of the 'nomothetic' claims-making and pragmatic universalism of crime science and mainstream American criminology. By way of contrast, the arguments presented in this book provide a more circumspect position on the claims for convergence in prevention, safety and control internationally. As Pollitt (2001) observes helpfully, convergence generally takes place at different levels and stages. For example, there may be convergence in debate and at the level of 'talk', convergence in reform 'decisions', through to convergence in actual 'practices' and ultimately convergence in 'results and outcomes'. Such a recognition of the complexity of the levels and stages at which convergence – or continuing difference or divergence – may operate also alerts us to the importance of the historical legacies of different localities and contexts, economic, cultural and political, and how these mediate the reception of policies exported from elsewhere (Newburn and Sparks, 2004; Edwards and Hughes, 2005c: 260). In the case of European criminology, the diversity of its traditions, contexts and languages may provide great scope for comparison and in particular for the testing out of the claims of grand sociological narratives about crime control and safety such as Garland and Johnston and Shearing. Much of the discussion and ground covered in this book has its origins in this acuity to the lessons that may be drawn from the comparative analysis of the diverse contexts of control and safety as well as the shared elements of such processes. This agenda for a theoretically informed, locally grounded comparative empirical research is concerned with 'the revelation, through comparison, of governable places and objects hitherto obscured by grand narratives and the drive for general theories' (Edwards and Hughes, 2005a: 260).

Comparative criminological research suggests that there are both convergent and divergent processes at play as a result of which there is a redefinition of the governance of security and crime control occurring across Europe and in particular at the local level (Theoretical Criminology, 2005). Institutionally there is now a growing number of new actors and emergent occupational practices involving new methods and technologies – not least through the technique of partnership – of 'policing' and 'security' across many European nation-states. Alongside these institutional developments there is the parallel articulation of new 'problems', ranging from the control of local disorders and incivilities and minor but persistent street crimes, to the management of the volatile mobilities of migrant peoples. And in turn, we see the rise of locality-based, 'reassurance policing' policies which attempt to get the public authorities closer to local populations and their 'fears' (Innes, 2004).

Among some of the key points of policy and political convergence across contemporary European nations then are the pluralization of local policing and the rise of multi-agency partnerships, the growth of crime prevention and reduction strategies alongside historically dominant 'repressive' criminal justice policies. We are also witnessing the common recognition of wider social harms and problems in addition to crime per se alongside technicist approaches to the management of risks. More worryingly for liberals and human rights supporters alike these developments co-exist alongside more popular and 'primitivist' communitarian appeals for order and safety etc. in the wake of the new global mobilities and the populist law and order and security conflation of 'migrant'/'asylum seeker'/ 'terrorist'. Perhaps, the latter is the most striking of all shared European 'nightmares' matched only by the demonization of the local and 'anti-social' outcast within (see Chapters 5–7 for a full discussion of these issues).

Having noted such trans-national trends, the 'European' story is not a simple one of political and policy convergence. There remain, for example, significant differences in the degree to which the rhetoric and practice of 'evidence-based policy-making', the 'whole of government' mantra and the technicist 'what works' paradigm of policy evaluation has crossed the Channel and the Atlantic from the United Kingdom and the United States of America (Domus, 2005). David Nelken (2000: 3) has also suggested that Garland's analysis of the ways in which the state in 'Anglo-American' countries is divesting itself of some of its responsibilities in crime control has less obvious and general application in 'the state-centred societies of Continental Europe where, in some respects, it is only now that the state's responsibility to protect its citizens from street crime is becoming a top priority'. Another key divergence between nations and localities is over the very vocabulary used to translate problems of 'crime reduction', 'community safety', 'social harm', 'public security' etc. in different European societies and regions. Susanne Karstedt's (2003: 19–20) comments on the different 'translations' of 'community' in Germany as against the UK and USA are especially instructive here:

> Crime policies comprise more than a technology, a practice or a strategy. They have to be conceptualised as integrated concepts, which have emerged in a particular institutional setting and in a legal and public culture of crime prevention and control. They are decisively local and national. Specific values and symbolic meanings are as much part of them as are particular institutional designs. The difficulty of even literally 'translating' these concepts ... make the problem of 'transport', 'import' and 'export' obvious. There is no proper term in German for 'community crime prevention' that can grasp its semantic, in particular not the context of the social fabric of a neighbourhood and community. The translation only refers to the political body of the municipality, but misses out on the sense it has in the context of the UK and the USA.

The implications of Karstedt's analysis is that crime prevention is therefore as much a matter of cultural meaning as what Nelken (2002: 175) describes as 'instrumental effectivity'. The conceptual and practical problems of translation thus remain central despite superficial similarity across nations (Newburn and Sparks, 2004). Nonetheless there is currently a fast growing 'export and import' trade and flow in ideas involving criminologists, criminal justice experts, policymakers and practitioners in this field. The 'policy transfer' debate on the question of 'how does crime prevention *and safety* policy travel?' has now entered the criminological academy (see Hughes *et al.*, 2002; Newburn and Sparks, 2004; Edwards and Hughes, 2005b). The collection of studies in Newburn and Sparks (2004: 5) lend support to the editors' claim that 'it is the socio-political and cultural context in which "transfer" occurs, or is attempted, that has the most profound effect on the eventual shape and style of the policy concerned'. Such debates open up the investigation of the *intra-* or *sub-*national and *trans-*national, as well as *inter-*national developments in the governance of public safety as one of the most exciting and challenging fields for criminological research. It is clear that we may learn as much from diversity as from uniformity, both within the nations, across Europe and globally. Once again, the discussion on some of the key new objects of governance in the field of safety and control in Chapters 5–7 explores the challenges for comparative research arising out of this sensitivity and acuity to the size and scale as well as history of different places and spaces.

The collection of local English case studies in Hughes and Edwards (2002) suggests that the intra-national politics of community governance is necessarily spatialized and its understanding needs to be 'place-sensitive'. Furthermore, it is contended on the basis of such local case studies that a crucial limitation of most commentaries on the national politics of crime control, with regard to Britain and other national 'surveys'[8] is that they ignore the effect that the diverse social, economic and political histories and the consequent cultural milieux of particular localities have on the generation of problems such as crime and disorder and on the governmental responses to these problems. As a consequence, such commentaries provide relatively indeterminate accounts of the actual conduct of crime control 'on the ground', given that all loci of political authority, whether supra-national, national, regional or local, encounter an 'implementation gap' between their legislative and policy commands and the practice of government. In particular, it may be argued that central authorities are dependent on sub-ordinate policy actors to enact their commands and it is in the interstices of this interdependent relationship that local actors can resist, contest and manipulate central commands to fit their own agendas and 'translations' (see also Chapter 4). In Newburn and Sparks' (2004: 9) words, 'Influential models and dictions meet resistances, counter-discourses and extant traditions and sensibilities.'

Understanding the importance of localities is, or at least should be, central to debates over the transferability of crime control and public safety policies across diverse social contexts. Furthermore, an appreciation of this effect is necessary if policy-makers are to anticipate and minimize any unintended consequences of emulating imported 'best practice' practices that have been implemented in very different contexts and circumstances elsewhere, ranging from, for example, New York ('zero tolerance policing') to Kirkholt, Huddersfield ('repeat victimisation'). Crawford's (2000) comparative research into victim-offender mediation initiatives across specific localities in France and England lends further support to the claims made above, given his finding that specific initiatives were 'pulled in different, and often competing, directions as they try to meet the multiple aims and objectives and satisfy the divergent demands of the different constituencies' (Crawford, 2000: 207).

Conclusion

This chapter began in the first section with an exposition of some of the most influential theses on the rise of the new preventive sector and its institutional forms internationally. In the process, the implications of Garland's, Johnston and Shearing's, and to a lesser extent Lea's, theorizing have been presented, largely uncritically. Following this exposition of the grand trans-national narrative about social control opened up by their work, the chapter then outlined the broad features of the governmental project on the preventive sector in England and Wales as one national case study in the second section. This outline of the recent history of the new institutional infrastructure for crime reduction and community safety in this national context implicitly qualified some of the international claims of the grand narrativists, suggesting there are likely to be particular and contingent factors at work at both the national and sub-national levels. Finally the chapter focussed in the third section on the evidence of both convergence and divergence in the meaning and implementation of local safety and control strategies comparatively across Europe.

Much of the discussion in this chapter should be read as an attempt to clarify the main contours of the preventive turn and its institutional forms across different geo-historical contexts. Having established this institutional overview, Chapter 3 which follows focusses on what may be termed the 'instabilities' of the new community governance as realized and implemented in specific localities. Following this, the potential for 'unpredictable agency' (Clarke, 2004) of the growing cast of actors now both empowered and constrained by the new modes of governing crime and safety will be explored in Chapter 4. The next two chapters may thus be read as 'tests' of the claims encountered in this chapter. In so doing the focus in Chapters 3 and 4 shifts to the understanding of the complex conditions that mediate between 'governing rationalities' and their 'outcomes'.

Throughout this chapter it has been argued that contexts are not just the superficial covering of the real stuff of prevention and safety practices, but instead are constitutive of the very structure and content of relations that emerge. The discussion in this chapter also confirms that crime-preventive and safety-promotive policies and their institutional forms are as much about politics and cultures and the normative and ideological as about debates over techniques that 'work' according to evidence-based evaluation. As a consequence, there cannot be in Nelken's (1994) terms 'a culture-free theory of crime' and nor can there be a culture-free theory of crime prevention. Furthermore, there is in Pat O'Malley's (2004b) words, a 'constitutive role for politics' in the governance of harm and risk. And just as there can be no 'pre-political' mode of risk management, so there can be no pre-political techniques of crime prevention and public safety. These important claims will be developed further in subsequent chapters.

3

Multi-Agency Partnerships and the Governance of Security

What counts is what works.

(Tony Blair, in Clarke, 2003)

Not everything that can be counted counts, and not everything that counts can be counted.

(Albert Einstein, in Clarke, 2003)

Introduction

The international criminological debate on community safety and the multi-agency partnership approach to crime and safety has been driven by the interlaced policy questions 'does the partnership approach work?' and 'what counts as success?' These are of course vital questions which cannot be ignored. However, despite their superficial simplicity they are also extremely complex and difficult questions which open up a whole gamut of 'wicked issues' which bedevil any attempts at the 'what works' evaluation of community safety as practice and outcome rather than rhetoric. Looking at the two quotations at the beginning of this chapter, it would appear that Albert Einstein's complex conclusion with regard to counting what counts, and by implication 'what works', is a more fitting position for social scientists to adopt in assessing policy 'success' than Tony Blair's pithy soundbite. In the following two chapters I will explore these questions primarily by a detailed sociological examination of recent trends in England and Wales across different localities and institutional sites supported by discussion of comparative trends 'elsewhere' where relevant. In this chapter the major claims made by Garland and to a lesser extent Johnston and Shearing with regard to the third sector of prevention and its emergent institutional infrastructure of multi-agency, 'community-based' partnerships will be examined critically. Compared to Chapter 2 this chapter provides a change of focus from institutional structures and formal powers to questions of policy implementation and delivery and processes on the ground locally. In particular the chapter will focus on the major instabilities of governance associated with the partnership approach to community safety-qua-crime and disorder reduction. In Chapter 4, the attention will shift from 'what works' to the less often asked question of 'who works' in this fast changing policy field.

In the previous chapter, an initial evaluation of the grand narratives of the late modern crime complex (Garland) and the new governance of security (Johnston and Shearing) was presented on the basis of a discussion first of the specific *national* context of England and Wales and second of the *inter-national* trends across Europe. In this chapter the focus shifts to the processes of *local* policy implementation and the performance of community safety partnerships. It is intended that both Garland's and Johnston and Shearing's admirable call for the detailed study of the enactment of the new ways of governing will be realized and accordingly their broad skeletal analyses given 'flesh and blood'. In particular, I explore in depth the following issues raised by Garland and to a lesser extent, Johnston and Shearing with regard to the nature of the new preventive sector in the four substantive sections of this chapter.[9]

- Performance management and the 'what works' paradigm
- Partnerships and the new community governance
- Partnerships and the demonopolizing of crime prevention
- The dichotomy of adaptive and denial strategies in community safety

Accordingly throughout this chapter the relevance of Garland's broad thesis on the new adaptive strategy associated with the preventive sector for the work of community safety partnerships is evaluated and 'tested' against recent research findings and analytical commentaries, including my own body of empirical work since the early 1990s.[10] In particular, the processes and practices of governance and implementation of the new community governance project are explored 'on the ground' in specific sites and localities. It is argued that there are profound 'instabilities' and much potential for 'unpredictable agency' and 'contestation' in the field of community governance which the grand narratives discussed in Chapter 2 tend to downplay. Much of the discussion in this chapter and indeed in the remaining chapters may be read as an attempt to realize Garland's ambition for a criminology that centres the problem solving efforts of institutions and actors *in situ* in specific geo-historical contexts. This is in my view a largely thwarted ambition on Garland's behalf due to the synthesizing priority in his work of narrating the 'big story'.

Throughout this book I draw on the work of John Clarke's (2004) Gramscian critique of the governmentality literature on neo-liberalism for inspiration. Clarke's work on contemporary welfare regimes draws attention to the contradictions and instabilities of the neo-liberal hegemonic project. Crucially for the aims of this book, Clarke suggests that thinking about neo-liberalism should foreground the 'unevenness' of the impact of this governmental project. In particular, attention needs to be paid to the difficulties faced by neo-liberal reforms in having to deal with 'stubbornly persistent or deeply sedimented policies, institutions and practices that refuse to go quietly' rather than the reforming processes being interpreted as a 'fluid spread across a flat landscape' (Clarke, 2004: 94–5). Clarke's conceptualization is important in alerting us to the risk of producing what he terms a 'symptomatology' (defined as an overview of symptoms as a whole) of neo-liberalism as a result of which there is a tendency to discover examples of neo-liberal political discourse and policy seemingly dominant 'everywhere' in the world. Rather the big picture looks more like an uneven and shifting set of accommodations at the regional, national and local levels between previously dominant political-cultural formations and that of neo-liberalism (Clarke, 2004: 98). In other words, whilst neo-liberalism may intend to subjugate the world, this is not the same as suggesting it accomplishes it. 'The world is also shaped by other forces, projects, ideologies and discourses, and we should be attentive to these alternatives (whether residual and on the defensive; or emergent and assertive). They are both what makes neo-liberalism's life difficult and the source of other imaginaries and futures' (Clarke, 2004: 105). Unlike the thrust of both much governmentality literature (Rose, 1999) and Marxist literature (Hillyard *et al.*, 2004b), the analysis developed throughout this book suggests it is vital to resist the temptation to bring about too fast a closure between a central government *intention* as represented in a strategy/legislation and *outcome* as realized in actions and practices by supposedly subordinate regional or local institutions and actors. In this way, 'governing can be approached in ways that treat instability and conflict as core issues (rather than residual additions after the "big picture" governmentality has been rolled out and subjected the world)' (Clarke, 2004: 115).

Let us now focus in the sections which follow on the four issues specified above which are vital to any understanding of the unstable and conflict-ridden working of the new community governance of crime and safety in contemporary late modern societies.

Performance Management and the 'What Works' Paradigm

The Audit Culture in Extremis

As noted in Chapter 2, both Garland and Johnston and Shearing are well aware of the pervasive influence of economic and managerialist logics (replacing forms of social expertise) in the field of contemporary crime control. Although such logics have their negative consequences, these authors wish to argue that there is much creativity and rationality in the managerialized, evidence-based endeavours of the preventive partnerships in the new institutional complex. It is difficult to deny that the ideology and practices of management has had some positive consequences for public services when compared to the older 'bureau-professional', institutional settlement of the welfare state. However, other commentators, including myself, have concentrated more critically on the 'down-side' of this managerialist 'turn' in criminal and social policy and have argued for its dominant influence over much of the work of community safety partnerships in Britain, far in excess of the largely rhetorical calls for 'community participation' and 'innovative local problem-solving'. Accordingly, we may ask whether in the long-term 'partnership' may be the framework and methodology through which a multitude of over-lapping disciplinary techniques such as performance management and auditing are being impressed upon criminal justice and community safety professionals from the dispersed but dirigiste state (McLaughlin *et al.*, 2001)? There is of course a long history of auditing as processes of financial accounting in relation to the provision of public services. However, since the 1980s and 1990s there has been an intensification and transformation of such processes. Tellingly auditing moved into the area of assessing organizational and professional achievement. Meanwhile, more generally auditing now appears to be the new incarnation of the 'public interest' in relation to public services (Clarke *et al.*, 2000).

In the world of Crime and Disorder Reduction Partnerships (CDRPs), Adam Crawford (1997) noted a decade ago the fixation with 'outputs', both organizationally defined and often stage-managed. This performance management culture has certainly not declined since Crawford's pioneering work in the mid-1990s. Rather since the end of the 1990s the process has intensified and become more rigid and centrally controlled whilst local CDRPs have been forced in the context of a competitive environment of league tables and selectivity to tell stories of achievement even, at times, in the face of declining resources and chronic problems of capacity. Is it surprising that the first two rounds of local CDRP strategies in England and

Wales (1999–2002, 2002–5) saw a concentration in strategy texts across the 376 local authorities on 'easy runs' or soft targets, largely derived from police data and targeted on conventional crimes (Tierney, 2001; Hughes, 2002b). It is likely that there will be a continuing marginalization of the 'qualitative', 'long-term' and potentially 'creative' measures and targets, given the pressure from the centre and the understandable local desire to deliver on national targets in the current triennial phase of local strategies (2005–8). In turn these strategies as policy texts appear emblematic of what Bottoms and Wiles (1996) termed self-referential 'paper tales of achievement' and of course 'performance' does have theatrical associations such as 'putting on a show' for an audience. As Layla Skinns (2005: 225) has observed in her comparative local case-study research on community safety partnerships in England in the first years of the 2000s:

> A member of the community safety team in Birmingham drew an analogy between eating food from McDonalds and projects implemented to attain PSA (Public Service Agreement) money; he suggested that the PSA projects satiated the hunger of every citizen because they were high visibility and yielded quick-wins but like cheap hamburgers, these projects would only temporarily satisfy citizens' hunger for community safety.

Service delivery meanwhile may often be sidelined by such 'performative' processes. Stoker has noted that managers across the public sector in the United Kingdom under the first Labour administration (1997–2001) were swamped by the volume of special projects, discretionary funding and demands to produce seemingly endless plans; the consequences of such examples of 'initiativitis' was that they 'hone up people's bidding skills but not much progress (is made) in tackling problems' (Stoker, 2004: 163). Skinns' (2005: 238) research again highlights this tendency and, crucially, the awareness of it among local practitioners in the following statement from a member of the Lincoln community safety team:

> You have to have performance management, yes, I don't disagree with that, you've got to have some way of measuring yourself ... but it should be on outcomes rather than all this bloody bean counting that goes on ... And they should be looking at quality, what we actually deliver at the bottom end, what service are the public getting ... and we don't do much of that, and we haven't got the time to do it because we're answering all these other bean-counting things, and it's getting worse. (Skinns, 2005: 238)

Drawing on the insights of Power (1997), Daniel Gilling and Adrian Barton (2005: 164) note that '[a]udits possess an aura of neutrality and technicality that really should not be taken for granted'. More specifically,

Gilling and Barton (2005: 171) suggest that there are two kinds of potentially negative consequence that follow from making things auditable. First, there is 'decoupling' where audit becomes a world unto itself and what comes to matter more is the collection of measurable, auditable data rather than much concern with what is being measured. The second consequence is that of 'colonisation': this occurs when the values of the audit penetrate so deeply into the organization that organizational action comes to be guided by such values rather than previously held ones. Gilling and Barton go on to explore how the colonization of audit is currently having a major impact on the voluntary sector and in particular in the field of drugs work and its 'shadowland agencies' which have traditionally sought to ensure 'distance' from the state and its formal agencies. On the basis of their research findings, Gilling and Barton show that the demands of the audit are creating pressures on 'outreach' drug workers to make their work more quantifiable. In turn what gets defined as 'best practice' in working with drug users has became benchmarked by what statutory agencies do, thus 'leaving little room in the process for the "difficult" working practices of outreach workers' (Gilling and Barton, 2005: 177). By way of conclusion, Gilling and Barton (2005: 179) note that this example of 'colonisation' by audit of voluntary drug work highlights the further marginalization of local practice that does not accord with the managerialized model of crime and disorder reduction favoured by the Home Office.

It is evident from the above discussion that the 'what works' performance management regime may give priority to quantitative information which may have negative consequences for other measures of creative community safety work. In turn the 'crime audit orthodoxy' may operate with a hierarchy of information sources. In particular, police statistics continue to provide 'both the skeleton and a good deal of the flesh around which the audit is hung' (Gilling and Barton, 2005: 167). In turn, a hierarchy of which crime issues will be addressed is evident, typically included are acquisitive high volume crimes (e.g. burglary and vehicle related crimes), violent crimes, drug-related offending and increasingly anti-social behaviour and hate crimes. The issues of corporate and white collar crime are noticeable for their absence (Levi, 2004). The hierarchy of crime issues to be addressed locally thus generally accords with central government priorities.

Across Anglophone, 'neo-liberal' countries such as the United Kingdom, New Zealand (Bradley, 2005) and Australia (Sutton and Cherney, 2003) a common ambition of national governments in recent years has been to replace 'old' criminal bureau-professional arrangements with multifunctional integrated partnerships whose performance will be dominated by the requirement to produce ever more arduous, measurable and quantifiable outputs and cost-effective outcomes. There is pressure to shift professional practice more and more towards a technical process in which risk assessment is determined by standardized statistical prediction models (Hughes and McLaughlin, 2002). At the same time there are resistances to these pressures, not least among the new 'technologists' of community governance (see Chapter 4). There is a paradox here in that partnerships only work well if the soft elements are in place, such as the willingness to co-operate, trust between partners etc., yet the manner in which they are being measured is through the easily quantifiable. This may lead one to speculate that such targets and measures may become a ritualistic, paper process and will thus score low on the 'integration' front.

Rethinking Evidence-Based Policy and the 'What Works' Paradigm

I noted above that the 'evidence-based', adaptive work of preventive partnerships was celebrated by Garland (2001: 131) in large part due to the 'high level of administrative rationality and creativity' associated with their problem-solving efforts. There is obviously much to be said for evidence-based policy and practice and 'what works' criteria will have a key role to play in the ongoing reform and improved performance of public services across contemporary societies (Wiles, 2002). And yet some cautionary observations are necessary. The governance of public services generally is increasingly focussed on questions of performance and in the process its management, measurement, evaluation and improvement has now become a major concern of a complex array of governmental practices, relationships and organizations, with the result that '... evidence has become a highly valorized idea – and its absence or abuse is a matter of serious concern. The fusion of evaluation and evidence in the management of public service performance marks a distinctive shift in the field of relationships between governments, publics and services ' (Clarke, 2003: 1). To paraphrase Clarke (2003), whose paper addressed a Social Policy audience, this conjunction of evidence, policy and practice in the development of improved crime control and safety services might be interpreted as a matter of celebration for the Criminology community in the United Kingdom following the years in the wilderness during the ascendancy of neo-right politics. Clarke (2003: 20) goes on to ask the following questions for social policy analysts which also speak to criminologists. 'Do we not hear ourselves being hailed in the commitment to a systematic programme of evidence-based reform?' 'Do we not hear ourselves being summoned to be useful to government – to assist and befriend?' I would add 'who could disagree with the challenge of rational, scientifically driven policy making conjured up by the new "crime scientists", "scientific evaluators" and the "new criminologists of everyday life"?'

Viewed positively the comparison between the vast amount of public information and data on levels and types of crime available in the United Kingdom, for example, with that in most continental European countries is striking and its potential use for 'enlightened' policy making should not be lightly dismissed (see Morgan, 2000). Nonetheless, it is suggested here that the Criminology community should be cautious and somewhat sceptical about this conjunction of 'evaluation, evidence and evangelism' (Clarke, 2003; Hughes and Stenson, 2006). There has not been a particularly creative and expansive notion of, nor debate about, 'what works' and what is to be counted in the United Kingdom. First, for understandable reasons, those working in the preventive field and in community safety partnerships in the United Kingdom have been largely uncritical, in public at least, of what is a highly prescriptive top-down approach from a dirigiste state (see Chapter 4). In the United Kingdom, the government's declared commitment to pragmatism, in the form of 'what works' and 'evidence-based' practice, is obviously a welcome relief from the New Right's dogmatic insistence on 'competition'. In addition, central departments such as the Home Office provide copious guidance and direction on how to measure 'what works', 'success' and 'progress'. But is this conducive to undertaking imaginative, long-term crime prevention, never mind ambitious, locally nuanced community safety work? Evaluation research remains politically and intellectually constrained and compromised. In turn it is linked to what may be termed the apparent 'technicisation' of government as illustrated above with regard to the 'audit explosion' (Power, 1997). It is becoming increasingly obvious that 'success' in the reduction of crime and disorder is, in the short term, largely synonymous with what can be counted, audited and easily targeted. The pressure to deliver 'what works' and to minimize risks ensures that 'tried and tested' (situational) crime prevention initiatives continue to be prioritized over potentially more ambitious social programmes of prevention and safety (for a fuller discussion of the implications of the 'what works' paradigm for a public criminology see Chapter 8).

Mike Maguire (2004) offers a compelling 'insider/outsider' account of the recent history of the most ambitious programme of evidence-based crime reduction ever undertaken in England and Wales between 1999 and 2002. According to Maguire, the Crime Reduction Programme (CRP) benefited initially from an unusual 'window of opportunity' when such a programme appeared attractive to a whole range of key players, from newly elected government ministers, administrators, practitioners to leading criminological researchers (including Maguire himself). This resulted in a level of funding for pilot projects and evaluations that was unprecedented in the field of crime prevention. Maguire then goes on to plot the less than happy unfolding of this story of an initially research-driven, evidence-based governmental experiment. In particular, Maguire shows how, although originally conceived as research-driven, the programme was sold rapidly to politicians as contributing primarily to the government's challenging crime reduction targets. 'Although initially conceived essentially as a set of *experiments*, or pilot projects, the CRP was sucked even as it commenced into the wider government reform agenda and expected to contribute significantly (and quickly) to the achievement of *performance targets'* (Maguire, 2004: 218; emphasis in the original). The ideal of 'evidence-based policy' became subverted by the political imperative of 'quick wins' , leading some to suggest cynically that the programme was an instance of 'policy-based evidence' rather than 'evidence-based policy' (Maguire, 2004: 227).

Since the demise of the CRP, Maguire (2004: 226) contends that there has been a retreat from innovative, research-based evaluations of 'what works':

> While the notion of 'evidence-based practice' remains very much part of these new performance regimes, in general it is based less upon continuing research and evaluation than upon sets of simple precepts about how to analyse and respond in the short term to local crime problems (typically, through the use of Anti-Social Behaviour Orders, target hardening, targeted policing, or surveillance by CCTV).

Alongside the limits built into the narrow conception of evidence-based practice in government circles, there are institutional and intellectual challenges around learning and training in 'what works' for practitioners and policy makers as 'change agents' (Cherney, 2003) facing strategic dilemmas in the field of community safety. It will be argued in Chapter 4 that the work of local agents is not just about techniques but also involves normative and political questions for every practitioner 'doing' community safety. To date much of the push on training in 'evidence-based practice' seems to emanate from 'above', is centrally driven and often comes neatly if simplistically packaged as 'toolkits' on 'what works'. There may be a need to move urgently beyond the 'off the shelf' or its latter day equivalent of 'off the web' naïve emulation and evaluation in crime reduction policy and practice. This is a specific area where Garland's (2001: 131) view that 'creativity' is to the fore in preventive work may require serious qualification. The extent to which this narrow approach to knowledge construction is being challenged by professional associations and related practitioner networks at times in alliance with academic researchers remains uneven and underdeveloped. This issue will be discussed in depth in Chapter 4 which follows.

Viewed cynically, the faith in evidence-based practice, the 'what works' paradigm, and the partnership methodology may be interpreted as a subtle form of denial about 'beating crime and disorder' or at least not be viewed as a politically neutral and purely pragmatic 'adaptive' solution, pace Garland. Hope (2005), for example, has contended that there was complex manoeuvring and political positioning in creating a politically 'satisficing' solution in England and Wales in the 1990s to the problem of the crisis of public policing and the growth of crime. According to Hope (2005: 374), the establishment and promotion of the multi-agency, community safety partnership approach as inscribed in the Morgan Report of 1991 may be viewed as a cynical exercise in providing a 'win/win' situation for the perceived 'failing' police given the new emphasis on sharing responsibility for crime prevention and thus off-loading the police of full responsibility. The Morgan model of multi-agency community safety through a partnership approach also ensured that local government had a role in the crime prevention field in a period when local authorities were almost an 'endangered species' given the then central Conservative government's hostility to local government. This model also provided a managerial solution for both senior local authority and police officers which excluded not just community leadership, however loosely defined, but also locally elected politicians and in turn side-stepped issues of local democratic accountability (Hughes, 1998a).

On the basis of the detailed exploration of how the performance management culture and the 'what works' approach have been embedded in the work of local community safety partnerships in England and Wales, Garland's claims regarding 'innovation' and 'creativity' in the third sector of prevention have to be tempered. Whilst not discounting the importance of seeking sound evidential bases for policy and practice (not least backed by social scientific research), the above discussion has pointed to some important disincentives to innovative, locally nuanced 'good practice' arising out of the combined logics of performance management and the 'what works' policy evaluation paradigm.

Partnerships and the New Community Governance

In Chapter 2 it was noted that Garland suggests that greater community involvement is unfolding in the preventive sector. In the case of Johnston and Shearing this emphasis is allied even more explicitly to a normative valorization of local, community-based networks such as when they argue that 'The mobilisation of local knowledge is fundamental to the construction of just and democratic forms of security governance' (Johnston and Shearing, 2003: 140). It will be evident to the reader from the discussion of 'radical communitarianism' in Chapter 1 above that I share much of Johnston and Shearing's hopes if not current optimism.

According to such optimistic assessments of the empowering potential of governance, partnerships are exemplary illustrations of 'networked community governance', built on relations of trust, interdependence and participation, rather than hierarchical command and professional control. However, the extent to which partnerships represent an ideal typical form of such networked governance is an issue that has to be resolved by close empirical investigation. I argue in this long section that both Garland's and Johnston and Shearing's positions run the risk of conflating empirical analysis with normative evaluation, with the latter appearing as both ' the endpoint of a historical sequence and the most desirable form of governance' (Clarke, 2004: 110). Certainly the current enthusiasm for *appearing* to govern in, through and by communities is particularly marked in the field of local crime and disorder reduction in both the United Kingdom generally (Crawford and Matassa, 2000) and across other Anglophone countries (Hughes and Edwards, 2002; Hughes *et al.*, 2002; Cherney, 2004; Bradley, 2005) and to varying degrees in Europe (Theoretical Criminology, 2005; Stangl, 2004).

On the basis of the growing body of research evidence to date I suggest in this section that a more accurate assessment of the realities of networked community governance 'on the ground' is that this type of communitarian participation, never mind community leadership, remains a lofty and often righteous aspiration that is very rarely realized in practice in the work of partnerships. Although there is a very visible partnership infrastructure across England and Wales, the prospects for genuine networked governance appear to be significantly hampered by the hierarchical interventions of the central state as well as obdurate local government traditions. Whilst these interventions of themselves (national targets, monitoring of performance, tight time-scales etc.) do not necessarily deny space for partnership working with local communities, they may often have the unintended consequences of undermining local trust formation, upon which effective partnership working depends (Gilling and Hughes, forthcoming). The research in Britain to date that has been conducted also suggests a tension between the sober and 'adaptive' evidence-based administration of crime reduction and the often more visceral political representations of the demand for order in specific localities (Edwards and Hughes, 2002; Stenson, 2005 and see Chapters 5–7). Furthermore, the grand narratives of change discussed in Chapter 2 largely side-step the major instabilities associated with community governance through the partnership approach. Let us now examine these instabilities associated with community governance; instabilities that are suggestive of both major obstacles to 'genuine' community empowerment in this field and the still open-ended nature of the opportunities for progressive and inventive governance through community empowerment.

: in the present conjuncture,
s the site of governance, the
effect of governance. They –
authority and capacity due to
hey also require the attention,
y and private governmental
essential repositories of values
: even 're-activated' – in the
hese new forms of local gov-
his section I contend that the
and effect of governance are
hallenge for all institutions,
nd harnessing such collective
participation. For example,
need them; it is difficult to
itimate' representatives; and
plural and contradictory en-
raphical place are often con-
and interests. On the other
emselves riven with divisions
entialized' identities and the
and representing these qual-
hold them stable for the pur-
rhetoric, communities are
ns, whilst being to varying
modern conditions. 'Despite
ntested and changeable con-
ntities)' (Clarke, 2004: 124).
ts contradictions than in the
increasingly indistinguishable policy fields of community safety and local crime control in recent decades.

Let's now examine some concrete illustrations of the instabilities associated with the reinvention of community as an 'unholy trinity' of site, mode and effect of contemporary governance. It is indeed paradoxical and comi-tragic that policies designed to tackle social exclusion often imply that 'community' is commonly prescribed to the poor, marginalized and 'excluded' and yet rarely to the more affluent and 'included' majority. As Mulgan notes, 'it is hardly progressive to distribute responsibility to the powerless' (in Taylor, 2003: 165). However, the people who live in high crime areas have generally been incidental rather than central to the practical enactment of 'community' crime prevention efforts. It has been noted, for example, that communities in partnerships across the public policy sector, even when they are (rarely) involved in programme planning such as the New Deal for Communities (NDC) in the late 1990s in the United Kingdom (see Chapter 7), have had little say in the establishment of the criteria by which such programmes are monitored. For example, in the case of the NDC in which 'communities' were involved in the projects from the beginning, Marilyn Taylor (2003: 124) notes that the monitoring criteria were pre-set by an external consultant and the 67 mandatory indicators were established at this point. To quote a 'community participant' in one such neighbourhood renewal project, 'it is about someone else's agenda. They just want you to tinker with this bit or that bit but you are never actually asked to set the priorities' (quoted in Taylor, 2003: 124). As a consequence, agencies charged with constructing community-based programmes have largely ignored the core constituency and then determine that it cannot be relied on as an agent of change (Hope, 1995, 2001). Crawford (1997: 224) has also noted that appeals to community and partnership do not necessarily undermine the expertise of specialist agencies:

> Despite the apparent critique of 'expertise' implicit in appeals to 'community' and 'partnership', the reality remains highly reliant upon expert knowledge which managerialises any significant community input or control. Rather than the end of professional expertise, 'partnerships' reconstitute a new model of professionisation.

Karen Evans' research (2004) suggests that often experts have accepted community involvement only on their own terms and that in the absence of trust in professional experts, people look to more familiar social networks and lay understandings. In some extreme but by no means unique cases, these local networks and understandings may involve reliance on the support of local 'organized' crime groups as a graphic instance of governance 'from below' (Stenson, 2005; Walklate, 2004). There are of course much lauded exceptions to these processes of marginalization of community involvement such as the award-winning Safer Neighbourhood Partnership Scheme in Birmingham in the 2000s which was focussed on 5 deprived and crime ridden neighbourhoods where it appeared that local people were not just consulted but were involved in 'steering' the projects (The Guardian, 5/1/05). What remains uncertain is 'which' local people were engaged and empowered and 'which' local people were perhaps excluded from community involvement.

Much of the critique of attempts to generate community-based preventive work and to involve communities in this work points to the problems associated with professional and bureaucratic/managerial interests in the agencies of the state at various levels. This of course runs the risk of both pathologising public agencies and valorizing the 'community' simultaneously as victim and potential saviour. In practice, things are usually more complex. In Shiner *et al.*'s (2004) study of 'community responses to drugs' in Britain, for example, important qualitative data was uncovered which highlighted the complex issues surrounding appeals to community involvement in this area. They argue that superficially at least, there is widespread support among the relevant agencies for the principle of community involvement but at a deeper level there was little agreement as to what this might mean or what form it should take. Many professionals in the drugs field were concerned about the hostility of local communities to the demonized drug-user and their seeming wish to expel drug users *tout court* from their midst. Shiner *et al.* (2004: 10) also discovered that many 'experts' such as drug and alcohol action team (DAAT) co-ordinators were acutely aware of the limits to genuine community involvement in the supposed community-based work of governmental agencies, including their own work. To quote one such co-ordinator:

> A lot of things fall down because of a lack of time and money, it's all about tokenism. We all say we involve the community and then go and do these tokenistic things – public meetings and consultation – but we don't go through a process where we educate the community, we don't think in terms of long-term investment to make the community more effective. (Shiner, 2004: 10)

Such views are perhaps expressive neither of a conspiratorial professional defensiveness nor a deliberate wish to 'managerialize' community input in partnership work but rather of the inherently difficult and demanding nature of attempting innovative, 'bottom-up' community-capacity building work.

Drawing on a Foucauldian analysis of local managers' deployment of the concepts of community, empowerment and sustainability in a community regeneration project in the North Midlands in Britain, Schofield (2002) suggests that managers in the public services did not treat 'community' as 'an already existing entity, a proper noun that refers to a solid and stable reality' – unlike the prevalent use of community both in much public policy texts and formal governmental pronouncements and equally tellingly in the 'reading' of community discourses by much of the critical academy (see for example, Crawford, 1997). According to Schofield (2002), community is not so much a descriptive term as a key concept of a managerial process whereby managers construct and mobilize selectively discourses of community and aim to make them conducive to the aims of government. In other words, there are instances of translations of community that literally 'make people up'. This is not to suggest that such translations of this capacious term will be necessarily progressive but nor should we assume in a radically pessimistic and essentialist manner that community will necessarily be articulated in regressive and exclusive ways which the work of both post-modern thinkers and critical criminologists have tended to assume (see Chapter 1 above). Schofield (2002: 680) remains normatively agnostic in arguing that 'what passes for "community" here needs to be viewed as a pragmatic, processual accomplishment that works by articulating discourse as a performative expression of the local and historical context ... Community ends up less a stable monument to the past or the future, but rather as a gathering around work-in-progress'. Meanwhile Adrian Cherney's research (2003) in Victoria, Australia on the policies and practices of community crime prevention also lends support to the thesis that the articulation of community/communities remains 'unfixed' despite the predominance of both managerialist and orthodox communitarian appropriations of these signifiers. In O'Malley's (2004b) words, 'these are the politics of knowledge exerted by expertises and their practitioners'. Such debate also raises the question as to whether there is a need for researchers to explore not just the important and contested variants of communitarianism but also the possible variants of managerialism, to varying degrees politically progressive or regressive. The power to name and interpellate subjects – including communities – suggests that power is not just restrictive but enabling. I would ask whether it is entirely fanciful to see 'holistic', 'community-based' crime prevention as one element of (at certain times and in certain places) progressive drives towards local capacity building and away from the traditional logics of reactive policing and criminal justice?

Researching the specific manifestations of community governance in particular geo-historical contexts and spaces also requires the development of analytical insights that facilitate the understanding of local differences. According to Stenson and Edwards (2004: 218), this necessitates two levels of analysis, one well-trodden and one still to be fully developed. The well-trodden level concerns the formal local politics of crime control involving state agencies and their forms of occupational 'habitus' (see Chapter 4). The less developed level involves that at which official agencies blur into more informal and communal sites of governance, for example the spontaneous, often angry gatherings, residence associations, and ethnic, religious and even 'criminal' collectivities. As Stenson and Edwards (2004: 218) observe wryly, these 'sites of governance do not necessarily minute their meetings but may, nonetheless, play a significant role in local governance'. Local ethnographic research is thus likely to open up the uneven ways in which political rationalities and community-based technologies are arranged in different localities-qua-communities by competing coalitions of actors. The case-studies by Lynn Hancock (2001) on Merseyside and Lisa Miller (2001) on Seattle, for example, represent empirical work which illustrates that the local is not synonymous with 'sites of tyrannical responses' (Hancock, 2001: 179) to crime, disorder and insecurity. Ranging across 'dramatic' examples of disorder and threats to stability, such as where to settle and house asylum seekers or paedophiles, how to control illegal drug markets, whether to zone or ban the activities of sex workers to more 'mundane' practices involving 'repair and maintenance' work in communities, we may expect to find struggles to translate issues into forms that will disrupt and forge alliances, both inter- and intra-communally (Edwards, 2005a). What evidence, for example, is there of instances of progressive communalist 'governmental savoir' – that is 'the intellectual instruments and substantive data that drive, shape and provide rationales for the governing process' (Stenson and Edwards, 2001: 211) – beyond both atavistic, communitarian moralism and the seemingly technicist, measurement-obsessed fixes of 'what works' modes of governmental savoir? These questions are beginning to be asked and complex answers unveiled in criminological research and normative analysis. They are also questions that the chapters that follow will seek to answer.

Local empirical realities and experiences of the work of community activists do, however, temper such optimism. Across the range of public-private partnership working, it is difficult for community activists to offer effective representation without the infrastructural capacity to ensure that representation and leadership are firmly embodied in the local community. It is unrealistic and unfair to expect community representatives to reflect the diversity of the views of a given community if there is neither the time nor resources to relate to the constituent communities or any forum in which to discuss the potentially different views. Whilst it is rare for representatives of the 'business community' to be challenged about their legitimacy or representativeness, representatives of officially defined 'hard-to-reach' groups such as disabled people may find themselves in a 'no-win' situation as described, for example, by Bewley and Glendinning on the basis of their research (cited in Taylor, 2003: 134): '[r]epresentatives for organizations of disabled people ... were sometimes dismissed by social and health officers as being unrepresentative of users because they appeared too articulate to be "real" users'. And of course community involvement and representation, particularly in the context of local crime and safety issues, may be a very high risk activity for local people in the most excluded communities, whether it, for example, be opposing the virulent intolerant othering of some sectarian 'host' communities or challenging the local organized crime networks around drugs and related crime markets. Taylor (2003: 141) observes that much of the work done 'with' communities is often described as 'capacity-building' which itself is a 'top-down' term that has been criticized time and again for implying that communities are empty containers into which information-knowledge have to be poured. Drawing on the work of Warburton, Taylor argues that community-based initiatives should not be viewed as involving the redressing of the inequalities of 'abilities' but rather of 'resources' and 'opportunities' to practice and develop those abilities that others in society take for granted.

Many of our most deprived and marginalized communities are witnessing a displacement of risk on to those least able to bear it. Indicative of such processes are such examples as the resettlement of previously convicted paedophiles in the most deprived and marginalized housing estates and the forced dispersal and settlement of asylum seekers in inner city areas in the first decade of the twenty-first century (see Chapters 5–7). The situation facing such 'communities of fate' is graphically captured in the following passage from the crime novelist Ian Rankin (2004: 5) describing a fictional run-down housing estate in Edinburgh and its latest inhabitants, newly 'dispersed' asylum seekers as encountered by the detective hero, John Rebus:

> Knoxland was not a popular estate. It tended to attract only the desperate and those with no choice in the matter. In the past, it had been used as a dumping ground for tenants the council found hard to house elsewhere, addicts and the unhinged. More recently, immigrants had been catapulted into its dankest, least welcoming corners. Asylum-seekers, refugees. People nobody really wanted to think about or have to deal with.

Although this is a fictional example it is one based on an all too real case of a killing of an asylum seeker in a run-down housing estate in Scotland and it speaks to other communities – 'hard places' of often trapped and hopeless people – across the United Kingdom and Europe (see Chapter 6). Such communities may be viewed as victims of top-down initiatives whereby significant numbers of vulnerable people, whether they be ex-offenders or refugees or mentally disordered people, are introduced into already vulnerable areas without either prior consultation or preparation for such settlement schemes. Not surprisingly the consequences may be a dangerously potent brew of defensive community activism. As Taylor (2003: 216) observes:

> In a shop-around society, those who can are increasingly choosing 'off the shelf' identities, politics and moralities, while those who cannot are seduced into exclusive sectarian, racist and fundamentalist politics which render the dispossessed and uncertain vulnerable as both followers and targets.

Taylor goes on to argue that even the most optimistic commentator needs to be cautious about the possibilities of 'bottom-up' community politics since the most deprived communities will always be a 'David' compared to the 'Goliath' of corporate capital and the state. At the same time, she suggests that cynicism is a luxury which abandons those who are excluded to their fate. Taylor concludes that the key challenge for advocates of progressive community change policies is 'to accommodate – and indeed celebrate – diversity and yet forge the common bonds which we need to survive. Community and civil society are the places where we want to have it both ways' (Taylor, 2003: 225).

Both Tim Hope and Ian Loader make important contributions to this broader debate on the challenges facing advocates of what Taylor (2003) terms 'progressive community change policies'. Hope (2005: 381) has argued that the New Labour government in the United Kingdom has shown a naiveté about the production of community safety in assuming that it could be guaranteed by reducing instances of crime and disorder rather than seeking to undertake the institution-building task of constituting a new security governance in the community. That noted, Hope sees a small glimmer of hope in the UK government's promotion of a civil renewal agenda (Blunkett, 2003) in that the latter appears to recognize the fundamental premise that citizens and statutory agencies actively co-produce (or rather *should* co-produce) community safety. However, when we examine the civil renewal agenda as articulated in the White Paper on police reform, *Building Safer Communities Together* (Home Office, 2004), the absence of any mention of democratic representation is striking. At the same time Hope notes that the key distinction made in the civil renewal discourse between 'active citizens' and others carries clear dangers such as creating bodies composed of the usual suspects ('local worthies') which are likely to be unrepresentative of the wider communities at large. Hope (2005) views the potential of the civil renewal agenda as decidedly volatile, offering both inclusionary and exclusionary consequences for communities. Let me quote Hope at some length on both the risks and progressive potential of this communitarian agenda:

> Communities that produce 'active citizens' already possess collective efficacy, especially the kinds of 'social capital' that enable voluntary groups to express 'voice'. Because these capacities are inversely related to the risk of crime ..., 'civil renewal' risks the possibility that those communities already possessing a degree of security will be able to command more of the support and attention of the police, thereby reinforcing 'security club goods' of their communities, capturing more of the police's resources for their safety, and diverting attention away from higher-crime communities that lack in local social capital ... There is real potential for the civil renewal agenda to create a new local governance of crime based on the notion that citizens and the state are co-producers of community safety. But there is also a danger that the communities most in need of community safety will end up doubly disadvantaged – enduring both high rates of crime

> and a deficit in their capacity to access the public services they need to ameliorate their difficulties. (Hope, 2005: 382–3)

A position somewhat similar to that of Hope is evident in Ian Loader's (2005) critique of 'reassurance policing' and its increasing importance in debates on police reform and civil renewal. Loader recognizes that the public police are both 'minders' and 'reminders' of community; they are involved in the production of significant messages about the kind of place community is or aspires to be. However, the danger of the broad 'security' mandate associated with reassurance policing, as the latest incarnation of community policing, is that it both panders to popular fantasies of total security – making it 'policing for the discontented majority' – and is likely to result in a targeting of teenage and minority groups as the objects of policing. Noting that the 'war on terror' is reminding us once again, anxious citizens make bad democrats, Loader (2005: 22) sees the challenge as follows:

> If policing is to be capable of recognizing, rather than denigrating or silencing, the security claims of *all* citizens, and in this way fostering a sense of common belonging, the task is to create what Charles Tilley suggestively calls a 'shared identity space' – institutional arenas in which competing demands can be listened to, argued about , and negotiated on a recurrent basis. Bringing the claims of anxious, disgruntled majorities, and insecure, misrecognised minorities, into common democratic processes of this kind may even help dispel the forms of *ressentiment* that fuel the contemporary cultural politics of pervasive security.

Both Hope and Loader's interventions throw up urgent questions regarding what may constitute a progressive and inclusive politics of belonging and recognition. It speaks to the broader public criminological debate on the rethinking of notions of the shared 'public' and 'social' that runs throughout this book. The worrying alternative to such rethinking of safety/security as a shared public good may in Loader's (2005: 22) words be a society that fractures into 'a world of markets and tribes'.

The extent to which governmental practitioners and local actors – including academic researchers and commentators – confront these issues routinely in their discourses and practices of governance needs to be fully examined and debated as a central question in this policy field. In concluding this lengthy discussion it would appear that Garland's positive characterization of the nature and extent of community involvement – not to say leadership – in the field of local crime control and community safety seriously underestimates both the instabilities and barriers to, as well as dangers of, local communitarian social control and needs to be tempered by a hard-headed realism but not fatalism. It is widely, and in my view correctly, agreed by many commentators, including Garland and Johnston and Shearing themselves, that the appeal to community is at the epicentre of major transformations in the relationship of citizens to political authorities in many advanced liberal democracies. Community-based governmental experiments certainly provide an acid test of policy-oriented learning about contemporary crime control and safety promotion. Meanwhile the very capacious character of community governance offers different political actors the opportunity for advancing their particular agenda for policy change. As Adam Edwards and myself have argued previously,

> The elusiveness of what 'community' actually means in relation to crime control, the absence of any clear consensus over what constitutes 'community-based crime control', 'community safety', 'community crime prevention' and 'community policing' etc., is a product not of intellectual vacuity but of the political struggles to define the responsibilities for, and strategies of, crime control. (Edwards and Hughes, 2002: 5)

These political struggles still await sustained and long-term empirical and normative scrutiny by criminologists and allied social scientists. However, it is hoped that the subsequent chapters of this book alongside the discussion here will help take this research agenda on communities forward in some positive ways.

Partnerships and the De-Monopolizing of Crime Prevention

Garland (2001) and Johnston and Shearing (2003) have claimed that the new preventive partnerships offer the rich promise of a de-monopolisation of expertise and responsibility for crime prevention away from the usual suspects (police and allied public agencies of the state) and increasingly incorporating and harnessing the forces of 'civil society'. In this section we ask the question 'how far has responsibilisation and de-monopolisation been realized in the processes of local implementation of the community governance of crime and safety? In the previous section we noted that community engagement, never mind leadership, of local crime control and safety strategies remains at best rhetorical in nature and is certainly a trend that continues to be restricted largely to the level of formal consultation in most community safety and crime prevention work. There is very limited evidence in the United Kingdom to date that the bottom-up concerns of differentially layered communities have been of much significance to community safety partnerships, other than in the formal requirement to 'consult' local communities, including 'hard to reach' groups (Hancock, 2001; Hughes and Edwards, 2002; Newburn and Jones, 2002; Gormally, 2004). Meanwhile the influence of private business is not overtly pronounced in local partnership work and especially in their public proceedings. However, much of the mobilization of private forces may occur 'behind the scenes' and may be of growing importance as Garland predicts (see, for example, research on 'urban boosterism', regeneration and safer city politics discussed in Chapter 7). The role of the private sector and capital may well differ depending on the specificity of local contexts and political and economic histories, particularly in the major cities of the west. That said, in the United Kingdom context the preventive-reductive sector is still largely a 'top-down', central state-driven project rather than being what Crawford envisages as networks of interlaced agencies drawing from the public, private and voluntary sectors as 'the bedrocks of the new governance' (Crawford, 2001: 60).

Almost all community safety partnerships across England and Wales and increasingly across much of Scotland and Northern Ireland in the first years of the new millennium may be characterized as duopolies managed by the police and the local council. Accordingly, there appear to be severe limits to the extent and degree to which responsibility and thus de-monopolization has been spread out to new actors and agencies. Indeed, 'responsibility' for developing and implementing local crime-reductive and safety-promotive strategies has routinely been left in the hands of beleaguered annd often demoralized local authority community safety teams, supported by the local police. Meanwhile the symbolic ownership of the crime reduction problem has remained in the hands of the public police in most localities. Genuflection to the public police's authority and wisdom is still common in the public performance of local partnerships in England and Wales, and, it would seem despite the paucity of research to date, in Scotland and Northern Ireland. Most partnerships remain dominated by traditional policing concerns and to a great extent, the work is targeted crime and disorder reduction rather than more expansive community safety promotion. That noted, local crime control and policing of disorder is a much more crowded space when compared to previous decades. One possible scenario in the future is the prospect that local authorities and their community safety teams will take on increasing amounts of the lower level local policing with the proliferation of community safety and neighbourhood wardens and anti-social behaviour order 'enforcers' (see Chapters 4 and 5 for a detailed discussion).

There is now a well-established body of research in England and Wales since the 1980s that has shown the limits to, and conflicts associated with, multi-agency working (Pearson *et al.*, 1992; Crawford, 1997; Hughes,

1996b, 1998a) and which has been confirmed by more recent qualitative research (Skinns, 2005). Indeed one of Skinns' (2005) respondents in the Birmingham community safety partnership described the local partnership as, 'a group of people with barely concealed mutual loathing, forced together in the never-ending search for money' (Skinns, 2005: 156). Meanwhile a member of the Birmingham community safety team interviewed by Skinns (2005: 131) again made the following comment:

> What are our priorities in this partnership, because currently it's like a big tanker isn't it, drifting on a sea of social issues, and everybody can see it, but nobody really knows where it's going. You stand on the sea-shore and you see this huge ferry going by, and it says community safety on it, and somehow it gets bigger every time you see it, but you have no idea really where it's coming from, and where it's going.

Many statutory agencies, for example, in large CDRPs have remained present only in a representational capacity. In turn the local authority departments that have proved to be the most difficult to engage with CDRPs, such as probation, social service and education departments, are those that might be more inclined, due to their occupational cultures and sense of core business, to question the legitimacy of the narrowly circumscribed crime and disorder discourse of many CDRPs. As Gilling and Hughes (forthcoming) have noted, crime prevention is characterized by a political struggle between the extremes of an inclusivist, pan-hazard and essentially liberal community safety approach and a more exclusionary, enforcement-oriented and potentially illiberal crime reduction. This struggle may be played out in interagency politics, with some agencies and their representatives wishing to have nothing to do with the police. There remain a number of agencies that do not feel that crime prevention is really their 'business'. Historically health agencies have maintained a detached position from the field of crime and disorder reduction. The 2003 Police Reform Act in England and Wales, for example, expanded the list of responsible authorities to include primary health trusts and the fire service, and it promoted the merger of CDRPs and Drug Action Teams (DATs) in an attempt both to overcome the autonomy of certain partners and to build greater interdependence (Gilling and Hughes, forthcoming). It remains a mute issue whether this expanded and 'extended family' of legally responsible authorities for community safety will push these agencies deeper into the 'criminalisation' of social policy or push the work of partnerships into a more expansive public health direction and encourage the 'socialisation' of crime control. My own research observations in the field in the first years of the twenty-first century suggest that both tendencies are unfolding with as yet uncertain long-term consequences for the performance of CDRPs.

Gilling and Hughes (forthcoming) have also observed that the breadth of the pan-hazard model of community safety may itself be a potential barrier to trust formation. This may explain why agencies more interested in community safety have tended to shy away from involvement with most CDRPs because of the latter's narrow crime and disorder reduction agenda. On the other hand, some local authorities have been able to sit comfortably with the police precisely because they have narrowed their vision to that of crime and disorder reduction and as more welfare and social democratic discourses of social regeneration have given way to market-led discourses of physical regeneration and 'urban boosterism' by city authorities keen to attract capital investment into the local economy (see Chapter 7). As a consequence they have also narrowed the field and created the foundation for trusting relations, albeit largely based on central government departments such as Home Office and Office of the Deputy Prime Minister (ODPM) agendas. Meanwhile, non-statutory, voluntary agencies are often pulled into relations of dependence on local and central government due to their efforts to secure contracted funding for their work. CDRPs are generally dominated by statutory agencies and one reason for this may be that they possess a high degree of institutional and cultural similarity: for example, they are large organizations with vertical structures of accountability up through senior managers to central government; they are staffed by front-line bureau-professionals etc. Agencies that do not correspond to such properties may find it more difficult to fit into CDRP business. This includes voluntary agencies and of course even more so the 'community' itself which lacks a clear structure into which statutory agencies can easily tap (Gilling and Hughes, forthcoming).

The discussion in this section has highlighted the difficulties in assuming – often on the basis of a textual reading – that partnership working in community safety and the new institutional infrastructure has brought about either the de-monopolization of formal agencies' authority and power or, concomitantly, the responsibilization of new forces and agencies outside the state. Accordingly, the thesis of a simultaneous de-monopolization of professional and public power and widening reponsibility and empowerment of non-professional, civil forces appears empirically questionable and conceptually over-stated.

Adaptation and Denial in Community Safety Partnerships

In this section of the chapter the final theme to my sympathetic empirical 'testing' of the grand narratives on the new preventive sector is explored. In the discussion which follows I contend that the seemingly contradictory and bifurcatory relationship between a pragmatic and adaptive strategy and an expressive and punitive strategy of the state highlighted most starkly in Garland's work may be subject to more complex forms of mutual hybridization than his thesis suggests. The contemporary politics of crime control and community safety in the United Kingdom are thus more complex and diverse than the choice of either a punitive politics of vengeance or a rational problem solving and adaptive strategy.

To return to Garland briefly (and echoing Johnston and Shearing's thesis), it is claimed that the new preventive sector is institutionalizing a new logic of prevention and risk managment:

> Its very existence exerts a small but insistent pressure that tends to push police away from retribution, deterrence and reform and towards a concern with prevention, harm-reduction, and risk management. Instead of pursuing, prosecuting and punishing individuals, it aims to reduce the supply of criminal events by minimising criminal opportunities, enhancing situational controls, and channelling conduct away from criminogenic situations ... Community safety becomes the chief consideration and law enforcement becomes merely a means to this end, rather than an end in itself'. (Garland, 2001: 171)

In the specific context of CDRPs across the United Kingdom in the first decade of the twenty-first century being cajoled and encouraged by both central and local political pressures to 'tool up' in increasingly coercive, enforcment-oriented and expressive ways following the government's orchestrated crusade against the anti-social in its myriad forms, Garland's broad conclusion above on the new preventive sector and the work of its partnerships looks prematurely and sadly optimistic.[11] Rather, a growing number of community safety partnerships and local authorities appear increasingly to be the new local branches of the 'culture of vindictiveness' towards the dangerous and 'awkward' members of the 'underclass' that Garland identifies elsewhere in the punitive strategy. As early as 1999, Rob Allen (1999) noted the punitive and coercive dangers associated with the CDA agenda before the 'big push' on the disorderly and anti-social following the Anti-Social Behaviour Act of 2003. According to Allen, there were tensions between the evidence-based approach and the call for the much greater involvement of local people in designing and implementing local solutions ushered in by a CDA described by the then Home Secretary, Jack Straw, as the 'triumph of community politics over detached metropolitan elites'. However, Allen (1999: 22) noted that more worrying was the prospect of local crime reduction strategies assuming an 'increasingly repressive edge'. Noting the well-acknowledged balance between social and situational measures, seeking respectively to prevent the propensity of people to offend and those looking to restrict opportunity by target hardening or surveillance, Allen discerned an emerging third preventive component which he terms 'coercive crime prevention'. This new component involves the local and flexible use of the police and the courts to deter or remove the seemingly intractable problems caused by difficult people. Measures first piloted in the CDA such as the Anti-Social Behaviour Order (ASBO), the local child curfew, the power to remove truants and so on all added to the armoury of existing local authority powers to deal with anti-social tenants. Writing in 1999, Allen noted that how these powers would be used in the aftermath of CDA remained unclear. With hindsight it would appear that initially and before the Anti-Social Behaviour Act of 2003, many councils declined 'the offer' to use repressive banning orders against anti-social behaviour available in the powers vested in them by the CDA. However, in the aftermath of the rushed through legislation of 2003, councils and CDRPs have been encouraged to develop their coercive crime prevention armoury, following the mandate to be much more visibly tougher on disorder. And of course there are resources available for investment in the new anti-social armoury and expertise which may sweeten this coercive pill for under-resourced community safety teams (for a full exploration of these developments see Chapter 5).

Further research on the ground and across different localities is still required to know if the problem-solving measures collectively known as social crime prevention will, in Allen's (1999: 22–3) terms, be squeezed between the situational and the coercive. However, much of the routine work of local CDRPs in the first decade of the new millennium has been associated with a narrow brief of controlling specific types of street crime rather than other harms, such as corporate crimes and incivilities. At times this has been allied to an authoritarian, quasi-communitarian posturing on controlling incivilities and disorders, arguably related to the problem of controlling the consequences of the long-term residualization of social housing in the most deprived areas of Britain since the 1980s (Hope, 1998). As Crawford (1997) has observed, partnerships may have the potential to encourage 'a stronger and more participative civil society' but it is just as probable, if not more so, that they will promote 'a defended exclusivity'. Interventions against crime and disorder provide acid tests of community governance because the emotive sentiments associated with victimization can easily segue into popular support for direct, and potentially vigilante action. In this context the empowerment of citizens to participate more directly in their own government presents a 'strategic dilemma', for just as the opening-out of decision-making processes to broader participation has the consequence of fuelling forms of 'street justice', so the insulation of these processes from popular concerns, as in bureau-professional models of governing, can result in the same consequence (Edwards and Hughes, 2002: 9–10).

Local developments associated with more coercive prevention strategies are also being influenced by an emerging grass-roots, populist 'community' politics around law and order which is often but not exclusively far-right in political orientation. Hope (2004) suggests that the CDA-inspired partnership ethos is unable to handle this but this visceral local politics of belonging and othering is pressing hard on local councillors who in the 'modernized' local government context of newly empowered and reformed political management and leadership, as elected representatives, are the local community's main political conduit (see Chapter 4). The growth of populist politics around crime and disorder and community 'belonging' appears to constitute a key process that is likely to shape the current politics of community safety. Particularly worrying is a revamped politics of 'race', ethnicity and immigration, mixed toxically with fears over asylum seekers, new migrants and terrorists, post 9/11, following the invasions of Afghanistan and Iraq, and post- 7/7 London bombings (see Chapters 6 and 8). Whilst the recent emergence of 'evidence-based' policymaking forms part of the attempt to 'modernize' public administration and suggests that policies ought to be premised on evaluative research findings, about 'what works' in delivering public services such as reductions in crime and disorder, this approach competes (within the preventive sector and its partnerships) with the long-standing trend in the political representations of the 'law and order problem' for short-term electoral and mass media advantage. In the light of the above, the prospects of a socially inclusive preventive and rights-based approach, never mind a genuinely 'pan-harm reduction' paradigm of community safety (Wiles and Pease, 2000), do not look promising. It may be that we are entering the era of 'governing through safety and security' in which the articulation of solidarity through, rather than counterpoised to, 'criminologies of the other' is an increasingly central theme, not just in local partnerships in the United Kingdom but also unevenly across contemporary European politics (Edwards and Hughes, 2005b and see Chapter 8).

Hope (2005: 380) has argued that the growing emphasis on the central role of statutory agencies in reducing crime and disorder is perhaps sapping the remaining reserves of informal social control in communities and civil society. The unintended consequences of this governmental approach may be potentially deeply damaging to community safety as a public good and may auger the rise of the coercive prevention approach that Allen identified and with which the discussion in this section began. According to Hope (2005: 380) the risk here lies in creating the following vicious circle. First we have a decline in tolerance (approximating to zero), caused by encouraging the public to invoke authoritative (i.e. statutory) controls at a higher rate. In turn this also increases demands for preventive measures against ever more mundane nuisances as more of everyday life becomes policed and regulated. Perceived gaps in provision and capacity then arise in the legal and other administrative measures available. And so on in an ever-increasing regulatory spiral. Rather than the strengthening communities, such strategies paradoxically contribute to the overload of the institutions of formal control by rendering more visible and public the problems with which they are required to deal. Meanwhile the subsequent failure of statutory agencies to deliver control and safety may further diminish public trust in statutory authority, while putting very little in its place.

Such a scenario cannot be easily reconciled with either Garland or Johnston and Shearing's optimistic claims about the new preventive sector. Instead it suggests that the dichotomous distinction between the rational adaptive strategy of prevention and the irrational denial strategy of punitiveness seriously downplays the influence of the 'punitive turn' on the work of preventive partnerships within the community governance of crime and safety more generally.

Conclusion

This chapter has provided a critical evaluation of the claims associated with the grand narratives of the preventive turn first encountered in Chapter 2. In particular the four sections of the chapter 'tested' these claims empirically in terms of the implementation and processes of delivery of community safety and the governance of security at the local level. In the first section the consequences of the dominant performance management culture was evaluated and questions asked as to the rational and innovative nature of this audit regime and its managerial practices. In the second section it was argued that the extent to which there was a genuine commitment to community engagement and leadership in partnership working had been exaggerated by both Garland and Johnston and Shearing. This section drew particular attention to the instabilities of attempts to govern through communities. At the same time these instabilities were not merely about constraints and limitations to more participative, 'bottom-up' governing but were also likely to throw up opportunities to inventiveness in local politics. In the third section it was suggested that the claims of a simultaneous de-monopolization of control and authority over the work of partnerships and dispersal of responsibility for community safety to new actors was exaggerated by Garland and Johnston and Shearing. For the most part preventive partnerships remain duopolies of the public police and local government. Finally in the fourth section Garland's thesis of a bifurcatory (twin-track) and contradictory relationship between a rational, pragmatic and adaptive preventive strategy and an irrational, expressive and punitive strategy was questioned. Instead the discussion in this section was suggestive of mutual hybridization across the two strategies in which a coercive form of crime prevention was possibly emerging.

Overall the discussion in this chapter suggests that the multi-agency partnership approach to the community governance of crime and safety is indissolubly linked to political and moral contestations about the nature of the relationship between the state, public authorities, citizens and communities. Accordingly it is reducible to neither good managerial practice nor to technical efficiency, however important these may be. Despite Garland's accentuation, and at times seeming seduction by, the neoliberal 'new criminologies of everyday life', his analysis stimulates criminology to re-centre cultural, political and social processes into the study of the field of crime control. At the same time, the discussion in this chapter has contended that there is a potential reading of both Garland's and Johnston and Shearing's theses which runs the risk of over-predicting and over-reading the determinate nature of the 'global' trends and processes at play in this fast moving and contested field of prevention and safety. This appears to be the case with grand narratives of the preventive turn that underplay the uneasy melding of governmental mentalities and the potent and volatile mixes that result. In accord with much governmentality literature, Garland shows a tendency to offer an over-integrated account of contemporary forms of governance. Furthermore, local studies of crime control by criminological 'water-carriers'[12] alert us to the limitations of broad theoretical theses which postulate coherent processes of ordering, whether authoritarian/progressive or rational/irrational in character, and which in turn underplay the sheer messiness and the contradictory character of crime control and safety practices on the ground. In recognizing these tensions between the general and the specific in research and theory, I have returned to Garland's own intellectual starting point and have hopefully made a small contribution to the further refinement of our thinking on crime control, community safety and social ordering in late modernity. The detailed exploration of the *new expertises* and *political agency* of practitioners of the community governance of crime and safety that follows in Chapter 4 aims to deepen further the work undertaken in the present chapter.

4

Expertise and Agency in Community Safety and Local Crime Control

The actual practice of partnerships can ... be understood as a contingent outcome of ... struggles to translate problems of crime control and the quintessential role of key actors who are capable of apprehending strategic dilemmas and acting as spokespersons for an imaginative repertoire of responses to these dilemmas.

(Edwards, 2002: 157)

Introduction

In this chapter the focus turns to the new actors employed and deployed in the field of community safety and local crime control. Several key questions structure the discussion that follows. What is the nature of the expertises associated with this seemingly increasingly pluralized field of work? What are the main areas of conflict and compromise between different actors? Is there a dominant occupational 'mentality' or 'habitus' shared by such socially situated actors? It is around the issue of 'who works and how' as well as 'what works' that this chapter is structured. There are two major sections to this chapter. In the first section, the detailed exploration of the habitus and the knowledge, skills and values of local government community safety experts in CDRPs is provided. The exploration in this section may be read as an empirical case study of the historical and collective 'career' of community safety practitioners. The discussion in this section concludes that Garland exaggerates the extent to which the community safety manager 'habitus' is constructed around the ideas of the 'new criminologies of everyday life'. The second section then examines the increasingly pluralized division of labour around local policing and the governance of security as well as the emerging influence of non-professional political actors in community safety.

The long-term criticism of local CDRPs has been that they have failed to deliver in terms of tangible 'outcomes' in reducing crime and disorder and increasingly *fear* of crime and disorder. This criticism has prompted the development of more 'bodies' on the ground ranging from community safety wardens, police support officers to private security patrols. Are such trends leading to a harmonious 'extended' policing family or more a case of antagonistic 'neighbours from hell'? As practitioners located in new, 'joined-up' institutional sites and working interstitially between both organizational and professional forms of authority and discipline, the practitioners of community governance have to manage themselves in an overlapping series of potentially contentious and politically infused relationships: between the local, the regional and the national; between agencies; between conflicting policy objectives and discourses ('regeneration', 'crime reduction', 'community safety', 'zero tolerance' etc.); and between conflicting representations of the community ('unitary', 'diverse', 'inclusive', 'exclusive', 'cohesive', 'divided' etc.). Policy advocacy coalitions and different ways of thinking are likely to emerge that will seek to 'problematize' policy and practice agendas in specific ways. During the last three decades across the United Kingdom, for example, there has been a massive proliferation in posts and teams dedicated to the pursuit of the by no means easily reconcilable goals of both community safety and crime and disorder reduction. The community safety manager and increasingly her team stand at both the tactical and strategic centre of this new institutional architecture. However, to date there has been a paucity of empirical research on these new workers in the emerging division of labour.

The following discussion aims to correct this empirical and theoretical silence in criminology first by an exploration in the first section of the knowledge and skills base and complex 'habitus' of one of the key new 'partnership' experts, the community safety manager-practitioner and then in the second section by comparing these experiences with those of other actors in the growing cast of partnership players and the so-called extended policing family (Crawford *et al.*, 2004). This discussion represents a provisional and tentative sociological exploration of a new institutional division of labour under construction before our very eyes. By the end of this chapter, a provisional sociology of 'who works' in the community governance of crime and safety should have emerged.

This chapter continues the critical conversation begun in Chapter 3 with Garland's ground-breaking work of synthesis on comparative trends in crime control in late modernity. In particular, the discussion which follows accords with Garland's methodological injunction for social scientists to adopt a Weberian, action-oriented approach and to focus on 'the real human stuff of disposition, choice and action' (Garland, 2001: 23). To quote Garland (2001: 26):

> Socially situated, imperfectly knowledgeable actors stumble upon ways of doing things that seem to work, and seem to fit with their other concerns. Authorities patch together workable solutions to problems that they see and can get to grips with. Agencies struggle to cope with their workload, please their political masters, and do the best job they can in the circumstances. There is no omnipotent strategist, no abstract system, no all-seeing actor with perfect knowledge and unlimited powers. Every 'solution' is based upon a situated perception of the problem it addresses, of the interests that are at stake and of the values that ought to guide action and distribute consequences.

Doing Community Safety Work

In the last two decades the typical job descriptions of the community safety manager in England and Wales have generally been worded as follows:

Example 1: 'co-ordinating effective policy and strategy developments in areas of crime reduction and community safety, working closely with relevant partners (particularly the police) in line with the statutory responsibilities'.

Example 2: (i). 'to enhance community safety in X by managing and co-ordinating the delivery of X Community Safety Strategy, ensuring effective partnership working and a holistic approach to community safety and the reduction of crime, disorder and the fear of crime'

(ii). 'to develop, manage, co-ordinate and promote effective community safety initiatives across the city'.

The centrally propelled, and hierarchically controlled development of creating CDRPs and the range of new expert officers has been strikingly apparent across every local government authority in England and Wales given their statutory duty since 1998 (together with the police) to develop local partnerships with triennial strategies for reducing crime and disorder. Similar initiatives are being developed in Scotland and Northern Ireland albeit with some differing 'translations' of these policies and practices (see McAra, 2006, Gormally, 2004 and see the web sites of the Scottish Executive and Northern Ireland Office). By the beginning of the twenty-first century there has been a growing number of community safety teams – of managers, officers, project workers, police secondees, co-ordinators employed in drug action and anti-social behaviour teams etc. – which form part, however uneasily, of local and regional governmental structures. The community safety team has usually been the 'engine-room' of both the full partnership – a 'talking shop' meeting 4–6 times a year – and of an executive group made up of the responsible authorities, which effectively sets the goals and tasks of the partnership. In turn in the larger urban contexts community safety partnerships and their teams have tended to develop sub-groups or working teams, geographically – based or thematically – focussed (for example, on anti-social behaviour, domestic violence and so on). Such developments raise major questions about where the new institutional expertise and its division of labour may be heading.

The 'Habitus' of Community Safety Experts

In attempting to decipher the contours of the new expertise of community safety practitioners, I draw on Pierre Bourdieu's concept of 'habitus' (1977). This engagement with the ideas of sociological theory also helps move the debate on the community governance of crime and safety beyond the dominant, narrowly technicist and tactical paradigm of 'what works' in crime reduction. The discussion here examines the contested nature of the knowledge, skills and values base of the work of community safety as currently experienced by practitioners across different locales. A crucial element to this argument is that the politics of articulation of what constitutes community safety 'work' remains unfinished. Indeed this work continues to slide uneasily and with contradictory effects between the at times conflicting and at other times collusive agendas of a technicist Home Office-based 'crime reduction' approach, a moralizing communitarian concern with 'disorder' and 'anti-social-ism', and the vestiges of a social democratic vision of 'social regeneration' and 'community safety' going back to broader social programmes of the welfare state.

I noted in Chapter 2 that both Garland and Johnston and Shearing make big claims for a new 'habitus' or 'mentality' among key players in the new crime control establishment. In turn it is argued this new mentality is based on the actuarial and situational, risk management-oriented, 'new criminologies of everyday life' and their techniques. According to Garland (2001: 127–9), crime is no longer seen retrospectively and individually but rather prospectively and in aggregate terms. The new focus for practitioners is not people but places and it is a 'supply side' criminology, concerned with shifting risks, redistributing costs and creating disincentives. In the following discussion I contend that such claims for the growing influence of the 'new criminologies of everyday life' and a 'risk management mentality' on the routine work and mentality of the new experts in community safety both in England and Wales and more generally across late modern, 'risk' societies, whilst important, may be over-stated.

What is meant by the concept of habitus and why might it be a valuable tool for the sociological study of knowledge and practices of community safety experts? The social reproduction and durability of dominant, and to a lesser extent oppositional, social relations have been famously explored by Bourdieu (1977) in his elaboration of the role played by habitus in institutional processes. Of late this concept has been employed to explore the field of public policing and its abiding occupational cultural forms (Chan, 1997). The concept is especially instructive in helping us explore occupational groups and their shared working philosophies in periods of transition. It also sensitizes us to the distinction between 'the institutionalized perceptions, values and schemas' (Chan, 1997: 92) of the particular occupation's work as against the 'field' (the formal rules that govern public services such as the police, probation or social workers) in which it takes place. The concept of habitus also alerts us to what may be termed the mediated internalization of the actor's environment and social location over time (Cooper, 2001: 124). As a consequence, habitus provides a useful way of explaining social stability, especially in its naturalization of past experience to form present preferences and interests in certain groups, institutions etc. It elucidates how routine practices are crucially shaped by the intersection between the present conditions within which action takes place and past conditions and experiences that shaped the way an individual's habitus was formed. In particular, habitus can draw our attention to three main things. First, the social constitution of 'good sense'; second, the ability of practices and commitments to 'outlive' the context in which they were formed; and third, the way in which new environmental conditions or institutional norms, such as legislative reforms, may both clash with the prevailing bias of particular actors' habitus, while also converging to produce new, complex, unpredictable subjectivities, rationalities and forms of purposive activity (Cooper, 2001: 125–6). Whilst theories of social reproduction have often been criticized for their inadequate recognition of agency, Bourdieu's concept of habitus provides one way of making space for agency without sacrificing the capacity of the social to reproduce itself. These insights are of obvious academic interest in terms of a sociological understanding of the experiences of a new occupation but they are also of importance for 'policy learning' in this case in the fast changing field of community safety.

The Post-1998 Experiences of Community Safety Practitioners

It is clear from the previous discussions in Chapters 2 and 3 that the watershed legislation of the Crime and Disorder Act (CDA) 1998 was not painted on to a blank canvas across the diverse localities in England and Wales. Some local authorities and their key local agents, either in response to the call-to-arms of governmental circulars, or for their own political reasons, had already established their own community safety capacities and sense of the 'field' a good deal earlier (including local authorities in Scotland, Crawford and Matassa, 2000). Again it is important to recognize that there are distinct and unevenly developed geo-histories of community safety across different localities in the United Kingdom. These also generate distinct policy coalitions of actors with different powers and liabilities (Edwards, 2002). The reality of a pre-existent community safety habitus among some partnership actors with their own constitution of 'good sense' was a consequence of this process. Furthermore, a majority of community safety practitioners in the immediate post-1998 period were previously employed by local authorities, and a large proportion of these had previous community safety experience (Hughes and Gilling, 2004: 138). The fact that a large proportion of current managers have had prior community safety work experience is significant for one particular reason. In the pre-1998 days, local authorities were not constrained by the statutory requirements of audit, consultation, strategy and so forth. Those who obtained their experience in such times inevitably had their expectations and habitus shaped by it, and thus there is a question of exactly how receptive such people were to the kinds of changes heralded by the CDA, subsequent practice guidance and further legislative changes outlined in Chapters 2 and 3. To what extent, for example, did the new institutional norms post-1998 both clash with the prevailing habitus and converge to produce new subjectivities and forms of purposive action? Just as probation officers in the United Kingdom in the 1990s exhibited some (unsuccessful) resistance to change in the occupational shift from social work to community punishment and risk management (Nash, 2004), so we might expect to find similar forms of resistance in experienced community safety managers. It is worth remembering that community safety developed in part as a more expansive alternative to hard-nosed (situational) crime prevention, and, on the basis of my own current fieldwork among practitioners it often appears to be regarded equally as a more inclusive 'replacement discourse' to the Home Office's narrower vision of crime reduction and enforcement. That said, there have been both experienced managers and more recently appointed members of community safety teams who took on the Home Office crime and disorder reduction vision, for both professional as well as pragmatic reasons. However, a 'health warning' is again in order given that we still await rigorous and cumulative, longitudinal research evidence regarding the precise nature of the changes taking place in the occupational culture or 'cultures' in this field (Hughes and Stenson, 2006).

At this point it is pertinent to ask whether the 'permanent managerial revolution' of the UK central admininistration (McLaughlin *et al.*, 2001) has reconfigured community safety actors' 'pathways' in a similar way to that which the 1988 Education Reform Act did for educational actors, despite the considerable ideological and professional opposition to the reforms at the time from the teaching profession (Cooper, 2001: 137). The jury must remain out on this matter and research findings to date have been largely restricted to just one of the key sets of actors, community safety practitioners, in what is an increasingly variegated and pluralized institutional field and division of labour. That noted, my own research with Daniel Gilling (Hughes and Gilling, 2004) on community safety practitioners is suggestive of competing and contradictory views being held simultaneously. What are we able to discern about the habitus of community safety practitioners, and in particular CDRP managers from the limited survey and ethnographic research evidence to date? Given that community safety is a relatively new domain, it is pertinent to note that community safety managers demonstrate a commitment to it, expressed particularly in terms of their aspirations for their work as a 'professional' specialism. In the national survey by Gilling and myself respondents were asked if they envisaged staying in community safety for the foreseeable future, and a response in the affirmative from 83 per cent of the sample was received. Given that the average age of respondents was 40, and that 70 per cent of them were qualified at least to undergraduate degree level, this showed a relatively high level of commitment from experienced and well qualified practitioners, who were more likely to have made a positive choice for community safety rather than simply 'fallen into it' as a job. Asked to indicate the extent of their agreement with a range of different statements, 65 per cent agreed that 'there should be a formally recognized professional association for community safety officers' (12% disagreed); 56 per cent agreed that 'there should be a national system of professional qualifications' (17% disagreed); and 55 per cent agreed that 'there should be a national set of occupational training standards and minimum standards' (18% disagreed). While the quest for professional status is always open to the allegation that it is self-seeking, the level of agreement with these statements appeared to suggest a recognition of the specialist and complex nature of the community safety task. This task requires a complex set of skills and knowledge bases, and perhaps these managers and officers recognized this in agreeing that there should be set standards and qualifications, and a recognized professional association that might be involved in discussions concerning the future development of community safety. If there is majority support for a professional identity, the question still remains as to precisely what that identity might look like. Is there a core professional ideology to community safety work? The survey did not paint a totally clear picture by way of an answer and more qualitative research studies remain to be done. For example, 19 per cent agreed with the statement that they should focus exclusively upon crime and disorder reduction, while 72 per cent disagreed; however, 64 per cent agreed with the statement that community safety should be judged on its contribution to social and economic regeneration as much as on crime and disorder reduction.

Arising out of this research evidence we need to be mindful of at least three futures for the occupation increasingly across the United Kingdom. First, there is a socially inclusive model that sees it as occupying a place within a framework of both preventive work with offenders and others 'at risk' and the broader goal of social and economic regeneration. Second there is a narrower model of it as a highly technical and managed form of crime reduction, responding to an agenda set by the Home Office and the police. Third there is the 'crusade' to turn community safety into the struggle over the persistent anti-social and criminal minorities in communities and for a moralizing twist on 'respect'. From the responses to Gilling and Hughes' survey in 2001–2, the majority view from within the occupation veered more towards the first rather than the latter two, thus confirming an impression of local practitioners as a potential locus of resistance to both the narrow crime reduction agenda and the moralizing communitarianism of the 'respect' agenda. However, there is a potentially big difference between what local experts *think*, and what local partnerships and community safety teams *do*, especially when it is not just the local authority agenda that managers have to contend with. Tales of heroic aspirations are doubtless easier to make claims about in the context of a questionnaire than when observed and interviewed *in situ*! However, there is support for this impression of resistance and 'paper compliance' in the views aired by practitioners in surveys I have undertaken under the aegis of the UK-wide National Community Safety Network (NCSN, see www.community-safety.net/) and in various fora which I and others (for example, Burney, 2005, Prior *et al.*, 2005, Hughes and Follett, 2006, Skinns, 2005, Parr, 2006) have observed in ethnographic research.

According to 'Third Way' thinking (Giddens, 1998), the old world of the local government professions was based on the pursuit of cognitive exclusivity, public deference and policy closure. Increasingly local authority organizational structures have supposedly moved from single profession/bureaucratic 'silo' departments towards larger, multi-disciplinary organizations. New patterns of governance are meant to take individual professionals into areas distant from their core disciplines. The decline of 'the discipline' has thus undermined the exclusionary strategies of the professions. In turn the public sector professions are no longer framers of policy problems. Government now looks to supposedly 'neutral' competence (especially of management and auditing) in trying to reclaim a lost objectivity, with the professions viewed as part of the problem rather than its solution. As Garland (2001: 273) notes,

> in the new field, it is not the case that all experts and professionals have been downgraded. Rather it is those professional groups most associated with the social rationality (probation offices, social workers, community workers, sociological criminologists) whose influence has declined, and the professionals associated with the new economic rationality (auditors, accountants, managers, information technicians) who are in the ascendancy.

Despite the broad truth in this claim, this is not to suggest that there is clear evidence of a strong de-professionalization thesis at the level of individual practice. In the specific case of the still aspirant community safety expertise, professionalism in the form of education, training, recognized body etc. remains an attractive route to both career and status. However, what appears particularly significant about the present period is that the professions are generally trailing rather than leading change. This seems broadly to be the case with community safety practitioners across the United Kingdom. Nonetheless, despite this 'hostile' environment there are indications in the first decade of the twenty-first century that practitioners in part by means of such advocacy coalitions as the National Community Safety Network have been making stronger claims to knowledge for themselves rather than accepting uncritically and passively the strictures and dictatorial 'guidelines' coming from on high from such central government bodies as the Home Office.

Mobilization of an Advocacy Coalition: the Case of the NCSN

Let's briefly focus on some of the policy and practice interventions of the National Community Safety Network (henceforth NCSN).[13] These interventions may be best understood as examples of the mobilization an 'advocacy coalition' which is capable of apprehending strategic dilemmas and acting as spokespersons for an imaginative repertoire of responses to the strategic dilemmas of community safety practitioners (see the quotation from Edwards at the beginning of this chapter). Between 2004 and 2006, the NCSN undertook a series of surveys of members and produced reports which may be viewed as attempts to give 'voice' to local practitioner concerns over the dominant though by no means monolithic central and regional governmental agenda[14] on measuring 'success' and improving 'partnership performance' and on the local management of 'anti-social behaviour'. Such reports also represented attempts to mobilize alternative policy and practice 'translations' of these issues that sought to reflect the predominant habitus of local practitioners.

Much of the work of the NCSN in giving 'voice' to the concerns of local practitioners focussed on the poor management of CDRPs and community safety work more generally. In this type of policy intervention, 'constructive' criticisms have been levelled at the central/national as well as regional and local levels of government. It is evident that in its reports NCSN have employed the language of new public managerialism, inventively, comfortably and self-consciously, and in ways that both spoke to the dominant policy discourse of our times but also challenged its specific manifestations and consequences. Perhaps most significantly to date, the NCSN undertook a survey of members' concerns over 'barriers to performance' (NCSN, 2004a) that preceded the Home Office's major review of the CDA in November 2004. Seven key barriers to improved performance and 57 specific examples (!) associated with these barriers were identified in the study. These barriers (supported by quotations from practitioners 'on the ground') ranged from

- 'legislation and guidance' (e.g. 'new strategies launched with little resource back-up'; 'often unrealistic timescales for implementation');
- 'organisational barriers' (e.g. 'partners lack commitment'; 'poor communication between partners and with the community');
- 'staff issues and capacity' (e.g. 'lack of top level commitment and leadership'; 'lack of recognized career structure');
- 'processes' (e.g. 'lack of project management'; 'poor communication and marketing');
- 'community engagement' (e.g. 'adverse impact on the fear of crime'; 'poor/no involving of the community in delivery');
- 'funding' (e.g. 'short-term'; 'complex application/allocation process');
- 'improving performance on individual crime types or in particular settings'.

This trans-local expert chronicling of the collective concerns of practitioners may be indicative of a growing confidence of this network of practitioners – as an advocacy coalition within the broader conditions of the new preventive governance – in attempting to respond proactively to rather than follow passively central government agendas. In its formal submission to the Home Office's Crime and Disorder Act Review of 2005–6, NCSN contributed a provocatively and ironically entitled report ' "A Vision of Paradise" – The Ideal CDRP in Ideal Conditions' (NCSN, 2004b).[15] This report had the formal aim of 'setting out a vision of the ideal partnership [that] will help us all to improve. We are committed to making a major contribution to raising the standards by lobbying Government and by supporting our members, and we intend to update and refine this vision as part of that contribution' (NCSN, 2004b: 1). In this report thirty features of the ideal partnership were outlined which clearly departed dramatically from the common experiences of CDRPs and community safety practitioners that the 'barriers to performance' survey had highlighted. Each feature was in turn cross-referenced to the Home Office's own template themes on 'guidance', 'structures', 'delivery', and 'funding and data' for CDRPs. The report may be read as a clear example of a discourse that 'speaks to power'. As a participant myself in the Home Office's Crime and Disorder Act Review, the insights associated with this intervention from a practitioner network and policy coalition, together with others such as the Local Government Association, were of influence in the review process despite the difficulties it raised, particularly for central government officials among others. Note, for example, the irresistible logic of the call for more 'joined-up' thinking and practice from central government departments in the light of the Home Office's strictures in the past for local joined-up work outside agency 'silos'!

NCSN as an advocacy coalition of local experts has also intervened in the debate on anti-social behaviour (NCSN, 2005), not least in attempting different policy translations of the problem from that of the Home Office's Anti-Social Behaviour (ASB) Unit. Again, drawing on the perspectives of local practitioners, the NCSN report detailed in clear managerial 'speak' four major areas which all statutory players, ranging from the Home Office's ASB Unit to local authorities and allied partners, needed to confront. In particular, the report suggested a number of specific recommendations for improved performance around 'priorities and target setting', 'resources and costs', 'definition and information issues' and 'consistent management of anti-social behaviour'. In the course of its exposure of some of the problems in implementing this new area of policy and practice, I suggest that a subtle ideological challenge was made to the dominant enforcement logic of anti-social behaviour measures associated with the ASB Unit. For example, we may note the translation of the issue of anti-social behaviour along more 'preventive' lines based on sound managerial good sense in the following extract, '[m]embers felt that the broad nature of anti-social behaviour and a lack of standardized anti-social behaviour data recording made target setting problematic and that targets were often vague and too focussed on enforcement at the expense of preventive work' (NCSN, 2005). In conclusion, a possible 'checklist' for more effective anti-social behaviour work was drawn up, involving:

- a standardized framework for actions and assessment;
- protocols defining roles and responsibilities across agencies;

- a range of preventive measures as an initial response;
- training and staff development plans;
- systems for relevant data to be collected and managed in an effective, pre-arranged manner (NCSN, 2005).

None of the above discussion on the work of the NCSN as an example of a trans-local UK practitioner network of course assumes that these interventions from a policy coalition will be 'successful' as projects for mobilizing new agendas on policy and practice in the area. Just like central government agendas, they represent of course 'projects' not 'outcomes'. However, the articulation of such agendas does appear to speak again to the instabilities of governance and the necessary 'power dependence' between central policy makers and local policy implementers (for a fuller discussion of strategies on anti-social behaviour and local/central governmental tensions and unsettlements, see Chapter 5).

To repeat the claim made in the introduction to this chapter, it will be crucial to explore in future research how the new local experts in community governance working interstitially between both professional and organizational forms of authority and discipline attempt to manage themselves in an overlapping series of potentially contentious and politically-infused relationships – between the local, regional and central; between agencies; between conflicting policy objectives; and between different representations of the community and such like. As 'professionals' mediating between the state and the public, the new experts in the community safety field are also potentially vulnerable to different senses of obligation and trust: to the state as employer and as 'collective/popular will'; to the client as embodied public, as need, as purpose; to the emergent 'profession' as specialist, colleague, peer; to 'rational' evidence-based approach to policy change and learning and 'democratic' responsiveness to popular fears over crime and disorder etc. (Clarke, 2002; Hughes and Gilling, 2004).

Risky Business? Knowledge, Skills and Values in Community Safety Work

If we follow the logic of the 'new penology' thesis (Feeley and Simon, 1992; Hughes, 2002c), the chief role of community safety experts in the next decade will increasingly be that of making the risks of crime and disorder more identifiable and visible and of advising and instructing others on their successful *management* (rather than their eradication and prevention). The expertise of such actors would thus reside in discovering, gathering and processing knowledge about in/security and risks of crime and disorder, not least through the techniques of the audit and performance management targets. This risk society thesis has been most famously applied to the police by Ericson and Heggarty (1997). If this diagnosis is viewed as being applicable to the public police, it could also be applied to the emergent role of the community safety managers and their teams in multi-agency, and increasingly inter-sectoral, partnerships. As noted in Chapter 3 above, it is evident that CDRPs are routinely and centrally involved in the collection of vast amounts of performance management information and data. Much of the coordination of the collection of the data, the calculative assessment of the success, the setting of targets for the management of risks resides in the office of the community safety manager and her team. Given this key position in the pluralized arrangements for policing crime and disorder, it could be argued that these managers and officers will be increasingly central as risk-knowledge brokers (potentially challenging the police's past and current ascendancy in crime prevention and community safety partnerships). Indeed we might speculate on the chances of community safety teams being seen as one of the 'favoured children' of central government's modernization project for both local government and criminal justice, given their remit to address 'wicked issues' through 'joined up', targeted 'problem-solving' approaches which carry none of the 'old baggage' of bureau-professional compartmentalization. Less heroically, the odds may appear to be on the community safety practitioner of the first decade of the twenty-first century being a mix of 'jobbing' auditor, facilitator of never-ending partnership loops, and competitive and entrepreneurial bidder for (often short-term) project funding from central government. As a consequence, much of their routine work may reside in developing increasingly bureaucratized audits and output-based strategies. The non-heroic twist here would be the absorption of community safety teams in the production of 'easy win' measurable performance indicators of success in crime reduction audits and strategies. In de Maillard's (2000: 17) expression (regarding France's local project leaders in the field of urban security), this image would reduce such actors to being a basic technician of public action ('un simple technicien de l'action publique').

Despite the appeal of such a vision of the future career of such preventive practitioners, the extent to which this makes them 'brokers in information on risk management' may have been over-played in both national and international overviews of developments in community safety in the 1990s and beginning of the new millennium, including my own (McLaughlin *et al.*, 2001; Hughes and McLaughin, 2002). It remains uncertain as to whether the tasks of community safety practitioners to date have been dominated by these risk management priorities. As Adrian Cherney (2004) has noted with regard to related developments in the state of Victoria, Australia, a more pressing imperative for community safety practitioners may be that of reconciling the difficulties of managing organizational change and not least, the shift to inter-agency working across still distinct, 'silo'-style departments and agencies (see also Bradley, 2005, on similar developments in New Zealand). Indeed, if we wish to understand the place of notions of 'risk' in the shifts in forms of both safety and security, it is crucial that researchers analyse the specific sites and the decisions and actions of the reflexive agents who carry the 'risks' associated with safety practices and policies and their implementation (and possible 'failure').

According to some critical criminologists, CDRPs are both emblematic of, and help constitute, the new neo-liberal mode of both entrepreneurial and a more dispersed, coercive governance (see, for example, Scraton, 2003 and Chapter 7). The tendency of much community safety work to fit this neat and compelling story of both change and new ordering is difficult to ignore. CDRPs clearly inhabit the audit-, and performance target-obsessed culture of the managerial state as indicated, for example, by any critical textual analysis of the second round of local audits and strategies since 1999 in England and Wales (Hughes, 2002b). However, the neo-liberal managerialist and actuarialist thesis does tend to foreclose the future and silence the unevenness and sheer chaos of much of the social regeneration and crime control practices 'on the ground' in differing localities and experiences in situ. O'Malley (2004b) has cogently argued with regard to the new governance of risk that the common assumption in much governmentalist literature is that disciplines and professions are portrayed as being passively operated on and selectively neutralized by the logic of actuarial justice/risk management. This assumption is not one that should be taken for granted as it underestimates the resistances and instabilities of governing through risk. Indeed, at all times 'there is the politics of knowledge exerted by expertises and their practitioners' (O'Malley, 2004b: 20).

It may be argued that Garland side-lines from his analysis of the preventive habitus criminological work which is not narrowly 'scientific' and 'administrative' in character, such as the critical, sociological traditions of theory and practice in criminology and analyses generated by the 'new social movements' (anti-racist, feminist, gay and lesbian etc.) (Young, 2003a). Contemporary community safety strategies, as texts, certainly speak to and through the discourses of the administrative and situational criminologies, often in heightened performance management forms. Indeed these same texts may be saturated with these ideas because they are part of the requirement of 'playing the (Home Office) game', fulfilling the required narratives of accomplishment of the prescriptive central state and acting in accordance with its in-house administrative criminologists' copious guidance on 'best practice' and 'what works'. Thus when we dig deeper and talk to actors in situ there is often an unsettling of this apparently dominant intellectual paradigm. For example, it is evident that the ideas of, and practices promoted by, the 'new criminologies of everyday life' certainly sit alongside 'quieter' work, for example, on hate crimes and the rehabilitation and resettlement of offenders. On the basis of my own research involving the new community safety experts, it is evident that social democratic and 'critical' narratives have remained institutionalized in the habitus of the new specialists, as 'habits of thought and action' (Garland, 2001: 161) often co-existing alongside the technicist, risk management narratives of situational reduction and administrative criminology. In fact the influence of feminist and related 'anti-oppression' discourses is evident in the local strategies for all to see in, for example, the prominence given to 'zero-tolerance' regarding (domestic) violence against women, children and other vulnerable groups. Similarly the attempts to target 'hate crimes' against minorities of various types also speaks to the anti-oppressive narratives of both critical criminology and new social movements (see Chapter 6). To take one illustrative example, it is telling that Blagg *et al.*'s (1988) early research on multi-agency crime prevention partnerships concluded that both domestic violence and racially motivated crime were rarely addressed in these fora in the 1980s. By way of contrast, Phillip *et al.*'s (2000) post-1998 survey discovered that 86 per cent of the community safety partnerships centred domestic violence as the most commonly cited priority. Furthermore, claims about the role of social deprivation and social exclusion as both causal factors in criminalization and narratives of concern have not been expunged as issues for partnerships and their key actors, despite the pressure for quick, situational rather than longer-term, structural 'wins' in most preventive and safety work.

One way of seeking to gain an impression of what community safety work is, or at least how it is interpreted locally and in situ as a competence, is to ask practitioners what knowledge and skills they use, and think *should be used*, in their day-to-day work. To return to the national survey by Gilling and Hughes, a range of knowledge bases understood to be central to the community safety task were uncovered. The ranking in terms of priority was ordered as follows by respondents, with the first ranked knowledge base standing out well in advance of all others, and the fifth, sixth and seventh bunched some way behind all others:

1. the causes and prevention of crime
2. the policy context of local government and community safety
3. communities (e.g. in terms of their social make-up and diversity)

4. organizational culture and behaviour
5. research methods
6. different approaches to management
7. public relations

The survey also listed a range of skills that were understood to be central to the task, and once again asked practitioners to rank them in order of importance. The ranking was ordered as follows, and as with the first knowledge base the first skill stood out well in advance of others, while the seventh and eighth lagged well behind the rest:

1. inter-professional working
2. communication
3. community development
4. management
5. evaluation
6. auditing
7. information technology
8. public relations

Respondents were also asked for additions that may have been omitted from the original list and once again, specific forms of management were mentioned, while refinements to inter-professional skills included a number of references to *negotiation, conflict resolution* and *political skills*. One set of skills not anticipated by the researchers but that were mentioned quite frequently were those of *dealing with complexity, patience* and *coping with stress*, all pointing to the heavy and sometimes unrealistic demands that may be made of managers and officers and in turn local partnerships (Hughes and Gilling, 2004: 141–2).

In interpreting the results of these responses to questions about knowledge and skills, it is clear that these practitioners appeared to de-emphasize what may be described as the *technical* sides of the task – hence aspects such as research, auditing, evaluation, IT and public relations all tended to occupy positions of less importance. The results of the survey suggest that practitioners tended to eshew the Home Office's idealized vision of the 'crime scientist', versed in techniques such as crime mapping and crime pattern analysis. More recent fieldwork observations in the mid-2000s suggest that this 'resistance' to the 'science of crime reduction' model has remained prevalent among these local experts. By contrast, what has tended to be emphasized are the *political* and *local* aspects of partnership work, giving the impression that the work requires delicate negotiation between agencies, within and between communities, and among local elected representatives; and that it needs to be closely tailored to variable local circumstances. These findings may come as a surprise given the ascendancy of technicist and performance management discourses in this policy field (see, for example, the proliferation internationally of governmental crime reduction web-sites, 'knowledge banks' and 'toolkits' for successful crime reduction). How might such resistances to dominant, technicist discourses be explained? A number of possible explanations suggest themselves. It may be that practitioners recognized that the demands that were placed upon them were unmanageable: quite simply, too much was expected of them, and consequently they had to prioritize certain aspects of their role, thus using certain knowledge bases and skills and elements of the pre-1998 habitus, and not others. In prioritizing certain aspects of their role, the technical aspects may have been the easiest ones to de-emphasize in turn for a number of reasons. For example, it was possible for them to offload technical tasks on to others. Similarly, local authorities or their police partners also have research or analysis capacities, so those difficult technical questions about auditing, crime analysis, monitoring and evaluation potentially could be left to others – or, as is often the case in crime auditing, external expertise could be bought in. Technical knowledge and skills (using complex computer software such as geographical information systems, analysing statistics, techniques of information sharing etc.) are in short supply more generally, and community safety officers and managers often lack them. With limited training in such areas, managers may have perceived such things to be unduly difficult, and thus worth avoiding. Finally, the de-emphasis on technical knowledge and skills may have been a more deliberate political strategy on the part of these actors. It remains uncertain whether community safety managers and partnerships more generally will – or should – be able to resist the undoubted appeal of new technologies for information gathering and sharing, such as the police's National Intelligence Model in England and Wales. The latter model has been increasingly employed in partnerships and may of course undermine the previous resistance of some local partners, particularly if the police provide the technical infrastructure for this latest technical 'silver bullet'.

It is arguable that the CDA, in its haste, assumed a level of infrastructure that simply was not there: repeating mantras of partnership and joined up government does not suddenly make them appear! Many community safety practitioners may therefore have prioritized the political and local side of their knowledge and skills because they were acutely aware of the fragility of local infrastructures. It must be remembered, after all, that community safety is a relatively new policy area for many, and it lacks the solid local political constituency of many other policy domains, compared to which it remains low profile. This resistance to 'technocracy' may be illustrative of the way in which new environmental conditions and institutional norms may have both clashed with particular actors' habitus, while also producing new complex and still unpredictable subjectivities and forms of purposive activity.

In the mid-2000s community safety practitioners inhabit a rapidly changing policy terrain that is contested, and occupied by political tensions and contradictions. They are aware of the very strong and hierarchical influence of the Home Office and to a lesser extent the Audit Commission: responses in the 2001 survey by Gilling and Hughes, for example, showed these two bodies to be the most influential by far, compared to other bodies such as the Local Government Association, the now disbanded Community Justice National Training Organisation (CJNTO) or the National Community Safety Network. Since the survey was undertaken, other central government departments, such ODPM, Department of the Environment etc., have had a growing influence on local community safety work although not, as yet, on the scale of the Home Office. On the basis of the research evidence to date, it would appear that most practitioners do not embrace the narrow technicist, 'what works' crime reduction agenda that has been promoted by the Home Office since the late 1990s; and the skills and knowledge bases that they concentrate upon in their own work would not necessarily greatly further this agenda. As managers and practitioners, most appear to aspire to a strategic, long-term, future-oriented and preventive approach suggestive in part of Johnston and Shearing's risk management mentality. But this mentality or habitus is not actuarially amoral but rather wedded to a more welfarist and socially causative framework. This may suggest a vision of community safety, for some, in keeping with the social regeneration agenda, where crime and disorder are indicators of the social dislocation that such regeneration seeks to address and help prevent. There are also complex safety policy projects emerging from central government departments beyond the Home Office. For example, the development of Local Strategic Partnerships and community strategies, combined with initiatives such as the New Deal for Communities Programme, the Neighbourhood Renewal Fund and Safer, Stronger Communities Fund from the national government in the United Kingdom may help to push local community safety down this 'regeneration' path (see Chapter 7).

There is, however, no smooth, uncontentious development of a long-term, social inclusion, strategic 'mentality' among these local workers. For example, community safety managers often express the short-term, 'tactical' view (Hough, 2005) that the police have been by far the best local agency to work with, while agencies such as probation, education, social services and health have been regarded as problematic and at best 'seat warmers'. We know from specific case studies (Phillips, 2002, Skinns, 2005, Follett, 2005) that there have been persistent problems trying to engage other parts of local authorities, less committed to a policing mandate. It is little wonder that the police have proved to be the best partners, since the local partnerships and strategies have provided the police with opportunities to 'share out' the problems of crime control and thus meet their own tactical performance management-driven objectives. The danger lurking here is that, despite the inclusive aspirations of local authority community safety officers, community safety is drawn into a police agenda centring on the crime-policing nexus, which may reflect narrow, short-term and managerially-driven crime reduction, or a bifurcation in which local authorities and their community safety units get 'lumbered' with the management of low level crime, disorder and incivilities, leaving the public police to target the serious crime, thus raising the distinct prospect of a form of two-tier local policing. These countervailing forces raise the distinction that goes to the very heart of crime prevention: namely is it better served by crime-specific strategies or by those that seek to create the general social conditions that might drive out crime and disorder and help build new institutions of a more inclusive civil society (Hope, 2001)? From the findings and analysis offered above, many practitioners in community safety appear to manifest a habitus which accords as, if not more, closely with the 'old' liberal social democratic mentality as that of the neo-liberal, technicist and risk-oriented turn of mind.

The Pluralization of Community Safety and Local Policing on the Ground

In the discussion that follows some of the most important issues associated with the new ensemble of actors, statutory and voluntary, public and private, regarding the implementation of local crime control, local policing and community safety are examined. The exploration of these interactions and likely new networks – as well as the common constraints and old networks across the field – may complicate any over-deterministic views of crime control and instead alert us the salience of 'agency, conflict and choice' (Stenson, 2002: 114) in this policy field. Once again, the discussion here should be read as an initial exploration of a political and policy terrain that still awaits a sustained body of longitudinal empirical research. I again focus largely on UK developments, although there are some important parallel developments across other advanced liberal democracies.

It is nigh impossible to accurately calculate the exact numbers of actors, old and new, whose work is now focussed on the increasingly intermeshed issues of local policing, crime control and community safety. In part this is a consequence of the necessarily porous nature of such local crime control and safety-promotive activities. It is also a result of the common tendency for community safety to appropriate other pre-existing practices under its name, for example, from youth outreach work to specific police initiatives. Partnership work may, to use an educational term, at times commit the crime of 'plagiarism', namely stealing the work of others whilst claiming it for oneself (Skinns, 2005). Despite the difficulties in arriving at an accurate calculation of the numbers now employed in the hybrid world of community governance of crime and safety, there is undeniable evidence that the new policy terrain has generated many new recruits into the 'extended' community safety/policing family. What remains as yet uncertain is whether the labour of the new occupations – community wardens, anti-social behaviour officers, DAT co-ordinators, community police support officers etc. in their interactions with more established occupations from the police, youth workers, registered social landlords, other specialist professions as well as voluntary and private bodies will be a case of 'teeth gnashing harmony', to use Althusser's evocative term (Clarke, 2004), rather than genuinely 'joined-up' inter-agency governing. Put tersely, is it a tale of 'happy families' or 'neighbours from hell'?

Across the 376 community safety partnerships in each local authority area currently in operation across England and Wales in the first years of the twenty-first century, the majority now have dedicated community safety teams, ranging from as few as two people in the small population authorities to whole departments with as many as 80 staff in some of the larger metropolitan boroughs. Although there is still a 'duopoly' of the local government and public police in most CDRPs (as noted in Chapter 3), one of the most important changes associated with the local crime and disorder reduction strategies following the Crime and Disorder Act Review of 2006 has been the growth of 'on the ground' service deliverers, in the shape of a mixed economy of visible security patrols involving community/neighbourhood safety wardens, community support officers, 'quality of life'/'anti-social behaviour' teams and such like. If the icon of crime reduction and community safety in the 1990s in the United Kingdom was the omnipresent CCTV, the icon for the 2000s appears to be human 'guardians'. Viewed positively, these developments may be a sign that partnerships are moving from the phase of 'process' focus to that of 'outcome' focus. As Crawford *et al.*'s (2004) pioneering research indicates there is now an established mixed economy of visible security patrols incorporating a range of sworn police officers, special constables, community support officers, neighbourhood and street wardens, other forms of municipal policing, private security guards and citizen volunteers. In particular, Crawford *et al.* (2004: 63) noted that:

> This research has revealed a growing economy of residential patrols, one that is likely to expand and become more established over the forthcoming years. The end to the police monopoly of reassurance policing in residential areas is now an acknowledged aspect of contemporary policing.

Officially, it is often claimed, for example, that neighbourhood or community wardens (established since 2003) have the potential due to their local presence and problem-solving brief to support local 'at risk' communities particularly in the reduction of anti-social behaviour. Crawford *et al.*'s (2004) findings again suggest that locally dedicated visible patrol personnel that do engage and work with local communities can have the potential to provide people with a stake in their own security, help foster 'social cohesion' and assist in the regeneration of areas. However, the extent to which these local 'guardians' will deliver what is increasingly termed 'reassurance policing' (Innes, 2004) or what may be termed the 'soft end' of community policing remains uncertain and largely unproven in research terms. Rogers (2005), for example, argues that community support officers do offer a visible presence 'on the streets' but have only limited effectiveness as representatives of authority. He argues that they are unable to assist effectively in the 'order maintenance' function of the public police due to the lack of legal powers and the public's uncertainty about their powers and duties. What appears more certain is that policing is becoming increasingly more fragmentary with sworn officers (the public police) focused on crime fighting rather than patrol duties that will be delivered increasingly by an array of local agents. According to Crawford *et al.*(2004: 60–1):

> Relations between additional policing and normal police range along a spectrum from co-production, co-ordination, indifference, competition to hostility ... Co-ordination deficits not only are a product of the nature of local relations between different policing organisations but are also structured by central government and the lack of, or presence of, genuine joined-up thinking.

With regard to the new social problem of anti-social behaviour, Burney (2005) has noted that the role of 'registered social landlords' has developed into a more explicitly regulatory and repressive one with difficult tenants. There has been a confluence of social housing and crime policy largely as a result of social housing in recent decades becoming a site of crime control. This development in turn is linked to social housing's status as a residual tenure for society's most marginalized groups. It is now not uncommon to find dedicated anti-social behaviour units, often located in local authority housing departments. In November 2002, the Home Office reported that it had found that over 90 local authorities had a named person to lead or co-ordinate action in the new specialism of anti-social behaviour. Just as we saw the emergence of the new occupation of the community safety officer in the 1990s, so we are now witnessing the rise of the anti-social behaviour officer as a potentially new career path in the local governance of 'problematic' behaviour in the 2000s. We are also seeing a growing 'two way traffic' between local police forces and local authorities in terms of secondments for such multi-agency work. It is now almost universal practice to have police officers' seconded to work with local authority community safety teams. Indeed most CDRPs have dual officer co-ordination of the partnerships work in the persons of a local authority community safety manager and police inspector or sergeant, reflecting the long-term duopoly of the local authority and the police in almost all CDRPs since the early 1990s. In some areas, such as Nottingham, area-based multi-agency enforcement teams have been established, driven by an overtly policing mandate, to deal with the worst 'hot spots' (Burney, 2005). In such teams, the process of secondment has gone the other way – still a comparatively rare flow – with local authority anti-social behaviour officers seconded to the police from housing.

Alison Brown (2003) has argued that anti-social behaviour is not so much a sub-criminal form of behaviour but rather a 'social construction', which indicates the creation of a new dimension of professional power and knowledge. Drawing on Cohen's (1985) work, Brown sees the new expertise on anti-social behaviour as a triumph of behaviourism but not in the psychological sense. 'Anti-social behaviour officers gather detailed knowledge about perpetrators, but the discourse is one of "common-sense" morality rather than psychology' (Brown, 2003: 207). Support for this claim is to be found in the ideas of the head of the Home Office Anti-Social Behaviour Unit, Louise Casey in 2004 in arguing '[t]here is absolutely no point in more legislation in the field, or extra money. We just need to bloody enforce things' (The Guardian, 26/2/04). However, Brown's interpretation relies too heavily on 'reading off' these possible developments from aspirational pronouncements and textual sources from government which of course do not necessarily match practices in situ. The complex relationship between central governmental intention/project and the local delivery and implementation in the area of anti-social behaviour management is examined in depth in Chapter 5.

Alongside the growth of 'on the ground' neighbourhood-based teams and specialists in anti-social behaviour, the terrain of community safety and local policing has also seen the development of local crime analysts, who are usually graduates versed in statistical and mapping techniques and indicative perhaps of the growing 'technicisation' of local governing via audits, National Intelligence Model (NIM) and such like. The rise of such technicians are perhaps indicative of O'Malley's (1998: 247) general claim regarding expertise in the emerging 'risk society' that '[i]nstead of training in sociology or social work, increasingly the new criminologists are trained in operations research and systems analysis. This approach is not criminology at all but an applied branch of systems theory'. Again, we still await rigorous research evaluations of the nature of the work of these new governmental technicians. The growth of these new technicist cadres is likely to be greatly promoted by those areas which take up the police NIM for information gathering and sharing (Maguire and John, 2006). However, it remains uncertain how these technicizing initiatives will challenge or alter the habitus and working practices of community safety officers and managers and in particular the difficult balance of resolving technical 'fix-it' solutions and a continuing commitment to what Foster (2002) terms 'the people pieces'.

Alongside and in a complex and at times uneasy relationship to the growing emphasis on both a more repressive enforcement-oriented mode of delivery of crime and disorder, there has also been a growing pressure to incorporate health service actors into the maelstrom of the community governance of crime and safety in the first decade of the twenty-first century. This pressure appears to come from actors in central government departments, probably outside the Home Office, as well as from academic researchers and public health policy entrepreneurs. It is too early to assess what the impact of public health-oriented, primary care trust representatives as legally responsible authorities on CDRPs since 2002 will mean for this work but there is some potential for new local public health and preventive agendas to emerge and perhaps challenge the narrow crime and reduction discourse. Increasingly, for example, drug action teams (DATs) and their coordinators are now an established part of the work of local community safety. It is likely that conflicts may emerge between the traditional and still dominant concerns of the police about the drugs/crime relationship – epitomised by a 'war on drugs' mentality – and DAT teams wishing to hold on to a preventive and harm minimization habitus. The following statements (taken from interviews undertaken in Shiner *et al.*'s (2004) research study) from a drug and alcohol action team (DAAT) coordinator and a drug/alcohol service manager respectively illustrate the concerns which such actors – reflecting their habitus as harm reduction and treatment-oriented experts – may bring to the multi-agency and 'community involvement' table:

> It's difficult because often the community has 'not in my back door' mentality and that would skew what we normally do. In communities we have to accept that there is a massive prejudice against drug users. I'm in favour of community involvement but there need to be protective mechanisms put in place (Shiner *et al.*, 2004: 10)

> If they say they want to lock up all drug users or run all drunks out of town well you can't do that. Community views are a part of what's needed but they need to be filtered by professional opinion (Shiner *et al.*, 2004: 10)

As well as these new specialist occupations, I have already noted in chapter 3 that other, 'unpredictable' lay actors (epitomized by the collective figure of 'the community') have also joined the drama, such as community volunteers and community leaders, including local elected councillors. Furthermore, it is also evident that the role of the academic researcher has also undergone important changes, not least from 'our' previous elitist insulation to being viewed as another flawed participant in the process of constructing a new 'governmental savoir'. We should note, for example, Maguire's (2004: 229) observations about the 'delusion' or 'collusion' of researchers in the over-ambitious, over-optimistic and with hindsight, indefensibly uncritical mood of the time around the Crime Reduction Programe 1999–2002 in England and Wales. As Maguire (2004: 228) notes:

> Understandably, many were genuinely enthusiastic about the sudden surge in importance and status accorded to their 'trade', which had had relatively little influence on government for many years ... rather than risk being left out, many were willing to suspend their doubts in the hope the potential problems could be overcome. At the same time..they were under institutional pressures of their own, a 'key performance indicator' and mark of esteem for university staff being success in obtaining external research funds.

There is of course a danger in exaggerating the newness and 'all is change' character of developments in partnership working. For example, in practice, local authorities have often allowed their community safety strategies to be directed by the police who in turn have 'presented themselves as "experts" and many of them feel deeply defensive about the possibility of some of their responsibilities being wrested from them' (Foster, 2002: 190). Looking back, this leadership role for the police working in association with other organizations and involving themselves in the life of the local community became the foundation upon which multi-agency crime prevention work throughout the 1980s and 1990s was based across much of the UK (see, for e.g. Monaghan, 1997, on Scottish developments in the 1990s). Indeed, according to Hope (2005: 374), the multi-agency partnership approach offered a 'win-win' solution to the police's difficulties in local crime control by bringing local authorities on board, improving their own image, offering an easy concession to community accountability and of course providing the police with another body to take, or share, blame if things went wrong. By the first decade of the twenty-first century Hope (2005: 377) argues that we have witnessed a recognition among the police that meeting the national targets established by the new Annual Policing Plan is its core business. Furthermore, senior police may be driving forward a 'scientific paradigm for crime control' based on the National Intelligence Model (NIM) which may have important implications for community safety. 'The intelligence-led policing movement privileges not only the goal of crime reduction over that of community safety but also the primacy of the police service as society's means of achieving it' (Hope, 2005: 377). If this policy movement is successful, it is probable that community safety – defined as local low-level policing – will become the prime task of local authorities along with the new actors in the extended policing family. Meanwhile the 'real' policing of serious crime will be reserved for the public police force. Crawford *et al.*'s (2004: 66) comparative research study on the extended policing family in the North of England again adds weight to the claim that a second tier of additional policing is increasingly a reality in contemporary Britain. However, the pressure to 'communitarianize' the police in the name of civil renewal and the new neighbourhood/reassurance policing paradigm and as reflected in the Police and Justice Bill of 2006 in England and Wales on police reform, may in turn unsettle the scientific management movement among senior police in ways as yet uncertain.

Following the detailed exploration of communities as unpredictable agents of governance in the second section of Chapter 3, the focus to date in this chapter has largely been on professionals -qua- experts actively working in the 'crowded house' of community safety. However, we should not assume that all professional partners wish either to be invited to play in the first place, or to participate fully in playing the multi-agency game. In particular the work of other statutory agencies such as education, social services, the youth service, probation and prison service (the latter two rebranded in the 2000s as National Offender Management Service [NOMS]) remain significant, resistant components of the melange, often due to their resistance to join the multi-agency game of community safety meets crime and disorder reduction.

Meanwhile, as a result of the Local Government Acts of 1999 and 2000, locally elected politicians are becoming increasingly important members of the crew on the Good Ship Community Safety and in turn lead us to examine what is happening in these local sites with regard to the issues of political authority and democratic accountability. Stoker (2004: 139) argues that such local politicians are a key element for any genuine expression of community governance:

> For networked community governance to work requires local politicians who can act to facilitate the expression of voice in diverse communities and reconcile

differences, develop shared visions and build partnerships to ensure their achievement.

This statement is of course aspirational in character and does not necessarily correspond to the actual interventions by many local politicians in the field of local crime control and community safety. Follett's (2005) research, for example, on a partnership in the Thames Valley in England suggests that the Local Government Acts of 1999 and 2000 have opened up a Pandora's Box which may be disturbing the hegemonic officer-coordinated, 'adaptive' and performance management-driven agenda of local community safety work. It would appear that there are votes increasingly in 'tough on crime and disorder' statements and positioning which have a powerful local as well as national resonance. The trump card available to local politicians is of course that of democratic representation and their role as the legitimate conduit for local people's concerns over ordering and crime and disorder. The resolution of tensions between local political leadership and expert-driven 'adaptive' solutions to community safety and crime and disorder problems remains a major challenge facing all experiments in community governance in the field across the world. It may be that Britain needs to look to both European and North American experiments in urban governance for lessons on community leadership, and in particular with regard to the potential leadership role of an elected mayor and its political and symbolic freight (Domus Project, 2005 see www.comune.modena.it/domus/; Stoker, 2004).

Conclusion

In this chapter the focus has been on 'who works' rather then 'what works' in the community governance of crime and safety. The exploration of the knowledge and expertise of local authority community safety practitioner in the first section opened up the world of these socially situated actors and the problem-solving issues routinely faced. The work of the community safety manager and his or her team remains a hybrid mixture of social and community-based crime prevention, social inclusionary and civil renewal work alongside more focused situational measures and largely police-driven targeted crime and disorder reduction. This section concluded that the habitus of the community safety manager in local multi-agency partnerships cannot be understood as simply reflecting the influence of the 'new criminologies of everyday life' and the risk management mentality. In the second section the increasingly pluralized division of labour in the field was examined. It was contended that there are now more different 'guardians' out there on the streets, most strikingly with regard to the new local mixed economy of visible security patrols. It was also suggested in this section that there was continuing resistance among some agencies to joining the community safety 'game'. Finally it was noted that local politicians may becoming an increasingly important source of legitimate authority and accountability in this field alongside non-elected community representatives. Taken together the two substantive sections of this chapter provide a sociological mapping of the main actors, professional and lay, involved in the implementation of community safety and crime and disorder control in localities across the United Kingdom.

We remain some way off the possible scenario of a radical inter-agency, non-police driven agenda envisaged by Ben Bowling and Janet Foster (2002: 1020) as '[m]ulti-disciplinary, area-based problem-solving teams, working out of combined offices of public service (integrating housing, health, social services and policing), perhaps even directed by non-police personnel'. Such a vision of new institution-building still appears a little idealistic. Nonetheless its very imagining may be indicative of the possible new pathways for policy, practice and politics in the field of local community safety. As Carson (2004b) notes, crucial to this possibility is a shared commitment among practitioners and researchers in becoming more reflexive both about their own practices and about late modernity's changing modes of governance.

Finally we may ask what is the likely role of the 'new model army' of partners in the processes by which new discourses of 'safety', 'crime', 'insecurity', 'disorder', 'community cohesion' etc. are articulated and fed into the ways in which the new governance of public or community safety will be constituted? Despite the ascendancy of a central government, Home Office-informed agenda across much of the United Kingdom in the decade of the 2000s, it is likely that there will continue to be competing advocacy coalitions of actors operating both at the different tiers of governance (supra-national, national, regional and local) and in different spheres of governance (formal and informal) and which will have different powers and liabilities (Edwards, 2002). Accordingly we can expect there to be tangled networks through which the problems of safety and crime control are governed. The differentiated UK polity – not least in the context of greater devolution to the regions and countries – may both enable certain 'translations' of public safety and crime control, whilst disabling others. Clearly this is not to suggest that the future fate of community safety lies in the hands of regional and local actors but there remains the stubborn fact of political agency, including the choices that local actors make in recognizing and acting upon the discretion that a differentiated system of governance opens up for them (Edwards and Hughes, 2002). There is no consensus among governmental practitioners in what Cohen (1985) famously described as the discourses of contemporary 'control-talk' or what we may rename today as 'security-speak', not because of intellectual vacuity but rather because of the continuing struggles to define, translate, settle and unsettle different strategies of public safety and crime control. These issues are explored in greater depth in Chapters 5–7.

5

The Management of the 'Anti-Social' in Communities

Britain has never been at a more insecure moment. I think my job is to provide some stability and order. Anti-social behaviour is actually at the foundation and root of insecurity'.

(David Blunkett, then Home Secretary, UK Government, 12 March 2003)

Anti-social behaviour was the hydra-headed monster that represented a spectrum of bad behaviour, from serious to merely irritating, afflicting neighbourhoods'.

(Burney, 2005: 16)

Introduction

Chapters 5–7 build on the earlier discussion in Chapters 2–4 of both the institutional architecture of the community governance of crime and safety and the attendant actors and 'expertises' associated with these developments. However, the focus now shifts more overtly to how new problems are being governed – even 'invented' – by the institutional infrastructure, governmental processes and occupational practices referred to above alongside the exploration of the broader underlying cultural and material conditions of their existence. There is a powerful, even visceral, political and moral vigour to contemporary debates around the three problems of the anti-social behaviour, asylum seeking and migration, and urban regeneration. Furthermore, with regard to all three policy issues, local communities tend to be framed both negatively (as metaphorically 'breeders' of crime and insecurity) and positively (as 'prophylactics' against crime and insecurity). As noted in Chapter 1 above, it is commonplace for social scientists to be dismissive of appeals to community. This is unsurprising given that the term is still often used 'as if it were an aerosol can, to be sprayed on to any social programme and give it a more progressive and sympathetic cachet' (Cochrane, 1986: 51). But is this verdict on community-based social programmes the most we can hope for in progressive social scientific analyses? Davina Cooper's (2004: 207) argument for a left pluralist engagement with the politics of communities suggests a more positive mode of engagement:

> Left rhetoric and discourses that see communities as marginal at best, but usually diversionary and self-indulgent, facilitate hostile forces in their effort to seal communities up. ... since communities play a key role in the creation of counter-normative practices – practices which not only posit alternatives but also provide a practical critique of the mainstream – how to strengthen and amplify their capacity to dig into the mainstream institutional and everyday life remains a key, underrated challenge.

If successful, the arguments that follow in this chapter and Chapters 6 and 7 will in small part contribute to this key if underrated challenge in the social sciences.

This chapter is structured as follows. The first section outlines the main argument of this chapter with regard to the 'new' social problem of anti-social behaviour. This section contends that we need to be attentive to national and local 'translations' of policies and practices. It is suggested that the empirical exploration of both the conditional exclusions and conditional inclusions of 'anti-social' people in the local sites of governance points to greater complexity and difference than either proponents or critics of the 'crusade' against the anti-social allow for. In the second section the intellectual and political roots of the problem of the anti-social in the United Kingdom will be plotted. Here particular attention is given to both the 'global' and 'local' origins of what may be a contemporary manifestation of the 'criminalisation of social policy'[16] and the social problem's mixed intellectual and political 'parentage'. Following this overview, the third section presents the key features of the raft of measures against the anti-social in the dominant political discourse in the United Kingdom in the decades of the 1990s and 2000s. In the fourth section the uneven institutional expression and consequences of such dominant but contested national tendencies are explored in specific contexts at the sub-national and local dimensions of the governance of crime and safety both in the United Kingdom and in other European localities. Finally in the fifth section I briefly discuss the morality of exclusion with regard to these indigenous outcasts of late modern societies, raising if not answering the urgent questions of tolerance and respect in divided and diverse late modern societies. Overall the chapter suggests that the contemporary management of the anti-social is leading to exclusionary outcomes for many internal outcasts of society but that this policy terrain also remains plural and contradictory in its forms when due attention is paid to the instabilities of governing strategies 'on the ground' in different localities and contexts.

What is 'Anti-Social Behaviour'? Navigating a Criminological Quagmire

The many guises of anti-social behaviour (nuisance, incivility, disorder etc.) now represent one of the most high profile 'objects' of the contemporary governance of crime, disorder and safety particularly across western Europe. Central to the criminological debate opened up by this contemporary sensitivity to, and seeming obsession with, anti-social behaviour among politicians, the media, and in turn growing numbers of the population, is the broader question why this 'new' social problem of anti-social behaviour has achieved such a widespread salience in recent decades across a range of late modern societies. Few can have failed to notice the almost incessant chatter about, panic over and clamour for 'tough' solutions to a growing array of potentially dangerous 'outcasts' and related threats to 'order and civilisation'. The contemporary crusade against the anti-social in the United Kingdom, for example, is characterized by an array of almost limitless representational forms – Burney's 'hydra-headed monster' (2005: 16) – from the villains' gallery of noisy neighbours, disrespectful youth in gangs, persistent and aggressive beggars, prostitutes and drug users to environmental signs of disorder such as the polluting acts arising from dog foul, abandoned vehicles and fly tipping. And it shows little sign of abating, not least in the United Kingdom with the launch of a Respect agenda by Prime Minister Blair immediately after the election of 2005. It is now impossible to discuss contemporary modes of governance across the spectrum of crime control and community safety measures without reference to the threat of the anti-social. Even potential terrorists have been associated with anti-social behaviour banning orders in the United Kingdom at the start of the new millennium.

The rhetorical power of what I have termed the 'moral authoritarian communitarian' discourse (Hughes, 1996a) on the anti-social is impossible to deny. In turn, it is widely speculated in critical criminological and human rights literature on the subject that profoundly exclusionary and damaging consequences for specific categories of the risky and at risk populations in contemporary societies are resulting. However the research evidence to date on what the consequences may be of this dominant discourse and its presumed policy and practice implications is by no means as clear cut as either supporters or opponents alike of this communitarian governmental experiment may wish to claim. A key task of this chapter is thus to navigate a judicious journey through this evidential quagmire by means of geo-historical analysis. As Adam Edwards and myself have argued elsewhere, there is a need for a comparative criminology that is sensitive to the origins (at national, regional, sub-national scales etc.) of innovation in the governance of safety and how these innovations are subsequently transferred cross-nationally to other localities (Edwards and Hughes, 2005a: 346). In navigating this journey I also aim to question the validity of two opposed but also 'mirror image' totalizing positions, namely that the new governance of the anti-social is either a righteous, commonsensical moral campaign of all good and right-thinking 'folk' against a dangerous, growing minority of deviants, or that anti-social behaviour policies represent a manufactured, moral panic supporting an unvarnished form of moral authoritarianism associated with the 'lock-down' state. In contrast to both of these positions, attention is paid throughout this chapter to the simultaneous governmental strategies of both 'conditional inclusions' and 'conditional exclusions' in the management and control of designated anti-social people in contemporary 'societies' of the West.

Much of the discussion which follows necessarily focuses on the consequences of the dominant national (UK) governmental drive to address the problem of anti-social behaviour in localities and communities across the country, and in particular the outcasts, young and adult, of the so-called 'underclass'. Indeed, the newly 'discovered' problem of anti-social behaviour appears to be increasingly re-coded as a social problem and public issue of young people in the deprived and marginalized working class communities and neighbourhoods across the country. The potentially exclusionary consequences of this process for young people so designated as anti-social will be explored through a careful interrogation of the by no means unproblematic evidence generated to date from often competing constituencies, researching variously at the national, local and regional levels. Alongside this attention to the exclusionary and 'othering' tendencies of much contemporary local anti-social behaviour policies across the country, it is also vital to note the continuing push and pull of the logic of 'conditional social inclusion', particularly for youth viewed as both troublesome and troubled, offender and victim.[17] The complex and uneasy interplay of these two logics (inclusionary/exclusionary) makes the evaluation of local governmental trends in the management of the anti-social complex and uncertain. This accords with Tim Newburn's (2002a: 453) conviction that 'the nature of youth justice and crime prevention under New Labour is somewhat tricky to characterize'. Such circumspection does enable us to recognize the messy instabilities of community governance which both ardent supporters and critics alike of the New Labour project in the United Kingdom on the problem of anti-social behaviour may have tended to downplay in their efforts to pin down the local implementation of anti-social behaviour measures either as a managerial, evidence-based and communitarian success or as a clear manifestation of a new institutionalized intolerance and populist authoritarianism

(Goldson, 2002). Nor should we assume that the New Labour message in the 2000s on anti-social behaviour, crime and communities is monovocal: rather we might expect to find ambivalences and contradictions expressive of competing networks and cabales even in this seemingly most 'presidentially'-ruled UK administration.

My central argument here is that there is a dominant national UK and increasingly international trend towards the punitive exclusion of specific categories of youth (often the most marginalized and already 'outcast' and angry young people) together with both damaged and damaging adults. In this current conjuncture, it is hard to deny the discourse and practices of anti-social behaviour control are playing an increasingly salient role with worrying long-term consequences for the rights of targeted 'risky' populations. At the same time, when we examine practices in depth and in situ in their specific geo-historical contexts, the picture is far from monochromal, visually clear-cut or finished. Compromise, contestation, even resistance, are all present in the institutional realities of the local implementation and delivery of community safety strategies on the persistent youth problem. As a site of governance, partnership work in the United Kingdom around anti-social youth thus remains 'unstable' and the actions of key actors are to varying degrees 'unpredictable'. Furthermore, despite the central government project to roll out a common approach to youth crime and disorder reduction across the country, the uneven development of policy and practice in distinct localities with their own distinct cultures and traditions of crime control and safety should not be underestimated by social scientists. As John Muncie and myself concluded in our overview of the changing and competing modes of youth governance under neo-liberal conditions at the end of the twentieth century:

> No reading of the future can ever be clear. The logics of welfare paternalism, justice and rights, responsibilization, remoralization, authoritarianism and managerialism will continue their 'dance' and new spaces for resistance, relational politics and governmental innovation will be opened up. (Muncie and Hughes, 2002: 16)

I suggest a similarly nuanced reading of the uneven developments around the management of anti-social behaviour may be necessary.

Intellectual and Political Roots of the Problem of the Anti-Social

From the outset it is vital to recognize that anti-social behaviour is notoriously difficult to define. Such definitional difficulties are even enshrined in the law. Thus, according to the first section of the Crime and Disorder

Act 1998 in England and Wales it is acting 'in a manner that caused or was likely to cause harassment, alarm or distress to one or more persons not of the same household'. Anti-social behaviour is often then about doing injurious things, or perceptions of such, in public places that may be acceptable when carried out at home (Cooper, 2004: 130). We also need to offer another health warning: there have always been concerns over the anti-social, nuisance and such like in certain places at certain times. Historians are keen to emphasize that social scientists should be wary of assuming the newness of both contemporary social problems and the responses to them. In recent history, for example, housing departments have regularly used civil powers to exclude troublesome home dwellers from public housing areas. Taking the longer historical view, what we now term anti-social behaviour has clear antecedents in, for example, the unrest and moral panics over mobile and disrespectful labour in post-plague, de-populated fourteenth-century localities across Europe or in the much recycled moral panics over troublesome youth, famously plotted by Pearson in *Hooligan: A History of Respectable Fears* (1983). Furthermore, the use of civil – rather than criminal – powers to control disorderly and troubling behaviour was the normal recourse for conflict resolution in eighteenth-century England. Accepting these qualifications, what may be most striking about the current national crusade against the anti-social, and the preferred means of managing it, is that they appear to depart radically from the recent and historically brief era of the welfare state and its collective risk management strategies for dealing with social problems, perhaps ushering in a new era characterized by 'governing through crime' (Simon, 1997) and, we may add, 'disorder'.

Why is there such a heightened concern and public debate over anti-social behaviour at the same time when the official rate of crime, including those associated with street crime, is going down in the United Kingdom and many other western societies? To answer this question we need to take note of both the broader socio-historical conditions of our times and the cultural sensibilities associated with late modernity as well as the conjunctural political developments in recent decades. Sociologically anti-social behaviour seems to be a clear instance of C Wright Mills' (1959) classic sociological distinction between a private trouble and public issue. It is both a real and pressing problem for certain people in certain localities and it also speaks to the broader fears over insecurity and (dis)order among significant numbers of groups in contemporary society, both in the most deprived and vulnerable communities and those less objectively at risk but fearful of seemingly juggernaut-like change. The culture of 'fear and loathing' towards those perceived and experienced as anti-social 'others' seems to have engulfed many communities – as collective victims – from the most affluent shires to those more objectively damaged by persistent nuisance conduct. According to sociologists such as Giddens and Beck (Hughes, 1998a: 131–4), it is the social insecurity of late modernity, which finds expression in increased risk consciousness and heightened fear of crime and in turn produces more punitive attitudes among significant sections of the public. This thesis is taken up most famously in Garland's (2001) analysis of the new culture of crime in which politicians grasp the political advantage to be gained by the espousal of tough law and order policies, albeit delivered by local, 'responsibilized' agencies. Allied to this potent cultural brew is the widely held view that the public police and by implication public authorities more generally are no longer able to deliver on one of their core mandates to citizenry – security and safety from criminal harms.

The social problem of anti-social behaviour is widely interpreted by social scientists as a classic moral panic (Cohen, 2004) stoked up by politicians and mass media campaigners who can rely on votes and improved readership figures by trading on the politics of fear, whether it be the 'stranger' both without and within the nation or in this case the anti-social 'outcast' from the indigenous 'underclass'. Within this context, 'youths hanging about' have become the almost universal symbol of disorder and more and more, menace (Burney, 2004a: 473).[18] Meanwhile, according to some commentators on the political right the crusade over the anti-social is indicative of a wider moral crisis in society around lack of respect for authority and inadequate socialization due to the decline of the 'traditional' family and allied institutions which have generated all too real 'folk devils' (Hitchens, 2003). For others on the political left the problem of anti-social behaviour is indicative of a political crisis associated with blighted communities and the ever widening divisions between the socially and politically included and the excluded and marginalized. For example such developments were noted by the left realist criminologists in mid-1980s and were closely related to their thesis regarding the implosion, internecine warfare and growth of parasitic crimes and harms in Britain's poorest and most relatively deprived communities. It is striking in retrospect that the manifesto of left realism *What is to be done about law and order?* (Lea and Young, 1984) ended with a chilling 'real life' experience of petty but unrelenting acts of incivility and anti-social disorder which might have subsequently been a scenario deployed by the New Labour spokespersons of the mid-1990s onwards in the United Kingdom. To quote Lea and Young (1984: 273):

> Let us conclude with a quote from Eileen Fairbrother's article which graphically sums up the predicament we face:
>
> 'In the street old Sal asks me "was I too woken by last night's shouting, the screams and then the sirens? What do I think of it all?" Useless to tell Sal that

> it's the slums and poverty which cause crime. She's been poor all her life and never hurt anyone. Useless even to tell her that the pros are her sisters in struggle. They jostle her in the street, shock her with obscene oaths, laugh at her little dog. "So hang 'em and flog 'em all!" cries Sal. She's become a Tory not because she's a reactionary, but just because she's so weak and so damned scared.
>
> Strong-arm solutions appeal when you are powerless and nobody seems to be offering anything else. ... I do now understand how the law of the jungle infests and corrodes even those who try to resist it. "The reason I want off the estate", a woman neighbour confides, "is that I swear to God it's turning me into a fascist. And I've been a socialist all my life"'

The concerns expressed by the left realist criminologists reflected local concerns in working class areas. Indeed it was in part local authority pressure which lay behind the New Labour government's introduction of the exclusionary 'anti-social behaviour order', expressing the concerns of councillors and housing managers who had to deal with a rising volume of complaints of un-neighbourly and predatory behaviour, mainly from Labour-controlled poor council estates in areas of high unemployment (Burney, 2004a: 470). In turn, the 'solutions' left realism offered in terms of multi-agency responses based on 'the planned, co-ordinated response of the major social agencies to problems of crime and incivilities' (Young, 1991: 155) also reflected developing local authority community safety work in certain localities that came to influence local policy debates in the United Kingdom and beyond. Much left realist thinking bears fascinating comparison with some of the elements of thinking behind both the Home Office-sponsored Morgan Report of 1991 (see Chapter 2) in which the discourse of community safety first gained a national profile and the subsequent pronouncements of New Labour politicians.

We should not assume that the left realist recognition of the importance of the anti-social and incivilities was a case of a lone wolf crying in the socialist wilderness. Concerns over the metaphorical crumbling of the bricks of civil society and of the criminogenic and anti-social consequences of rampant marketization of the 1980s and 1990s across working class communities were voiced by others on left too (see, for example, Davies' (1997) journalistic exposé). There has also been a growing body of quantitative social scientific research which had shown that the most deprived area suffered to a massive extent disproportionate levels of repeat victimization from crime (Hope, 1998). It is difficult to deny that social housing is increasingly a site of crime control as it has become a residual tenure for the most disadvantaged and marginalized groups. Furthermore, it is not an unjustified claim to note that people living in more comfortable circumstances often have no idea of the havoc that even 'petty' crime and disorder can wreak on the most deprived and marginalized 'communities of fate'. Such commentaries and diagnoses fed into and played a role in helping shape the New Labour agenda of re-launching the party as 'tough' on law and order from the mid-1990s. However, the strong connection made between poverty and deprivation and high rates of victimization from crime and anti-social behaviour which those on the left articulated, including the left realists, was generally expunged from the public pronouncements on the matter by New Labour politicians.

These indigenous influences were of major importance but it would be misleading to assume that the roots of the new political, policy and moral salience of the crusade against the anti-social in the public imagination were reducible to either purely indigenous UK influences or leftist analyses. A lively export trade in ideas and practices of crime control from across the Atlantic and onto British shores has been starkly evident for several decades (Newburn and Sparks, 2004). Indeed, the current hegemony of exclusionary, anti-social behaviour measures in neo-liberal policy discourses more generally is justified intellectually by the most influential criminological essay produced in the last decades of the twentieth century: JQ Wilson and George Kelling's (1982) *Broken Windows*. This essay has been translated and deployed – at least rhetorically – by local policing and safety strategies across many western societies. And many policy makers in the United Kingdom are no exception in following the seemingly commonsensical logic of the thesis that minor sub-criminal misdemeanours, incivilities and acts of anti-social behaviour need 'nipping in the bud' by means of 'zero-tolerance' community policing and the rigorous cleansing of the streets and public places. Put simply, the 'Broken Windows' thesis suggests that if cultures and climates of disorder are allowed to develop and take root, then more serious crime will grow as surely as night follows day. The importance of this New York-inspired discourse for policy and practice, travelling trans-locally across the globe, cannot be denied in providing powerful ammunition for the burgeoning neo-conservative 'criminology of the other' which demonises the criminal and the anti-social as a threat to order and to the morally upright community of the good and respectable. Indeed it is perhaps the simplicity of the thesis which makes it practically attractive, whatever its conceptual flaws (Matthews, 1992; Taylor, 2001). It also needed no crime-reduction justification to gain public support for the visible effects on the streets of New York: rather it was its visible sanitizing effect that had the most appeal internationally (Burney, 2005). Although Burney (2004a: 473) has cogently observed that 'the well-documented features of neighbourhood decline are mainly correlations, not causes, with a common root in poverty, structural weakness, and lack of social cohesion. ... [And that it] becomes increasingly hard for government rhetoric to blame individual nastiness for the destruction of communities', nonetheless proponents of the 'Broken Windows' thesis within governmental circles in localities across the world continue to do so!

The hybrid intellectual and political roots of the increasingly high profile public problem of anti-social behaviour reflect its broad ideological appeal. It was, however, the arrival of New Labour as the national government in 1997 in the United Kingdom that proved the crucial tipping point in establishing anti-social behaviour both as an increasingly popular and heightened focus of public consciousness and the rationale for a raft of legislative and policy measures.

New Labour's Communitarian Crusade and Anti-Social Behaviour

1998–2003: Ideological and Legislative Flood; Implementation Trickle

Specific policies and their subsequent 'careers' develop a momentum for a complex number of often contingent reasons and factors. Burney (2005: 16–17) has pointed, for example, to the pressure to deal with identified problems; often there are interested parties who put pressure on the government to try and ensure that their ideas appeal; there are usually leading politicians whose own concerns make them predisposed to take policy in a specific direction; and there are international influences which may seem to offer new answers and provide new rhetoric. In turn, these factors impinged upon the contemporary political culture that during the 1990s was moving in a more punitive direction. Such factors and influences were evident in New Labour's adoption of anti-social behaviour control as one of its unique and most high profile features.

By the mid-1990s, leading Labour politicians from Blair, to Straw and Blunkett increasingly espoused at the level of political rhetoric an exclusionary and moral authoritarian version of communitarianism (Hughes, 1996a) in which there were to be 'no excuses for crime' and people were to be made morally responsible for their actions. Commenting on Blair's communitarianism, Burney (2005: 23) notes that these beliefs might have taken a different turn whereby the importance of families and of communities could have been the focus for social support and regeneration (elements of which did later make their way into neighbourhood renewal programmes, see Chapter 7). However, instead the culture of censure and blame took over for both parents and their miscreant children. Since the 1997 election, a raft of legal remedies aimed at holding accountable and punishing the perpetrators of anti-social acts have been introduced by means of several major acts of Parliament – the Crime and Disorder Act (CDA) 1998, the Police Reform Act 2002, the Anti-Social Behaviour Act 2003 and the Police and Justice Act 2006. In turn as 'the choice of legal remedies designed to deal with anti-social behaviour has widened, so has the range of behaviours and potential offenders liable for prosecution ... Now a touchstone of the New Labour Government's policy- making agenda, it is increasingly difficult to remember when anti-social behaviour was not a familiar policy concern' (Parr, 2005: 1). The importance of the CDA in the populist communitarian discourse of New Labour is best captured in the speech made by Home Secretary Jack Straw during the Crime and Disorder Bill's second reading:

> The Bill represents a triumph of community politics over detached metropolitan elites. In the early 1980s, my party lost its way, not least by failing to listen to those whom we claimed to represent, and by failing to learn from them. My right honourable friend [P.M. Blair] broke decisively with all that and ensured that our policy making would be inspired above all by our constituents. Among many of the other things, that led us to a serious examination of how to reverse the apparently inexorable rise in anti-social behaviour and teenage crime. (Quoted in Parr, 2005).

By the mid-2000s it was regularly and loudly proclaimed by ministers, the Home Office and specialist Anti-Social Behaviour/Respect units that anti-social behaviour had become a widespread and increasingly urgent problem across the United Kingdom. In turn, tackling this problem was viewed by government as one of the greatest challenges facing 'our' victimized communities, alongside and increasingly in tandem with the 'war against terrorism'. For example, the Home Secretary in 2003, David Blunkett, portrayed anti-social behaviour in distinctly apocalyptic terms, claiming that 'Britain has never been at a more insecure moment ... .Anti-social behaviour is actually at the foundation and root of insecurity' (Blunkett, 12 March 2003). Meanwhile, in an attempt to reveal the 'true' extent of anti-social behaviour across the country and accompanied by a blaze of publicity, the Anti-Social Behaviour Unit commissioned a national day count of reports of the phenomenon across all 376 CDRPs in England and Wales. The data gathered between midnight Tuesday 9 September and midnight Wednesday 10 September 2003 by a range of local actors (many of whom in passing were deeply sceptical of the accuracy and purpose of the count on the basis of my own fieldwork observations) resulted in 'dramatic' figures which in turn were given much national media publicity. 66,107 reports were gathered, equating to more than one report every two seconds or around 16.5 million reports per year. On the basis of these figures, it was calculated that the estimated cost of anti-social behaviour equated to around £3.4bn per year (Parr, 2005: 2).

Despite the deficiencies of the count, the seemingly alarming figures that were constructed provided valuable 'sound-bites' (and an example of 'policy-based evidence'?) in the publicly heightened politics of fear and insecurity and in turn eased the passing of the Anti-Social Behaviour Act 2003.

The radical nature of the CDA lay in mandating local partnerships to undertake a statutory duty to reduce crime *and* disorder. In the context of anti-social behaviour, the inventiveness of the 1998 Act lay in it making available new civil orders and powers that could be made other than as a sentence. This civilianization of law may be viewed as moralizing in tone and as an example of 'defining deviance up' rather than the 'defining deviance down'. For example, child safety orders, local child curfews and ASBOs do not necessarily require either the prosecution or the commission of a criminal offence. Similarly an ASBO is a civil order that can be made by the police, local authority (and several other agencies since 2002) on anyone over the age of ten whose behaviour is thought likely to cause alarm, distress or harassment. Such an order lasts a minimum of 2 years in England and Wales but only 6 months in Scotland) and breach is punishable by up to 5 years' imprisonment (see Figure 5.1 for examples of typical ASBOs). In the build-up to the implementation of the CDA 1998 youths were not a prominent part of the 'anti-social' paradigm from the Home Office and in the draft guidance material immediately after the CDA, orders being made on under-18s were specifically discouraged. However, Burney (2004a: 473) argues that this was not 'what local authorities wanted' (or I should qualify this by suggesting *it was not what a powerful lobby among some local authorities wanted*). In the final version of guidance on ASBOs published in March 1999, young people aged between 12–17 were targeted as appropriate groups for their routine application. In the first two and a half years of ASBOs, 58 per cent were made on under-18s and a further 16 per cent on people aged 18 to 21 years (Campbell, 2002). However the total numbers of ASBOs nationally remained relatively low and in many CDRPs they were hardly employed at all. Across the total number of 376 CDRPs in England and Wales between April 1999 to March 2001, only 317 ASBOs were taken out for the whole population, with a third being served on young people (House of Commons Select Committee Inquiry into Anti-Social Behaviour, 2004). The overall picture then across the country – up to 2003 – was not one in which there was a local authority consensus over the desire to employ ASBOs. In order to explain this lack of local take up of ASBO powers we need to remain alert to the uneven appeal of ASBOs across the often very different contexts of local community safety work and Burney (2004a: 475–6) has noted that the first years of the ASBO (1999–2003) saw relatively high numbers of orders recorded by a few areas. It is sanguine, for example, to note that between 1999–2004 approximately a sixth of all ASBOs taken out were in the Greater Manchester area alone.

1. Prohibits from:
- entering onto the whole of a named council estate,
- engaging in conduct which causes or is likely to cause alarm, distress or harassment to others, or inciting others to do so,
- causing or attempting to cause criminal damage,
- engaging in behaviour which is or is likely to be threatening , abusive or insulting to others, or encouraging or inciting others to do so. (January 2000, Huddersfield Magistrates' Court)

2. Prohibits from:
- shouting, spitting, using verbal/physical and/or racial abuse, swearing, drinking alcohol,
- smashing bottles, throwing eggs, stones or other items at vehicles or property in any street in the LB (local borough) of Haringey including inciting or encouraging others in the commission of any of the above,
- entering the Park Ward of Tottenham (other than to remain at his house address) for one hour before and after the scheduled kick of time of any football match held at White Hart Lane football stadium,
- leaving his home address between the hours of 8.00 pm and 7.00 am unless under the direct supervision of a youth worker for the LB of Haringey on an organized event,
- for two years.

(May 2000, Haringey Magistrates' Court)

(Adapted from Burney, 2004a: 476–7)

Figure 5.1 Examples of Anti-Social Behaviour Orders.

- Fixed penalty fines for a wide range of low-level disorder, including insulting behaviour, graffiti, fly-posting and litter. The power to fine held by the wider 'police family' such as street wardens, community safety officers, private security guards as well as the police.
- Powers to confiscate noisy televisions and stereos.
- Police power to disperse groups of 2 or more young people on the street.
- Fines and parenting orders for parents of disorderly or truanting children
- Begging made a recordable offence
- Ban on airguns and replica guns
- Ban on selling spray paint to under-16 year olds
- Local authority powers to close noisy pubs and clubs
- Media allowed to name anti-social children
- Closure of 'crack houses' within 48 hours

(Adapted from Muncie, 2004: 237)

Figure 5.2 Powers of the Anti-Social Behaviour Act 2003 in England and Wales.

National Overviews of the Outcomes of Anti-Social Behaviour Powers and Measures post-2003

Since the 2003 Anti-Social Behaviour Act, both the classification of what constitutes anti-social behaviour have been extended (see Figure 5.2) and the legal powers of local authorities and CDRPs for dealing with anti-social behaviour have been extended and their implementation made simpler and speedier. In retrospect it would appear that this piece of legislation was brought in to try and make the generally resistant local CDRPs, police, and local authorities – outside a number of prominent metropolitan authorities – comply with the new exclusionary statutory powers which central government had given them.

Not surprisingly the use of ASBOs has attracted much intense criticism from legal academics, human rights lawyers and members of the so-called 'metropolitan liberal elites' for its all-embracing and subjective basis; deliberate confusion of civil and criminal law; potential criminalization of non-criminal conduct; for allowing evidence from "professional witnesses"; potential disproportionality; and for its stigmatizing and exclusionary effects (Ashworth *et al.*, 1998). More generally, Cooper (2004: 129) has noted that normative organizing principles work through law as well as policy and discursive claims of nuisance to consolidate and reinforce unequal social statuses. We should thus expect that the normative principles refracted by anti-social behaviour in this case will embed relations of inequality.

What does the available research evidence tell us about the actual processes of implementation accepting that the public rhetoric around the anti-social has resulted in a moral panic, particularly over anti-social youth? Locally and with some notable exceptions, CDRPs largely avoided using their anti-social behaviour powers between 1999–2003. The talk was tough but the local practices and actions were somewhat softer in actuality in the years up to the 2003 Anti-Social Behaviour Act. Commenting in 2002 on the use of such powers in youth justice, Newburn (2002a) observed that in practice, 'there has been a remarkable reluctance on the ground to use such powers'. We should also note the attraction of more conditionally inclusive, individually contractualized tactics such as Acceptable Behaviour Contracts (ABCs) which prescribe a range of 'responsibilizing' activities designed to help the 'miscreant' avoid exacerbating their anti-social behaviour and be re-socialized into 'acceptable' ways of behaving. ABCs were pioneered by the Islington community safety partnership and subsequently widely disseminated across many CDRPs across the country. With the privilege of hindsight, the period between 1999 and 2003 now appears to be a phase characterized by what Garland (2001) has termed 'adaptive' pragmatic preventive responses led by officers/practitioners which in turn appears to reflect the 'habitus' of such quasi-professional groups (see Chapter 4).

In the first years of the new millennium, local CDRPs have been under increasing pressure from central government to deliver on the 'tough' aspects of the government's crime and disorder reduction agenda. Added to this pressure there is a more visible presence for local elected politicians with portfolios on crime and safety as a result of the 'modernizing' agenda on local government and the new legal powers institutionalized in the Local Government Acts of 1999 and 2000 (Hope, 2005). There are then new powers and liabilities for local councillors who are often under pressure to respond to local concerns and who of course can make a successful political career out of addressing these concerns. In many localities the espousal of a 'tough on anti-social behaviour' agenda may be a 'win/win' situation not just for a growing number of councillors but also for beleaguered community safety teams (including the police) given the very high profile of anti-social behaviour work and such tough responses being indicative of local authorities 'at long last' doing something tangible with new repressive powers to assuage the concerns of the often most vocal local constituencies. Such a tendency appears to be indicative of a potentially new phase of expressive, symbolic politics of local crime control driven by the threat of expulsion and resulting in what may be termed majoritarian 'reassurance' policing and the segregation of the 'undesirables'. Indeed whereas only 466 ASBOs were made in the first two and a half years since 1999, 2633 were issued in the 12 months between October 2003 and September 2004 alongside 5383 ABCs in the same period. The Anti-Social Behaviour Unit and Respect Task Force, both led by the 'policy entrepreneur', Louise Casey, have been the main promoters of the new 'crusade', with its own award ceremonies for those individuals courageous enough to 'stand up to the nuisance neighbour or the intimidating group of people on the street corner' (Casey, 2004: 7). To the sceptical observer this award ceremony may appear akin to a stage-managed tactic of communitarian dramaturgy representing in turn the alter-ego of the public 'naming and shaming' of offenders. On the other hand, it may be argued that this central governmental 'push' represents an innovative focus on behaviour, particularly of young people, that may not be liable to criminal prosecution but is nonetheless considered anti-social. Alongside its regression back to a narrow focus on recordable crime, this behavioural focus on the incivilities of groups and measures to prevent persistent offending represents an *attempt* to eclipse 'the social democratic interventions in local structures of social inequality and exclusion that had previously been pursued by certain municipal authorities in England and Wales' in the 1990s (Edwards and Hughes, 2005a: 356). Across Europe to varying degrees, we may note the neo-conservative interest in the 'remoralisation of society', the 'ethnicisation' of belonging, and calls for the 'banishment of outsiders/foreigners' (Edwards and Hughes, 2005a, b). This new politics is perhaps most graphically captured in the seeming transformation of Holland's culture of control from one of toleration to one of punitive populism based on what Rene van Swaaningen (2005) describes as 'governing through safety', first developed in Rotterdam and 'exported' to other localities in Holland. Nevertheless, the extent to which this ideological shift has occurred across the sectors of the state and in different localities in Holland still requires further empirical substantiation (see Burney, 2005: 146–55).

At both the national and sub-national levels of governance across Europe, the exponential rise of governmental anti-social behaviour agendas would not seem to be about finding 'evidence-based' measures which can be shown to 'work'. Instead they may serve more complex and less easily measurable political ends. According to Burney (2004a: 482) in Britain:

> The ASBO saga provides a microcosm of the political processes in the contemporary governance of crime and disorder. The electorate is seen to suffer to an unknown extent from tangible objects of censure and fear – local bullies, noisy neighbours etc. Laws are passed subsuming these grievances into an all-embracing category – anti-social behaviour – with intangible properties and proportions.

Meanwhile Roger Matthews (2003: 8) noted that the general level of vagueness and lack of specificity in the then proposed legislation in the White Paper of 2002 was essential since it rationalized a wide range of sanctions which otherwise would have been difficult to justify. He also observed that there was an assumption that 'if a large enough armada can be mobilized then the offensive will be successful, even if it is not sure where it is going or what it should be aiming at' (Matthews, 2003: 8). However, what seemed clearer to Matthews was that the nationally orchestrated crusade against the anti-social was 'not going to be directed at those who pollute our environment for profit, those who recycle foodstuffs and inject meat with additives or those involved in multi-million pound pension swindles. This is an offensive aimed at the feckless, the marginalized and the poor' (Matthews, 2003: 6). Rod Morgan (2006), chair of the Youth Justice Board, has noted that the symbolic crusade against the anti-social is unlikely to disappear off the radar screen of politicians. In particular, Morgan suggests that Cabinet Ministers in the first decade of the twenty-first century are convinced of the psephological evidence that such tough measures against anti-social behaviour are very popular with potential voters. It may be wise to note, however, that, like any armada, military offensive or crusade, its chances of success are never certain or known in advance. To continue with the naval analogy, armadas after all may be blown off-course, get ship-wrecked and end up as a chaotic flotilla, if not flotsam and jetsam.

The Production of Behaviour Control in Specific Local Contexts

Despite this broad national and growing international shift towards a more overtly repressive criminality prevention (see Chapter 3), the nature of the new practices and their actual outcomes for those identified as anti-social remain complex and as yet has not been adequately and thoroughly evaluated by a sufficiently substantial body of criminological research. Indeed, there is a paucity of detailed empirical research, particularly of longitudinal evidence, to date regarding the implementation and consequences of these anti-social behaviour measures. However, on the basis of the limited research undertaken outside government-sponsored surveys and evaluations, the story that is emerging across different locations and occupational contexts appears to be an uneven mix of local enthusiasm and co-operation alongside wary compliance with and 'gentle' contestation of the national government's communitarian and popular punitive agenda and rhetoric. This situation would seem to support my argument (with Edwards) for the importance of reframing criminological thought more comparatively in terms of a broader conception of who governs, where and to what ends, and in recognizing the specific contexts in which problems of order and social reactions to them are constituted (Edwards and Hughes, 2005a: 346).

Local Youth Crime Prevention and the Anti-Social

Accepting the lack of a strong research evidence base on outcomes, what is evident locally is that the problem of youth 'hanging around' and causing 'trouble' has been a persistent area of concern for local partnerships generally and the issue of 'anti-social youth behaviour management' a priority in almost all local community safety strategies. For example, Hill and Wright (2003), on the basis of their ethnographic research on two estates in the West Midlands, suggest that community safety on the ground and in practice is predominantly about the local management of crime and incivilities, and not about issues of youth empowerment and inclusion. ' "Community" becomes a setting in which only the interests of adults are identified, interests which underpin a moral authoritarianism which operate to exclude marginal groups such as "dangerous" youth. "Safety" becomes a notion to be secured by blaming, isolating and silencing youth' (Hill and Wright, 2003: 291). Whether this damning conclusion can be generalized across the practices of most CDRPs is more difficult to say and I would contend that there are important qualifications to such a blanket foreclosure on the admittedly embattled possibilities of more inclusive, youth-oriented work (Newburn, 2002a). Indeed, even Hill and Wright themselves noted that on one of the estates they studied, parents did recognize the need for the authorities to take account of their children's views. This is in accord with Girling *et al.*'s (2000) finding in Macclesfield that confirmed that adults are willing to take account of the needs of 'their' youth whilst simultaneously perceiving youth from different areas as the dangerous 'other' (Hill and Wright, 2003: 295). In a research study on 85 youth offending teams (YOTs) and the use and impact of ASBOs, it was discovered that there was uneven use of such excluding orders by YOTs across the country, with many quite sparing in their use; whilst officially ASBOs are not considered to be a measure of last resort, many practitioners preferred to use other approaches first. The most common alternatives employed were ABCs, warning letters, interviews and referral to youth inclusion and support panels. More worryingly they found that the breaching of ASBOs, itself a criminal offence, was common, with more than half of ASBOs being breached. Half of breaches were for criminal or anti-social behaviour but a quarter were breached for lesser matters such as associating with named individuals. Furthermore, the release of publicity about the individuals on ASBOs appeared to be the norm, to this end employing local newspapers, leaflets to local residents and posters. Finally it was found that the main priority of local authorities and the police in applying ASBOs and addressing anti-social behaviour more generally was to respond to the concerns of local communities and provide reassurance that their problems would be reduced rather than changing the behaviour of young people.

Although rigorous data remain in short supply, there is evidence that ASBOs across Britain have been used disproportionately against the most vulnerable and 'troubled' as well as 'troublesome' young *and* adult people across the United Kingdom (Morgan, 2006; McAra, 2006). For example, Campbell's (2002) research discovered that more than 60 per cent of the ASBOs examined in the survey were associated with people manifesting very obvious social or mental problems, chiefly linked to drug or alcohol abuse. The pressure group, ASBO Concern, has observed that anyone who dares to criticize ASBOs is immediately accused by government ministers of being out of touch with those being 'terrorized' on housing estates. Yet ASBO Concern points to some telling examples of the orders being used against people who have never 'terrorized' anyone. It has cited many examples of people with mental health problems for whom ASBOs appear highly inappropriate such as a 23 year old woman who repeatedly threw herself into the River Avon being served with an ASBO banning her from jumping into rivers and canals, with the possibility of a prison sentence if she breached the order (The Guardian, 5/4/05). As Krudy and Stewart (2004: 11) note, the anti-social behaviour by young people associated with ASBOs is very often behaviour influenced by a matrix of underlying problems that include lack of suitable educational provision, poor parenting, social exclusion and drug dependency. It is not entirely fanciful to read such measures as attempts by some public authorities to clear the streets and public spaces of 'worthless', 'unproductive' and 'unpalatable' human detritus (see Chapter 7).

Research undertaken under the auspices of the UK government's Youth Justice Board (Morgan, 2006) provides some important evidence as to which young people are likely to be subjected to ASBOs. It has shown that most orders are taken out against already persistent and prolific offenders with over a third already having served a custodial penalty. The research suggests that ASBOs are generally used as a last resort across England and Wales but that ASBOs have too many restrictions and too long a period of exclusions on average. Morgan (2006) has noted that the typical youth in custody and subject to an ASBO is generally in age terms chronologically 16 years, with a street age of 20+ and a numeracy/literacy age of 9. Put brutally these young people are the children with no chance, having been failed by their families and the care and control system. This bleak picture is captured by the late great comedian, Linda Smith when she ironically claimed 'it's easy to knock ASBOs but they are the only qualifications some of our kids will get'.

These findings highlight disturbing trends in the use of excluding and repressive orders for controlling anti-social behaviour, often among 'at risk' and vulnerable young people and adults. Clearly this unease is not the preserve of academic commentators and human rights activists as Morgan's views as Chair of the Youth Justice Board confirm. As noted in Chapter 4, the UK-wide practitioner network, the National Community Safety Network, has advocated publicly that local practitioners are concerned that anti-social behaviour targets set by central government have been 'too focussed on enforcement at the expense of preventive work' (NCSN, 2005). The uneasiness over the use of ASBOs among local practitioners and managers is also evident in the case study research currently being undertaken by Matthew Follett (Hughes and Follett, 2006) on a new town in the Thames Valley area. For example, Follett's study illustrates graphically how the YOT manager on the local CDRP under scrutiny self-reflexively sought to broaden out the partnership's debate on ASBOs and youth and children. To quote this manager,

> The problem with ASBOs in ..., and elsewhere is that the context around anti-social behaviour has been driven around the crime and disorder silo, and there hasn't been a child-centred perspective. And yet all the services in place that deal

> with kids who are involved in anti-social behaviour are children's services – health, ed, social care etc. So I try and make sure that crime and disorder and children's side are talking to each other ... Principally the whole ASBOs thing is about protection of victims and public confidence. We are about that too, but you have to do something with the kids involved, you can't just shut them away somewhere.

The same partnership's community safety manager also expressed concerns over both the national government and local elected members' agenda on anti-social behaviour. In turn he spoke to a pragmatic but also social democratically-inspired social preventive discourse. To quote this manager:

> I don't object to the government's leading view that it's antisocial behaviour that blights lives. I think it does, probably more than anything else ... it's got to be dealt with. Where I slightly part company with the government is in their rather simplistic way of dealing with it ... I'd like to work towards a much tighter definition .... I mean you know in the extremes that some kinds of behaviour, that the alcoholic that comes so dependent on alcohol that their kind of violent or aggressive behaviour to others, urinating on the walls and this sort of thing, is causing a major concern and you know it's wrong and by any kind of analysis you've got to deal with that. But then, most of the referrals we get [are] things like kids kicking balls against garage doors and because this is what concerns people, that's what members are always referring or even the MP ... The other thing I really object to is that if we're going to deal with anti-social behaviour, it starts from education, it doesn't start from ASBOs.

While such 'talk' cannot be read as being unproblematically translated into local strategy and practice, the CDRP in question foregrounded preventive 'problem-solving' tactics on anti-social behaviour, including a long-established mediation approach, and has developed in its latest strategy (2005–8) what it termed a 'pyramid approach' to anti-social behaviour in which ASBOs are the last final stage following a series of preventive stages. It is possible that such local measures might lead to a 'widening of the net of social control' of which Cohen (1984) warned in the 1980s and which has become a common 'catch-all' mantra of many commentators on the left. The measures in question may even be viewed as constituting one element of what Phil Scraton (2003: 31), commenting on CDA legislation, foresaw as 'a strategy of "lockdown" leading inexorably and inevitably to differential policing, discriminatory targeting, universal surveillance, criminalization and an escalation in the prison population'. However, I would argue that this totalizing and dystopian prediction remains one that seriously downplays the uneven and uncertain implementation of such a 'strategy' across different sites such as the case study cited above, despite the general shift towards greater punitiveness in and politicization of local crime control measures across the country. Perhaps Newburn (2002a: 480) captures the current situation more adequately in suggesting '[T]here are clear tensions between some of the inclusionary aspirations of community safety and some of the exclusionary potential of criminality prevention.' To date in the local authority area covered by Follett's research (unpublished) 13 ASBOs had been taken out between 1999–2004. How long this minimalist 'adaptive' position might last is uncertain of course, given that 'in the eyes of politicians, and increasingly, the public at large, "success" in dealing with perpetrators of anti-social acts tends to be seen entirely in terms of ASBO statistics' (Burney, 2004b: 4). Furthermore, Burney notes that the exponential growth in the use of ASBOs since 2003 has been largely attributable to changes introduced in the Police Reform Act 2002. 'Most importantly they [ASBOs] can be obtained on top of a criminal sentence if proof of anti-social behaviour ... can be shown. The police have seized on this opportunity to extend control over persistent offenders and thus have sharply driven up the total of orders granted' (Burney, 2004b: 4). It has been estimated that of the 16,670 ASBOs granted between December 2002 and March 2004, 43 per cent were obtained on the back of conviction. Increasingly ASBOs have become 'just another policing tool' (Burney, 2004b: 5): against street gangs, disruption of drug markets, cleansing of public spaces of street drinkers and beggars, and against prostitutes.

Problem-Solving and Enforcement: Local Contexts and Cultures

It is evident from the discussion to date that the national governmental project in the United Kingdom on anti-social behaviour has been characterized by complex, even contradictory impulses combining both preventive ('adaptive') and punitive enforcement-oriented ('denial') tendencies, albeit with the latter usually pushed to the fore (see Chapter 3). Perhaps the most apt way to describe this national project is one of 'tough love' in which conditional social inclusions have been promoted based on both voluntary responsibilization of citizens and, where and when necessary, on 'compulsory social inclusions' (Hughes and Little, 1999) and potential social exclusions for more recalcitrant members such as 'anti-social families'.

At the local level this complex project on behaviour control has been manifested in forms that mean that the relationship of prevention and enforcement has remained more uncertainly balanced. Accordingly, even in the context of building potential ASBO cases, a preventive problem-solving agenda may emerge. The survey work of both Hunter *et al.* (2001) and Campbell (2002) on anti-social behaviour measures, for example, indicated that agencies placed great value on the time-consuming case conferences. In particular, they found that some social landlords found the process of developing ASBO cases particularly useful due to the 'problem-solving' component involved! Indeed, once a case was looked at from a multi-agency perspective, solutions at times emerged that rendered it unnecessary to pursue an ASBO. In many cases the behaviour complained of arose from social and health-related problems that needed addressing. Despite the rightly notorious and newsworthy cases of punitive exclusionary measures against vulnerable people noted earlier, there is some emerging evidence that harm reduction and rehabilitation initiatives have often been developed with regard to anti-social behaviour, particularly given the key role played by alcohol and drug abuse in many such cases. Sadie Parr's (2006) research in Sheffield on the Home Office-sponsored piloted intensive family support projects for homeless or at risk of eviction families, which have been associated with a history of anti-social behaviour, suggests that welfarist-rehabilitative interventions have by no means disappeared. Parr (2006: 13) tentatively concludes that such intensive, long-term projects stand as alternatives to ASBOs and related excluding measures and may be 'fertile grounds for local agents to be creative and open up possibilities for genuinely positive interventions built on mutual trust and respect instead of fear and suspicion'.

Burney's research has suggested that many local CDRPs and corresponding professional bodies across Britain have remained unimpressed by the central government criticisms of their perceived failure to use ASBOs. Her conclusion in 2004 was guardedly optimistic, arguing that some local partnerships were developing their own ways of dealing with their own problems – 'exactly what the partnership structures were to be intended for' (Burney, 2004a: 482). In turn 'responsibilization' or government by proxy runs the risk that the methods adopted by the local proxy agents such as CDRPs, given the encouragement and means to develop their own 'local solutions to local problems' may diverge from the central vision. There is clear evidence from surveying the published local community safety strategy texts across the country that all local community safety strategies do prioritize the reduction of incidents of, and fears about, disorder and anti-social behaviour. However, the specific form such work may take in practice results at times in the continuing promotion of preventive approaches to anti-social behaviour, albeit it often low profile and *sotto voce* in nature. The alternatives to ASBOs do not have the political weight of being seen to be doing something very publicly and symbolically to tackle persistent misbehaviour. They also tend to suffer in comparison to coercive, excluding orders due to the dreaded claim of being 'soft' options. Nevertheless, there is also a long history of diversion, mediation and restoration in local youth justice practices which, whatever their limitations and dangers, have potential reductive capacity in terms of both re-offending and avoiding the resort to custodial penalization (see Hughes *et al.*, 1997; Crawford and Newburn, 2003; Gelsthorpe and Morris, 2002).

The latest government initiative to improve the local performance of local authorities and their community safety partnership arrangements in Britain at the time of writing (2006) is the Safer, Stronger Communities Fund resulting in mandatory 'local area agreements' (LAAs) between local authorities and the central government. What are its likely consequences for community safety tactics and strategies targeted on youth anti-social behaviour? In this emerging institutional context, which was selectively tested and pioneered across the country in 2004–5, the complex 'centring and decentring' tendencies of the local governance of crime (and disorder) (Crawford, 1997) have again been evident. There is no denying the centralizing mission of the state in this latest phase in the career of 'community safety'. In particular, several nation-wide public service agreements and outcomes have been prioritized which all LAAs must meet, namely: (i) reduce crime and reassure the public by reducing the fear of crime and anti-social behaviour; (ii) promote cleaner, greener public spaces; (iii) improve the standard of life for people in the most disadvantaged neighbourhoods and ensure those service providers are more responsive to neighbourhood needs and improve local delivery; and (iv) empower local people to have a greater voice and influence over decision making and delivery of services. Even a superficial reading of this central government, 'joined-up' across departments, initiative (Home Office, 2005) cannot fail to reveal the persistence of a performance management logic alongside a communitarian-inspired civil renewal and community cohesion project. It is also clear from this 'new' policy of the mid-to late-2000s that the 'crusade' against anti-social behaviour has remained a key driver which sits in the first and most prominent public service agreement which all local areas must meet as a condition of receiving LAA funding. However, when we begin to examine how the broad community cohesion project may be realized and implemented in specific localities the picture becomes more complex, more open-ended and more sociologically and politically intriguing than a tale of one-way traffic 'rolling out' from the centre to the local. The 'rolling out' of the project may necessarily have to reflect the diversity of both socio-economic geo-histories of localities and extant administrative and political cultures within local government and local police forces despite the possible amalgamation of police forces and concomitant de facto 'nationalisation' of policing in the next decade. Let's look at the initial approach developed in one of the chosen 'experimental' sites in 2004–5, namely Barnsley.

In taking up the 'challenge' set by national government, it may be contended that key players in the Barnsley Community Safety Partnership and Borough Council were not simply responding passively to a central government initiative but, given the experimental nature of the work entailed, were also involved in an attempt at a quite specific 'translation' of what a 'safer, stronger community' might entail for 'their' city. According to the Chief Executive of Barnsley Metropolitan Borough Council (One Barnsley, 2005),

> Local Area Agreements have the potential to transform the relationship between central and local Government by recognising the characteristics of individual localities and breaking out of the one-size-fits-all mindset of national policy. They are based on open dialogue, mutual understanding, commitment, trust and partnership. Barnsley is willing to share those qualities, in abundance, with the Government.

There are of course many possible interpretations of such a statement. From reading both the formal textual pronouncements and interviewing one of the leading local actors, I suggest tentatively that this one example may be illustrative of the continuing local struggle to articulate problems of safety and crime, disorder and the anti-social in ways that may temper if not disrupt the dominant punitive and enforcement-oriented push which most national overviews of trends in the local management of anti-social behaviour point us towards. In particular, a commitment to both a preventive discourse on crime and disorder reduction and social inclusion agenda around the slippery concept of 'community cohesion' appeared evident in this local experiment in joined-up 'community governance', articulated through the required performance management language. 'Overall the aim of the Local Area Agreement, as with the Community Plan, is to deliver effective public services to overcome disadvantage and improve people's quality of life' (One Bansley, 2005: 5). For example, one of the provisional outcomes envisaged for the first three year time span of the LAA (2005–8) was to 'reduce anti-social behaviour but link (this) to positive activity with young people'. More specifically the local strategy aimed to include 'the YOT taking a lead on connecting with the local police teams to balance out enforcement with prevention and providing interventions to tackle anti-social behaviour working positively with young people'. It was also argued in the Barnsley strategy that the key issue around anti-social behaviour was the public perception that the problem was worsening. Throughout this particular LAA strategy the aspirational narrative of achievement centred and 'translated' children and young people as positive members of the local community. 'We want to use the Local Area Agreement as a catalyst for accelerated change to release creativity, intelligent innovation and build community capacity to deliver change for children, young people and their families in Barnsley. We want to raise aspiration, ambition and achievement through the development of personalized multi-agency provision at a local level.' There are of course as many dangers in 'reading off' outcomes from local policy texts such as the 'One Barnsley' Local Area Agreement 2005–8 as there is in doing the same from central government texts. However, the combination of text, talk and practice in this specific locality, with its own geo-history of growing disadvantage and exclusion particularly since the decline of the mining industry, suggests the possibility of creative spaces opened up for and by community governance. The LAA story in Barnsely like that of other places and spaces of community safety of course remains unfinished and uncertain in its long-term outcomes but we should not rush headlong into dystopian interpretation of such local responses to the call for 'safer, stronger communities'.

Measures aimed at reducing anti-social behaviour are now trumpeted loudly and clearly across all CDRPs across Britain. There is virtually no local community safety strategy that does not centre this area of work as a key object of the new governance through partnership. And yet despite the unfolding of the central state's policy agenda on anti-social behaviour, we have seen that the manner of the local implementation has by no means been a simple tale of growing authoritarianism and institutionalized intolerance despite the latter's ascendancy in the 'tough talk' of both central and local government actors. In her comparative research on the nature of anti-social behaviour policies and practices in two urban authorities in England, one an affluent, low crime 'new town' (Milton Keynes) and one a classic post-Fordist, high crime city with significant areas of deprivation (Nottingham), Elizabeth Burney (2005: 124–41) highlights what we may term the 'localities effect'. In particular, her work highlights the influence of the political economies of both places and the different cultures of their respective local authority and police institutions on their respective approaches to anti-social behaviour. Burney suggests that enforcement was the 'response of first resort' in terms of behaviour control in Nottingham and central to its strategy was the establishment of four police-based 'task force' teams on 'group disorder' working closely with housing enforcement and representing 'an overtly policing system'. Given that crime and anti-social behaviour are often two sides of the same coin, Burney (2005: 126) notes that it is no surprise that 'behaviour control has a much higher profile in Nottingham than Milton Keynes'. That noted, Burney then suggests that the differences between the two places was not simply down to crime and disorder rates and their differing problems of inequality and exclusion, however vital these were. In particular, Burney suggests that Milton Keynes' 'problem-solving' approach to behaviour control was also greatly influenced by the restorative justice culture that the Thames Valley police force had developed (see also Hughes et al., 2006; Stenson, 2002). Milton Keynes was viewed as being unusual in the national context in placing mediation at the heart of its strategy for anti-social behaviour. In conclusion to her comparative case study, Burney (2005: 140) suggests,

> It is clear from the two study areas that a 'one size fits all' approach when dealing with bad behaviour through legal and administrative remedies is not sustainable. Given the lack of consensus as to what the term 'antisocial behaviour' means in practice, it comes down to local responses to local problems. In the case of Nottingham, this means a focus primarily on activities that are clearly criminal, but also on street disorder such as begging and prostitution. In Milton Keynes, with its much lower crime rate, 'quality of life' is central to the strategy rather than ancillary to crime control, and enforcement is approached in a more circumspect way.

In summary, localities and their specific geo-historical contexts clearly matter and these sites need to be subject to long-term criminological research which can inform the debate on the complex relationship of rhetoric and practice as well as consequences of 'power-dependent' relations between central and local levels of governance and their respective actors.

Nuisance, Tolerance and Respect in Late Modern Societies

The dominant discourse on 'youth' and 'community' in contemporary crime and disorder reduction policy and allied measures of behaviour control in the United Kingdom views the latter ('community') as needing protection from the former ('youth'). This tendency of course risks rupturing the always tenuous links and bonds between the generations. This may be contrasted to a politics of both redistribution and recognition whereby young people are seen as both victims as well as perpetrators of crime and disorder and citizens 'in waiting'. The 2005 news story of a teacher in Manchester, England being sentenced to six months gaol for shooting at a group of young people, accused of persistent bullying and harassment of her family and vandalism towards her property, may be indicative of this 'othering' process towards anti-social young people. Once again the category of 'offender' and 'victim' became confused in the ensuing public debate and, in much media coverage reversed whereby the teacher was represented as the victim driven to the end of her wits by long-term sub-criminal behaviour by a gang of 'unruly teenagers' apparently 'terrorizing' the morally upright community. Whatever the particular merits of the case, it represents the staple diet of contemporary moral tales about loss of order and of mutual respect. For most social scientists it is easier to read the reaction to this case as a further fanning of the flame of a media-manufactured 'moral panic.' It is more difficult for social scientists to view it as potentially indicative of a moral and political crisis but we are surely obliged to look to the material and cultural conditions of existence for such a social problem and object of social control. In turn, we do need to look to the high level of crime (rather than class) consciousness in which '[t]he daily tribulation of minor crime and disorder easily slides into a concern with crime "as such" which in turn connotes violent predatory crime' (Garland, 2001: 164). The Observer newspaper columnist, David Aaronovitch, perhaps captured the widely held, yet uncomfortable and deep ambiguity around the problem of mundane but persistent nuisance in his commentary on the issue of ASBOs in noting,

> They [ASBOs] are problematic because they're new and could be abused. But one quote from my local paper last week shows Lanchester (*a critic of New Labour*) why so many people support them. A resident of King's Cross, until recently a gigantic al fresco drugs mart, told a reporter: 'If you look at the difference where I live it is massive. Two years ago people's doorways were constantly being used by drug dealers and users, but the problem has dried up.' The man felt, perhaps for the first time in years, that the law was on his side and protecting him. (The Observer, Comment Extra, 3 April, 2005, p. 22).

Despite the widespread currency of such views on the urgent need to do something about such local and persistent problems of anti-social behaviour, it is possible that the political heyday of the ASBO may be on the wane given the mounting pressure against the inappropriate use of them, their often excessive consequences and the uneven way that the orders are used in different parts of the country. Whatever the subsequent 'career' of the ASBO, the continuing political salience of fears over insecurity, often epitomized by incivilities, is unlikely to be a brief episodic issue. At the same time the nature and possibilities opened up by any new ordering of mutual respect and what may be termed a 'new civics' for a more diverse and less deferential society still requires serious attention from social scientists.

Within the New Labour project we have a seemingly contradictory espousal of both an evidence-based policy associated with the adaptive, pragmatic strategies of local preventive strategies and partnerships alongside a continuing recourse to a symbolic, visceral and expressive politics of penal segregation, banning orders and exclusion. It is difficult to deny that we are witnessing a concerted political drive to 'define deviance up' which has also had the paradoxical result that public tolerance to incivility is progressively lowered and public fear of young people, as well as other adult 'outcasts', is significantly increased. Positive communication between the generations is put in jeopardy (Muncie, 2004: 238–9). That noted, the populism associated with a 'zero-tolerance' approach to anti-social behaviour cannot be viewed as pure political and media fabrication from 'above'. As Stuart Hall (1988: 56) noted, ' "Populism" is no rhetorical device or trick. Its success and effectivity do not lie in its capacity to dupe unsuspecting folk but in the way it addresses real problems, real and lived experiences, real contradictions.' It may be argued that the issue of tolerance remains a crucial missing dimension in the populist discourse on 'respect and responsibility' from an increasing number of national governments and among which the New Labour government in the UK appears to be a front-runner. In the UK this has potentially serious unintended consequences for the national government's ambitions to build modern forms of 'community cohesion' and 'civil renewal'. As Matthews (2003: 8) observes:

> A society characterised by greater diversity and difference requires increased tolerance and respect for the lifestyle of others. A decrease in tolerance therefore signifies a *decrease* in respect. By the same token increasing the range and intensity of formal sanctions decreases the responsibility of individuals and neighbourhoods to regulate their own behaviour.

Following Matthews' logic, the current governmental drive against the anti-social is thus likely to encourage a decrease in public tolerance and thereby *reduce* levels of respect and responsibility (see also Chapter 3, pp. 79–80 for a similar argument by Hope, 2005). This a worrying exclusivist scenario for a diverse and profoundly unequal society such as the contemporary UK which may herald what may be termed a 'subtractive' dystopia in which the 'othering' of the outcast and the stranger become the communitarian *sine qua non* for constructing 'safe and strong communities'.

Cooper (2004: 137–8) has noted that the meaning of anti-social behaviour has been interpreted conservatively by British governments of the 1990s and 2000s, where sociality was anchored in terms of individual rights, public and domestic order and economic freedom. But Cooper rightly observes that anti-social behaviour also has more solidaristic connections. It is perhaps time that such terms as 'nuisance' and the 'anti-social' also became connoted with behaviour of all sorts – beyond the usual suspects – that disrupt the capacity of people to live in peaceful if not harmonious relations with one another. This would of course open up a veritable can of worms relating the widespread corruption and corporate harms and perceived anti-social behaviour that characterize even the most 'respectable' members of the population.

Conclusion

In this chapter we began by suggesting that the social scientific analysis of anti-social behaviour and strategies for its control was a more complex and multi-faceted phenomenon than both government proponents and critics alike tend to acknowledge. In the second section the rise of the social problem of anti-social behaviour in the United Kingdom was plotted. In the course of this discussion it was argued that the historical construction of this 'new' social problem was associated with popular concerns and mediated by intellectual claims-making from the political left and right. The discussion then explored in the third section on the legislative changes and new statutory measures developed as the flag-ship features of New Labour's project against disorder in many communities. In the fourth section the discussion then focused on the nature of the implementation process locally of strategies and tactics of anti-social behaviour management. Finally the unintended consequences of the growing intolerance to anti-social behaviour were tentatively explored.

More generally throughout the discussion in this chapter it has been argued that any accurate social scientific interpretation of the broad trends at work in the social control and management of anti-social behaviour must centre the following issues:

- The distinction between rhetoric and actual practice, or the gap between the intended governmental project and actual outcomes at the stage of implementation;
- The power-dependence of would-be 'sovereign' actors on other actors and institutions at different levels of governance;
- Alongside dominant national trends and discourses, localities have distinct geo-histories that make a difference.

It is clear that much of discussion in this chapter has focussed on the processes of 'othering' of outcasts from the troubled and troublesome populations of the indigenous disadvantaged of late modern societies and the place of these processes in the wider context of the community governance of crime and safety in the United Kingdom and beyond. In the next chapter we again examine processes of 'othering' of outcasts but our attention turns to those seeking refuge and asylum in affluent western societies from other conflict-ridden and poor areas of the world.

6

Strangers and Safe Havens? Asylum Seeking, Migration and Community Safety

The world has now come to the island because the island first went to the world.

(Garton Ash, 2004: 5)

In addition to representing the 'great unknown' which all 'strangers in our midst' embody, these particular outsiders, the refugees, bring home distant noises of war and the stench of gutted homes and scorched villages that cannot but remind the settled how easily the cocoon of their safe and familiar (safe because familiar) routine may be pierced or crushed and how deceptive the security of their settlement must be. The refugee, as Bertolt Brecht pointed out in Die Landschaft des Exils, is 'ein Bote des Unglucks' ['a harbinger of ill-tidings'].

(Bauman, 2004: 66–7)

Introduction

This chapter aims to contribute to the breaking of the general silence in European criminology on the connections between asylum-seeking and migration, and community safety and social cohesion. There is a large and growing body of important criminological research on asylum, detention and the criminalization of forced migration. However, there is much less research and analysis on how issues of asylum seeking and migration relate to questions of community safety and social cohesion in the increasingly diverse, unequal and globalizing late modern societies. This chapter will seek to make a small contribution to opening up this pressing and exciting area of both inquiry and intervention for a public criminology which is constituted in debate rather than existing as a uniform science of governing. In order to achieve this goal the following issues are explored in the main sections of the chapter. In the first section a preliminary case is made for the importance of the study of asylum seekers and refugees[19] (the 'strangers' of the chapter title) both for criminology as an academic discipline and more specifically for the study of the local politics and practices of the community governance of crime and safety. In the second section an overview of the new global context of the contemporary mass 'forced migration' (Castles, 2003) and asylum seeking is presented. In section three the political and policy consequences of the international as well as national and local 'moral panics' over asylum seeking and forced migration and their connections to crime and disorder are then explored. In particular, the features and consequences of the simultaneous 'securitisation' and 'criminalisation' of forced migration across an increasing number of states of the affluent, 'developed' world are discussed. Underpinning most progressive or critical scholarly commentaries on these developments are compellingly catastrophic, grand sociological narratives. In the fourth section a critical evaluation of such visions, with their emphasis on 'critique' and often implicitly abolitionist policy alternatives, is offered. The discussion in this section then moves on to try and provoke a less closed and less pessimistic analytical reading of the possibilities regarding 'what can be done', normatively and politically, about the problems of belonging and identity in an age of diversity when viewed through the lens of forced migration and asylum seeking. Finally in the fifth section, the chapter focusses on the instabilities and volatilities of governing migration and asylum seeking in particular spaces and places, drawing once more on geo-historical explanation of the complex translations of crime control and safety policy and practice and the volatile adaptations associated with these processes.

Criminology, 'the Stranger' and Asylum Seeking

It is now sociological commonsense to point to the growing diversity and insecurity in the ever-more globally inter-connected world with all its criminological consequences. Richard Sparks (2003: 152), for example, opines that 'the sense of exactly where our bodies lie and how they can feasibly be defended and by whom remains increasingly unclear'. He goes on to contend that the dangers and contagions of this endemically uncertain world are expressed in a growing obsession, at the multiple levels of the person, locality, region and nation, with 'dangers on the borders'. Many of the issues raised in this chapter emerge out of a debate between the author and Kit Carson with regard to the embattled possibilities of a progressive realist politics around communalism in the field of crime prevention and the politics of safety more generally (Carson, 2004a, b; Hughes, 2004a, 2006a). In a rejoinder to Carson's powerful critique of communitarianism in this policy field (Hughes, 2004a) I suggested that a major 'provocation' for a critical realist criminology was the issue of how to imagine and 'translate' (Callon, 1986) a replacement discourse around the volatile politics of safety and belonging in the shadow of the new, often forced, mobilities and diasporas of late mobility. The relationship of migration, belonging and citizenship has attained possibly an unprecedented high profile today across many western nations.

In this chapter, I argue the problem of the 'stranger' or 'outcast' on the real and metaphorical borders in the contemporary politics, policies and practices of crime control and community safety is a vital issue for criminologists to engage with in their public role (see Chapter 8). It is clear that the problem of the 'dangerous/criminal' immigrant stranger has been a significant one for criminological discourse historically – from that of the Irish immigrant in nineteenth-century UK (Curtin, 1971) to that of Afro-Caribbean youth in post-war UK (Hall *et al.*, 1978; Lea and Young, 1984). Nonetheless this chapter presents a case as to why the figure of the asylum seeker/refugee needs to be centred today in criminological theory and research due to the iconic role such figures are increasingly occupying in the politics of safety, securitization and criminalization – nationally, internationally and locally – across many late modern societies. Matthew Gibney (2004: 1) has noted that over the last twenty years 'asylum has become one of the central issues in the politics of liberal democratic states.' In the light of this fact, it is surprising that European criminology for the most part has been silent until late on the issue of asylum, migration and its crime control and public safety implications.[20] As Jo Goodey (2002: 140) wryly notes, '[w]hile the subjects of "migration" and "crime" are usually treated as separate disciplines in academic circles, politicians and policy-makers do not hesitate to connect one with the other and to act accordingly'.

The notable exception to this general rule of criminological silence is the largely over-looked essay by Leanne Weber (2002) *The detention of asylum seekers: 20 reasons why criminologists should care*. In this synthetic essay, Weber draws on examples from her own empirical research in the United Kingdom on asylum detention. According to Weber, there are many theoretical, practical, methodological and moral reasons why the issue of asylum seeking should fall within the broader domain of criminology. Specifically she outlines five broad areas of connection within each of which there are more specific reasons for connection cited. To summarize Weber's account, let us look at each area of connection in turn. First, there are the links to 'broad theoretical debates', specifically 'globalisation, risk and the exclusion of the "enemy without" ', 'the regulatory-punitive state and the exclusion of the "enemy within" ', and 'human rights and the limits of state power'. Second, there are links to 'specific criminological themes', such as 'detention, deterrence and deviancy amplification', 'asylum seekers as the new "Black muggers" ', 'administrative detention as "procedural criminalisation" ' and 'risk management and the drift towards preventative detention'. Third, there are comparisons with the 'criminal justice system', including issues of 'procedural safeguards and the separation of powers', 'discretion and occupational culture', 'the construction of official statistics' and 'stereotypes, discrimination and ethnic monitoring'. The fourth area is that of 'asylum seekers within the criminal justice system', specifically 'asylum seekers as offenders', 'asylum seekers as victims', 'asylum seekers and the police', 'asylum seekers, courts and bail' and 'asylum seekers in prison'. Fifth and finally, there are the connections with 'debates about the scope and purpose of criminology' covering 'redefining crime, detention as "state crime" ', 'new forms of regulation: transcending administrative criminology', 'the issue of relevance: contributing to research-led policy' and finally 'criminologists as political activists and moral entrepreneurs'. This essay makes a compelling case for the importance of asylum and immigration control for the contemporary criminological enterprise. In her conclusion Weber (2002: 26) argues that asylum seekers occupy an ambiguous conceptual space where 'criminal-justice-like powers' have escaped the confines of the criminal justice system and where the permeable boundary between the administrative and criminal spheres becomes increasingly blurred. In drawing up signposts to a new frontier of criminological enquiry, Weber's work breaks with the general criminological silence on asylum seeking and questions of contemporary ordering and control. At the same time her focus on detention (see also Welsh and Schuster, 2005) leads both to a concentration on the permeable boundary between the administrative and criminal justice but also a concomitant downplaying of the important connections between the study of asylum seeking and that of the broader trends in the community governance of crime and safety, developments in the preventive sector, and the leaky boundaries between social policy and crime control terrains which are the main concerns of this book. My key argument here is that we still lack the conceptual tools and empirical research findings on the shifting position of the asylum seeker and forced migrant – as strangers and guests – in the broader politics and policies of security and community cohesion, and the questions these issues raise for contemporary debate on diversity, identity and solidarity in western 'societies'.[21] It is to this area of enquiry that this chapter aims to make an original contribution.

Brief Excursus on the Words 'Community Safety' and 'Stranger'

Some conceptual clarification about the words 'community safety' and 'stranger' may be helpful to the reader at this juncture. As argued in previous chapters, it is unlikely that the term 'community safety' will ever be easily, adequately or finally pinned down. Indeed its history as a policy idea in the last three decades appears to confirm its status as a moving target, oscillating from a social and criminal policy 'Cinderella' to 'Belle of the Ball' (Hughes, 2002a). Its very capaciousness and contested character, like that of its older sister 'community' and younger cousin 'community governance', may in part explain its continued and growing appeal in political and policy circles. Throughout this book I have argued that governing community as object, site and agency is arguably the new communitarian mantra across many Western states. Community-based solutions to various social ills – including inter-ethnic conflict and intolerance – are now enshrined across Anglophone countries as the 'new', 'joined up' and 'empowering' means of modern governance. Yet sitting alongside these potentially inclusionary appeals, the resort to an often explicitly exclusionary politics and culture of community safety and security by affluent nation-states has rarely been more pronounced. In this register, threats are viewed as coming from outsiders/strangers against whom communities need to defend themselves or be protected. To quote Crawford (1998: 245):

> this vision tends to assume an 'us versus them' attitude, which feeds into, and is reinforced by, the existence of an 'ideology of unity'. Here, crime and criminals are external 'others' and 'community' becomes something under attack from the outside … . This insider/outsider dichotomy taps deep-seated fears about social identity and otherness, particularly given the tendency of crime to bifurcate the 'rough' from the 'respectable'. Given the anxieties that crime evokes it can feed fears. The external threat, whether actual or imagined , can become both the reason for , and the means of sustaining , 'community'. Its collective past and future can be defined by reference to a perceived external threat.

When all else fails for the embattled sovereign state the promise of delivering some measure of safety and security to a fearful citizenry from various threats to its borders and order provides the late modern policy balm or panacea. And one of the acid tests of such contested policies of community safety is increasingly linked to the question of what to do about the problem of the stranger or outcast in local communities, both 'imported' (as with the asylum seeker/migrant) and 'home-bred' (as with the anti-social deviants discussed in Chapter 5).

The word 'stranger' here also needs some discussion given the specific uses of the word in sociological theory, past (Simmel, 1950) and present (Bauman, 1991, 2004), which have been closely linked to questions of estrangement and urbanity. The use of the term 'stranger' in this paper is also different from the manner in which it is used by Young (1999) and Carson (2003) when it is argued 'we are better described in the main as a society of loosely connected or lightly engaged strangers rather than in terms of the old (and itself questionable) idea of the traditional community' (Carson, 2003: 2). It is hard to dissent from this judgement although there is also a danger in exaggerating the looseness and lightness of our mutual connections (Hughes, 2004d), not least in terms of the experiences and material constraints at work on different social classes, movements of people and strata in our contemporary diverse and unequal societies. More importantly for the argument here, however, it is contended that we are not all equally regarded as 'mutual strangers'. Reflecting back on the work of Elias and Scotson (1965) on the 'established' and the 'outsiders', a key claim of this essay is that the asylum seeker/refugee in countries like the United Kingdom, Australia and much of Europe remains represented in dominant discourses as the stranger coded as the dangerous and polluting 'outsider' in the eyes of the established 'host' communities. This is illustrative of what may be termed 'stranger fetishism' in the politics of othering whereby 'migrants', in this case, are reduced to essences. The term 'the stranger' is thus employed to capture how the 'outsider' and 'outcast' are categorized, managed and controlled as well as the uncertain contestations of such processes by various actors, both of 'strangers' themselves and others engaged in encounters with 'them'. The specific type of stranger discussed in this chapter is the mobile migrant often forced to seek refuge and asylum in affluent western localities. In a real sense such people may be understood as being both mythic in part (as the dehumanized subjects of moral panics) and achingly real (as survivors, victims, criminals, strugglers, adaptive 'guests' and so on). Along with the less mobile outcast of the 'anti-social underclass' who may often live 'cheek by jowl' with new immigrants and a range of damaged and vulnerable people (see Chapter 5), the master status of the asylum seeker increasingly across Europe, Australia and the United States of America has been that of the vilified 'Other' and threat to order, safety and 'civilisation' as 'we' have known it. The recognition of this dominant tendency of often virulent othering appears a necessarily realistic starting point for the development of a more 'inclusivizing' and progressive replacement discourse which may turn these 'nomads' into 'guests' of late modernity.

'Bringing it all Back Home': the Outcasts of Globalization

According to UN figures there were 3 million refugees in 1975 as compared to 11.7 million by 2000 and these figures excluded the 10 million not satisfying either UN standards or who were displaced in their own country (Gibney, 2004: 4). These post-colonial mobilities are peopled by a complex array of outcasts of globalization. In the context of countries of the affluent North, such outcasts and victims of the changing global and local concentrations of power in commercial organizations and political authorities are varied in nature, including both 'the sedentary inhabitants of the most deprived districts, which have been deserted by the abler and more resourceful former co-residents; and the migrants from abroad, who have arrived in affluent countries without proper immigration status' (Jordan 2004: 177). As Gibney (2004: 5) notes, refugees and asylum seekers are merely the vanguard of a world where life chances and economic inequalities are distributed with great inequality. Mixed together with those fleeing political persecution are the growing numbers of 'forced' economic migrants. Indeed, all over the world, economic globalization has led to mass migration of labour from the Second (i.e., ex-Communist Bloc) and Third Worlds. It is widely acknowledged that we now stand at the cusp of one of the greatest eras of mass migration in our history – particularly from the poor countries to the rich countries and regions of the world. 'We' (the rich and western/northern) are now reaping the consequences of 'our' own success in the process of globalization (Carson, 2003). Accordingly, the peoples of the poorest parts of the world now wish to endorse the globalization logic by moving to live in the more affluent parts of the globe. In Bauman's (2004: 66) chilling term, refugees, asylum seekers and illegal migrants may be viewed as 'the waste products of globalisation' but we should add they are also products that are also recycled and put to use (as hyper-exploited labour and human bodies).

Across Europe, it is evident that the new processes of migration and the formal response to them are placing a heavy overlay of racialization on local and national control and security systems. More and more migrants are getting caught up in these systems both as perpetrators and as victims and at the same time most 'irregular workers' in the 'shadow economy' develop their own complex strategies of resistance and survival. The emotionally labile issues of security and exclusion continue to sweep across Western Europe and add further to the fuelling of what may be termed Europe's nightmares over cultural identity. It would appear that the conflation of 'migrant'/'asylum seeker'/ 'terrorist' is fast becoming one of the most striking of all shared European (and more broadly western) nightmares, matched only by the demonisation of the immobile 'anti-social' outcast within the durable 'homeland' communities of fate. With regard to contemporary European nightmares over migration in the specific context of Britain, Timothy Garton Ash (2004) has argued that Britain faces a 'Janus dilemma' today. According to Garton Ash, Britain has four faces. 'The back and front faces can be labelled "island" and "world"; the face on the left says "Europe" and that on the right "America". No wonder Britain's headaches' (Garton Ash, 2004: 4). Island and world appear opposites (as virulently articulated around the new migrations and mobilities) but the connection, particularly given the past of Empire also, is direct and simple. To paraphrase Garton Ash 'the world *and the post-colonial* has now come to the island because the island first went to the world *as Empire*' (Garton Ash, 2004: 5; italicised words added). This peculiarity is not unique to Britain but is shared, with important national differences, across most if not all Western European countries. As Garton Ash (2004: 6) again notes, 'Every other European country has its own version , though usually less extreme, of island versus world, if one takes "island" to mean not the mere condition of being land surrounded by water (a physical fact of ever-diminishing importance) but the nurtured peculiarities of a real or claimed exceptionalism'.

The Politics of 'Othering'

Of Folk Devils and Moral Panics

The concept of moral panic is both one of the most influential and overused concepts in modern sociology. However, there appears little doubt that an international moral panic as well as more provincial panics across many affluent nations have been generated over refugees and asylum seekers 'flooding our country, swamping our services' (Cohen, 2004: xviii) by a wide array of moral crusaders, politicians and the mass media. Drawing on Cohen's theory of moral panics, Vaughn Robinson (2003: 167) concludes that Western Europe appears to be in the grip of a moral panic about the extent to which it feels it is losing its ability to maintain the 'purity of space'. In similar vein, Valier (2002: 322) notes, 'The discourse of faceless predators lurking in our midst ... [is] deployed in the construction of asylum seekers as both violently criminal and as a grave threat to national security'. Following the terrorists attacks of 9/11 and 7/7, the result of this moral panic at European national levels appears to be a visceral and racialized politics over the unholy trinity of illegal immigration, asylum-seeking and terrorism. According to Kundnani (2001), a new 'common-sense racism' towards asylum seekers has largely replaced the now unacceptable racism against settled ethnic minorities (I would add, until 'they' generate indigenously grown terrorists). Certainly asylum seekers/refugees are represented as 'bogus', undeserving and threatening in much popular imagery. Furthermore, as a result of refugee and asylum seeker 'concentration' in specific localities across Europe established as an accepted fact of being a 'problem', the common policy responses among the European Union states has been that of deterrence and forced dispersal (Robinson, 2003: 23). Cohen (2004: xix) notes that the repeated and ritualistic distinction made across Europe, North America and Australia since the 1990s between 'genuine' refugees (entitled to compassion) and 'bogus' asylum seekers (no rights, no entitlement to compassion) has resulted in the once morally untouchable category of the political refugee being deconstructed. In turn a 'culture of disbelief' penetrates the whole system.

What is the basis of such fears other than Bauman's (2004) fear of the 'great unknown' cited at the beginning of this chapter? Gail Lewis and Sarah Neal (2005: 427) suggest that across the West, the political and social tensions associated with the new migrations revolve around two main clusters of issues. First there is the perceived effects of asylum seekers, refugees and illegal immigrants on social cohesion and forms of social solidarity expressed through welfare systems; and second, an anxiety about the effects of the migration of people who are clandestine or claiming asylum on strategies of multiculturalism aimed at the further integration of minority ethnic or settled communities of earlier groups of immigrants. Furthermore, policy prescriptions reflect these fears and accordingly policy convergence across individual nation states may be growing.

In the UK context the new politics of 'race', insecurity and criminalisation is associated with the prominence given to the volatile mix of new ('illegal') immigrants and asylum seekers, international terrorism from political Islam and the small but high profile numbers of fundamentalist radicals among British Moslems which together ensure that this sense of dread is thoroughly 'racialised' (Rattansi, 2004). In this visceral climate, we may also note the different representations of victimhood associated with the iconic tragedies of Britain's 'own' children (from James Bulger to the Soham murders) compared, for example, to the drowning of over 30 Chinese 'illegals' in 2003 whilst cockle picking at the once quintessentially Lancashire holiday resort of Morecombe Bay (perhaps to be re-imagined in the future as an unlikely space of tragic and fateful globalisation). The latter tragedy and 'crime' was in part notable in the popular imagination for the racist jokes it provoked (such as sharks in the Irish Sea 'fancying a Chinese take-away'). These different responses to stories of tragedy and crime may be crucially influenced by notions of childhood innocence of course but it is important to note that the personal tragedies of child asylum seekers such as the traumatized ex-child soldiers of Somalia in Britain's schools and such like rarely disturb – never mind reform- the popular stories and narratives around asylum seeking in the United Kingdom.

The above comments are not intended to suggest that interventions to reframe this exclusivist politics of community safety – framed as the 'British/Englishman' and 'British/Englishwoman's secure homeland (because exclusive, tightly bounded and bordered)- are not being articulated by local and national coalitions and networks. However, the dominant national 'obsession' associated with Spark's (2003) 'insecure states' and populist media campaigns makes different translations of the issue of the new global mobilities difficult to realize. Clarke (2004: 64) captures the nature of the regressive nostalgia summoned up by migration as follows:

> Mobility, migration and mixing evoke a (colonial) nostalgia for when peoples knew their places: the land, the climate, the culture and the people in their 'traditional' and proper alignment. This imperative is articulated by governments (as they confront asylum-seekers and migrants), by nationalist and racist political forces as they dream of ethnic/racial purity, and by populist media discourses that persist in eliding race, nation and place. The wish that people would stay 'where they belong' is the primitive geography that informs this conception of how race and place are aligned.

The Securitisation and Criminalisation of Forced Migration

Across a wide number of liberal democratic states, the last three decades have witnessed what Gibney (2004: 2) describes as 'a remarkable array of restrictive measures'. For example, policy initiatives in EU member states since the 1990s have focused on restricting entry through asylum by making conditions less advantageous for those claiming and seeking protection on the grounds of political persecution. In turn, reductions in benefits, dispersal as 'normalized' into remote districts or camp-style accommodation and rapid processing of claims all would seem to have the aim of cutting numbers, both for the sake of saving state expenditure and to dampen 'populist' and 'racist' campaigns (Jordan, 2004: 178).

Across the West a new dominant trade in policy ideas has been developed: namely what may be termed the 'securitisation of migration' (Huysmans, 1993, 2000). Illustrative of this new state strategy, the US Immigration and Naturalization Service was reorganized in 2003 as part of the 'Orwellian'-sounding US department of Homeland Security. In this new political and policy context immigration becomes defined and represented as a matter of security, and, as Coutin (2005: 15) notes, special alien registration programmes have singled out non-citizens from Middle Eastern nations as particularly suspect. Such developments are also evident across much of Europe in the increasingly harmonized and draconian EU policies on security and the control of terrorism alongside illegal migration. The possibility of a pan-European convergence predicated on 'integration through security' has been highlighted particularly by critical scholarship in criminology and social policy. Thus, according to Mike Grewcock (2003: 114–15), across the EU the official 'smuggling/trafficking' discourse with its focus on law enforcement as the core element of border protection reflects the development of a 'European Security Zone' in which the issues of national security and immigration policy are increasingly fused. For example, Grewcock notes that the European Council in 1998 called for 'solidarity among members states and between European institutions' in the face of 'the transnational challenges presented by organized crime and migration movements'. More broadly, critical scholars such as Grewcock (2003) and Marfleet (2001) argue that at the European level, the smuggler/trafficker is seen as the vehicle by which irregular migrants crash borders and threaten a European identity increasingly formulated in terms of cultural differences. It would seem that those who engage in any aspect of the smuggling/trafficking are not just criminalized because they have broken the law but 'because they challenge the basis of national and European identity' (Grewcock, 2003: 116).[22]

Meanwhile, at the national level, for example in Britain, it is not uncommon to hear politicians and state officials alike in the first years of the 2000s basking in the glory of achievements in reducing the intake of asylum seekers and in establishing deliberately harsh benefits and accommodation regimes (where asylum seekers receive 70 per cent 'normal' benefit levels and have no choice in accommodation allocation). It is difficult to see how this official culture of disbelief and deliberate severity maintains a comfortable balance with the stated aim of government policy to also address and counter racism against minorities, including asylum seekers. According to Sales (2005), the trend in Britain since the Nationality, Immigration and Asylum Act 2002 has been a deepening of the trend towards the repression of asylum seeking. 'Tackling fraud', 'border controls' and securing a 'seamless' process from induction to removal are now at the centre of British national asylum policy.[23]

It may be suggested that a form of schizophrenia pervades Western responses to asylum seekers and refugees in which great importance is attached to the principle of asylum but enormous efforts are made to ensure that refugees never reach the territory of the state where they could receive its protection (Gibney, 2004: 2). As noted above, this hostile political and policy context has further 'chilled' in the post-9/11 and 7/7 conjuncture where national security is increasingly viewed as being antithetical to asylum-giving. The consensus among states, post-9/11 may be described as follows: that refugees constitute as much a threat as an asset; that there are major dangers posed by asylum seekers, related to their increasingly diverse and variegated nature; and that there is a need for international co-operation to deal with these new security risks (Gibney, 2004: 256). Migration is thereby often transformed into a security concern (Huysmans, 1993). As we shall see later, the consequences of this securitisation and criminalisation of migration are often grave for those people 'settled' in often hostile and unwelcoming places.

The overall picture, however, with regard to European states' policies on migration more generally is more complicated and contradictory than a one-way process of exclusionary criminalisation/securitisation, involving both conditional inclusions as well as exclusionary practices. For example, Lewis and Neal (2005: 428) note that many European states in the first decade of the twenty-first century are attempting to develop policies in the wake of their own ageing and declining populations that simultaneously loosen, in a regulated way, the control of labour migration, tighten the control of asylum and clandestine migration, and establish a framework for the promotion of social cohesion and an inclusive national identity around a set of core or irreducible values. Like many other affluent European states with ageing 'indigenous' populations, the United Kingdom government in the 2000s has attempted to balance the challenges and what it sees as the economic benefits of globalization with those of domestic, inter-communal tensions. It is evident that the national government views the securing of borders and boundary maintenance as the pre-condition for harmonious social relations in a multicultural United Kingdom. Crucially, the work of preserving a national collectivity is viewed as requiring intervention in various forms of cultural practices of established migrants, as well as the policing of those who are allowed to enter and eventually become citizens. 'And so immigration policy in its inclusionary and exclusionary practices acts as the first step in determining who has the possibility of belonging and becoming a future citizen' (Yuval-Davis *et al.*, 2005: 517). 'Social (or community) cohesion' represents a central motif of contemporary UK government policy, and more broadly across many liberal democracies, for alleviating the conflicts between different ethnic groups in society. It also dovetails closely with the pressure for greater 'civil renewal' that may invigorate the local political engagement of the citizenry. Whilst accepting the dominant trend towards the overt securitisation and criminalization of migration, the public debate over belonging, social integration and cohesion between and across diverse ethnic groups – despite undoubted tendencies towards an emphasis on sameness and assimilitionism – may also be suggestive of complex, contradictory and uncertain processes and outcomes for governing safety in communities. Much of the critical criminological and social policy literature on migration and asylum has downplayed these tendencies, yet they remain difficult questions that social scientists cannot easily eschew. I return in greater depth to this argument later.

What is to be Done About Asylum Seeking in the Politics of Community Safety?

In this section the discussion focuses on the relationship of criminological inquiry to what I termed 'the normative turn' in Chapter 1. In particular

I focus initially on the strengths and limitations of the current critical criminological 'canon' on the politics of asylum seeking and forced migration. Following the evaluation of this body of work, I present arguments for what I have termed a critical realist perspective in criminology.

Take 1: Critique and the Grand Narratives of Catastrophe

Sharon Pickering (2001) and a growing body of critical scholarship in Australian criminology (Current Issues in Criminal Justice, 2002) have made the most sustained argument for a political and public role for criminology in the debate on asylum, migration and human rights. The growth of such critiques from Australia no doubt reflects in part the extremity of the Australian state's policy of compulsory detention for illegal migrants in the decade of the 2000s as well as critical criminology's relative stronghold in the academy there. According to Pickering, the most important contribution to be made in this context is to the criminological study of 'state harm' or state crimes. Pickering (2001: 221) goes on to argue that the mandatory detention of unauthorized arrivals represents the backbone of strategies to criminalize people who seek Australia's protection. The broader thrust of critical scholarship internationally on the contemporary politics of forced migration across affluent western societies is to suggest that it has developed into a security issue cynically invoking dangers to public order and stability brought by criminal and terrorist abuses. In turn it is contended that deterrence has been 'an enabling discourse of a refugee policy in which affluent western democracies pose as beleagured victim and those in need of protection are positioned as the ultimate deviant' (Pickering and Lambert, 2002: 83). The supposed dangers from migration and asylum seeking allow for the suspension of human rights and at times indefinite imprisonment. Furthermore, it is widely argued that such contemporary trends are 'part of the general technocratic and political surveillance and militarisation of migration' (Yuval-Davis *et al.*, 2005: 515). Commenting on pan-European trends, Green and Grewcock (2002) argue that the 'war' against illegal immigration has in fact become part of a deliberate political project to create an exclusive new European identity (after the Cold War) premised on opposition to the Muslim and Third worlds. According to these authors 'the new Europe is not just a fortress, but a bastion of state crime' (Green and Grewcock, 2002: 98). The broader cultural consequences of this trend are viewed as being the rise of 'defensive identity communities' and 'ethnic fundamentalism' to meet the threat of 'unassimilable strangers, draining state resources' (Yuval-Davis *et al.*, 2005: 516).

The powerful thrust of the claims presented by this burgeoning body of critical scholarship is that of moral and political condemnation – critique writ large – of the Western-wide strategy of exclusion of asylum seekers through the fused logics of securitization and criminalization. It is less common to see such scholars engage in normative and political arguments that address what may be both alternative and practical ways of addressing the 'real' problems associated with mass, forced migration from the poor to rich countries. However, Grewcock (2003: 115) does address the political and normative dimension of his critique in arguing for an alternative discourse to that of the simultaneous criminalization and securitization of irregular migration based on 'understanding the social dynamics of migration and developing forms of analysis which embrace the right to free movement'. In turn, an abolitionist position is presented:

> To be worthwhile, a critical discourse must locate smuggling/trafficking as a manifestation of state control, rather than a justification for state sanctions; and elevate the rights of the migrant above the illusory permanence of border controls. Suggesting these controls should be abolished – and therefore removing the state's capacity to criminalise all those connected with irregular migration ... offers a route through all the contradictions to which the smuggler/trafficker discourse gives rise. (Grewcock, 2003: 132)

The radically de-constructionist argument here is for the abolition of all border controls and for the free movement of all migrants. Unfortunately we do not find out how we get from 'here' (security states and the obsession with borders) to 'there' (a world free of border controls).

Intellectual support for these grand narratives of repression of human rights for migrants alongside a seemingly totalizing, convergent movement towards the securitization of safety and migration across affluent western societies is apparent in the increasingly influential interventions of the public intellectual, Zygmunt Bauman and, to a lesser extent, others inspired by his diagnosis of our times, such as Jock Young. As Bauman (2005a: 119) dramatically and typically notes:

> A spectre hovers over the planet: the spectre of xenophobia. Old and new, never extinguished and freshly defrosted and warmed up tribal suspicions and animosities have mixed and blended with the brand-new fear for safety distilled from the uncertainties and insecurities of liquid existence ... Indeed, throughout the world ruled by democratically elected governments the sentence 'I'll be tough on crime' has turned out to be the trump card that beats all others, but the winning hand is almost invariably a combination of a promise of 'more prisons, more policemen, longer sentences' with an oath of 'no immigration, no asylum rights, no naturalisation'.

Bauman's work is of axial importance in opening up a broader public debate on criminological consequences of the new global mobilities for the politics of safety and questions of identity, belonging and diversity in western late modern societies. At the same time, Bauman's conclusions have tended to be profoundly pessimistic and have entered into the mind-set and commonsense of critical scholars and liberal journalists and broadcasters alike.[24]

Meanwhile, Jock Young has plotted the bleak tale of exclusion and 'othering' of the new immigrants as a universal outcome across the West. 'In every instance a social and spatial process of exclusion has occurred in the host country and, concomitant with this, the cultural "othering" of the immigrant population' (Young, 2003b: 455), for example, as folk devils associated with crime, drugs, prostitution and violence. Although Young denies that this process of othering is a 'cultural universal', much of his ('in every instance'?) diagnosis, like that of Bauman, appears to offer a quasi-universal explanation associated with the allied thesis of the 'exclusive society' and the 'great transformation' (Hobsbawm, 1995; Young, 1999). Such an historico-sociological narrative clearly captures much of the dominant tendencies at play in the politics and policies of asylum control and immigration across many late modern societies. In turn it would be dangerously naïve and optimistic to downplay such potentially globalizing processes of victimization and demonization of 'outcasts'. In this current climate of fear and exclusion, the asylum seeker commonly occupies the deviant 'master status' of being not only the unwanted stranger but also increasingly that of 'stranger danger'. However, the dystopian narratives of catastrophe and of the great transformation in much sociological theory may underplay the contested character of these processes in the lived experiences of different communities and their variegated and unstable spaces and histories both inter-nationally and, as crucially, sub-nationally. In such sociological work then, there remains insufficient attention to the actual practices of governing in specific localities and in varying geohistorical contexts.[25]

Take 2: Beyond Critique and the Normative Turn of Critical Realist Criminology

Whilst recognizing the urgency of a critique of currently dominant discourses and practices of state and allied institutions in the management and control of migrant populations, I wish to argue that critique alone is insufficient. New possibilities and spaces for progressive interventions also need to be articulated, particularly if commentators such as Crawford (2002: 37) are correct in observing that '[w]hat we share is fashioned increasingly by our fears and concerns'. Or is the ever onward movement towards a 'culture of fear' unstoppable and inevitable?

In making this argument 'beyond critique', let's return briefly to Sayer (2000 and Chapter 1) whose ideas open up the possibility of a radical 'normative turn' in debates on safety, belonging and the 'stranger' in contemporary society. Sayer (2000: 157) has observed that there is a remarkable imbalance between our ability to think about the social world scientifically, as something to be understood and explained, and our ability to think about it normatively or even how it might be. For all the important work critiquing and deconstructing the processes of criminalization and securitization and questioning the legitimacy and legality of state processes, there are few sustained attempts at constructing alternative 'imaginaries' on the solidarity/diversity debate in the existing critical criminological and policy analysis literature on asylum seeking and forced migration. This is surprising given the fact that any criticism of existing social relations and institutional forms presupposes the possibility of a better way of life. Criminologists wishing to intervene in debates on asylum seeking, crime control and community safety might gain much from looking to the engagement with normative theory by such commentators as the political theorist Gibney, the human geographer Vaughan Robinson and the sociologist of law, Carson. These interventions range from the pragmatic and middle range theorizing of Gibney and Robinson to the self-consciously 'utopian' and speculative re-imagining of Carson.

Let's begin with the gritty, humanitarian realism of Gibney. Gibney (2004: 15) argues that adequate prescriptions for the responses of states must possess both ethical force, informed by a convincing value or furnishing a credible moral ideal, and have practical relevance, taking account of the character and capabilities of the agents at whom it is directed and of the public consequences of their actions. Gibney, for example, suggests there is a duty among academics to challenge the current constraints often facing national governments and to re-shape the political space in which they find themselves. More specifically Gibney points to several ways in which this might be achieved such as by reshaping public opinion and challenging the currently narrow view of how politicians' vulnerability might be reduced. In turn, the current public volatility regarding asylum and immigration may be best tackled by increasing people's sense of the moral value of the institution of asylum and the ethical, humanitarian importance of saving strangers from persecution and danger. Meanwhile, the work of Robinson (2003) challenges the widespread policy assumption that the 'concentration' of asylum seekers and refugees is necessarily a problem for which forced 'dispersal' is the solution. Dispersal, with its denial of a basic human right to choose where to live when no harm or crime has been committed, is viewed by Robinson as a 'knee-jerk' response to the moral panic previously noted. The rationale for dispersal is viewed as being attractive to politicians in that it appeases 'a bigoted but vocal minority of the indigenous population' (Robinson, 2003: 166). In contrast to this dominant rationale, Robinson (2003: 161) suggests the clustering of asylum seekers and refugees may be viewed and articulated as a 'natural process arising out of man's (sic) desire for a sense of belonging, security and companionship'. In making this argument we might note that there are few policy concerns over the emergence of affluent 'gated communities' of like-minded people in the United Kingdom or over the clustering of ageing British 'expatriates' in enclaves in Southern Spain! If the real issue is thus the soothing of the fears of 'white' voters who want to feel immigrants and those 'strangers' allowed to live in 'their' cities are under control, rather than the expense of clustering or the strain on services, then alternative solutions may be imagined. Among the different solutions proffered by Robinson (2003: 172–6) to make clustering less threatening and to soothe insecurities, the following appear to be potentially integral to future, inclusivist local community safety strategies on asylum seeking:

- asylum seeking needs to be re-legitimized as a distinct channel of migration, separate from that of labour migrants;
- the tone of both the national and local debate needs changing, noting that some governments have encouraged a debate on legal labour immigration but not on asylum seeking itself;
- greater attention needs to be given to the management of the media, both local and national;
- public perceptions may be changed through concerted educational programmes;
- and greater community involvement, active engagement and sponsorship policies may help overcome the predominant assumption that asylum seeking is 'someone else's problem'.

The articulation of such components of a 'replacement discourse' around asylum seeking and community safety would also lead to a questioning of the act of exclusion on security grounds as self-justifying and engender a call for the necessity of applying rigorous criteria for determining the validity of security threats.

Carson's (2004b) intervention in this debate begins with a pressing question, namely how do we address the issue of otherness, difference and diversity with their negative exclusionary connotations potentially endemic to any form of solidarism and acutely present in processes surrounding the world of crime and its prevention? Carson suggests one alternative way of thinking in this respect, drawing on the work of Pavlich

(2002), is by recourse to a discourse around *hospitium*, from which hospice, hospital, and especially importantly here, hospitality are derived. The language of *hospitium* envisages possibilities of persons, places and processes where hosts welcome strangers without surrendering control or identity and where a threshold 'simultaneously opens the limit of that threshold to otherness and accepts an undecided negotiation of the host relationship' (Pavlich, 2002: 126). The great advantage of the language of *hospitium* for Carson is that it attempts to conceptualize a process of coming together without the unitary, negative and exclusionary tendencies of 'community' or 'social capital'. Discursive shifts of these kinds – including Gilroy's (2004) emphasis on celebrating the 'everyday practices of conviviality' – could have far reaching implications for crime prevention and community safety writ large.

The debate on *hospitium* (hospitality) certainly offers one way of re-articulating and challenging the paranoiac and inferioritizing populist discourses around new migrants in the wealthy societies of the world as well as the fears of 'host' peoples and their own vulnerable neighbourhoods. Carson's tentative espousal of 'hospitium' when allied to a reinvigorated collective commitment to human rights may play a helpful role here. But there is perhaps even more potential for inclusivist and realistic ways of imagining belonging, respect and deep civility in late modern conditions to be found in the celebration and recognition of the *diasporic* – rather than the multi-cultural – as part of the new commonsense. As Sallie Westwood (2002: 430) observes, 'Diaspora foregoes the difficulties of naming populations, of producing essentialized "communities" of race, colour or ethnicity, and it allows for identities in process, rather than as finished products which adds to the sense of the normality of difference, even a celebration of difference and diversity'. Brubaker (2005: 12) also confirms that diaspora is best understood not as a bounded entity but rather as a category of practice used to make claims, to articulate projects, to formulate expectations, to mobilize energies, to appeal to loyalties. 'It does not so much *describe* the world as seek to *remake* it.' In turn, the promotion and celebration of the diasporic does appear to have an elective affinity with the urban world perceived and experienced as both coalescence and collision. At the same time it is vital to note that the diasporic is not a cosy world of the newly commodifed 'world music' and 'global foods' but rather the diasporic is embodied, lived and travelled as discontinuous, with massive psychic costs that relate very directly to racialised modes of power (Westwood: 2002). Furthermore, we need to be sceptical of grand claims about epochal breaks such as a new age of diaspora given that even if there may be as many as 120 million migrants, this amounts to less than 2 per cent of the global population. And we need to remember that the mobility of the great majority remains severely limited by the morally arbitrary facts of birthplace and inherited citizenship and by exclusionary policies of states (Brubaker, 2005: 9).

Local Safety and the Stranger: Volatile Processes and Places

Throughout this book I have argued that both neo-Marxist and Foucauldian governmentality literature have tended to conflate governmental 'strategy' and 'intention' with 'outcome' and 'consequence' in their analyses of the neo-liberal governance. In contrast the centring of contestation (over logics, forms and practices of governing) as a critical dynamic in the development of governance has been prioritized in much of this book's analysis. Analyses thus need to begin from an attention to the contested, contradictory and unstable qualities of social formations. As noted previously, Clarke's (2004) neo-Gramscian position is one endorsed throughout this book despite the risks that it may encourage a certain romanticisation of resistance and may overstate the spaces for the manoeuvre and the downplaying of the weight of dominant tendencies. That said, the non-total nature of domination and subjection 'makes a difference' (Clarke, 2004: 159). Accordingly, the instabilities of governance and the unpredictable agency associated with governing are not just the awkward background noise surrounding the policy process; rather such contextual processes are constitutive of governing itself. This final section of the essay is thus devoted to an examination of the unstable and unpredictable processes of the community governance of the new migrants and asylum seekers in 'host' (and often hostile) localities in the UK and Europe on which my recent comparative research has focussed.

Much of what local practitioners, policy makers, political actors and even researchers 'do' in the field of community safety crosses the increasingly leaky boundaries between social policy and criminal justice policy. We live in hybrid times with more and more hybridized actors. The policy maelstrom that is the community governance of crime and safety opens up new challenges and 'wicked issues' that are not easily insulated by firm legal definitions and institutional barriers. Working with 'communities' on the protection, settlement and integration of refugee and asylum seeker populations, and problem-solving initiatives associated with 'host-newcomer' relations in different localities, may represent a key new space for potentially innovative, progressive community safety work. At the same time, dominant contemporary tendencies tend to imply that community safety may become increasingly recoded as 'repressive criminality prevention' and as part of crusades against 'anti-social' chaos and for exclusive, nativist and majoritarian security zones in states across the West (see Chapters 5 and 7). Accordingly, Crawford's (2001: 32) warning about the exclusivist potential of community safety as part of the desperate assertion of state sovereignty across European localities cannot go unheeded:

> 'community safety', in so far as it is concerned with 'quality of life' issues is saturated with concerns about safety and 'ontological insecurity'. It evokes a 'solution' to crime, incivility and disorder, thus enabling the (local) state to reassert some form of sovereignty. Symbolically, it reaffirms control of a given territory, which is visible and tangible. The current governmental preoccupation with petty crime, disorder and anti-social behaviour reflects a source of 'anxiety' about which something can be done in an otherwise uncertain world.

Crawford's claims regarding the governmental preoccupation across Europe with 'petty crime, disorder and anti-social behaviour' may have easily been supplemented with the closely aligned preoccupation with the dangers and threats associated with illegal immigrants, 'bogus' asylum seekers and potential terrorists.

Local Politics and Struggles for the 'Community Integration' of Asylum Seeker and Refugee Groups in the United Kingdom

Looking across the United Kingdom in the first years of the twenty-first century, it is evident that the both tactical and strategic policy dilemmas associated with asylum seekers and refugees are unevenly distributed and varyingly articulated in local community safety strategies. Nonetheless it is increasingly common that the problems of both criminalisation and victimisation of and 'hate crimes' against asylum seekers, or presumed asylum seekers, are now routinely addressed in many such strategies (NACRO, 2003). Concurrently the broader issues around 'community cohesion' and the integration of such new groups have also now become key and often volatile concerns for those localities with often enforced 'dispersed' concentrations of asylum seeker and new migrant communities. It is not uncommon to hear local practitioners describe the situation in many of the most deprived, inner city areas where such concentrations of asylum seeker/refugee peoples have been decanted without much, if any, local consultation as 'tinderboxes'. The political volatility of such local contexts is captured in Stenson's (2005: 278) observation that in many UK urban areas, 'inter-ethnic relations, defined in terms of both visible, racial and cultural markers of difference, are the most sensitive bio-political issues for community safety'. On the basis of his research, Stenson (2005: 266) suggests that there are pressing problems and conflicts associated with rising rates of crime and anti-social behaviour which are in part related to, or as importantly perceived to be related to, the effects of inward migration on inter-communal relations and social cohesion in poor urban neighbourhoods of increasingly complex demographic composition. It is, for example, evident that there have been growing conflicts in some of the most deprived localities in Britain around both 'turf wars' over which groups, 'new' and 'established', may control certain illicit markets such as prostitution and drug use. In turn there have also been conflicts over seemingly more mundane questions of social ordering in localities such as what is perceived to be appropriate public decency and respect between groups in demographically complex neighbourhoods. 'Hence, complex inter-communal relations, often coded in terms of crime and anti-social behaviour, are the products of struggles over values, beliefs, lifestyle, sexuality and sexual partners, as well as the financially measurable material conditions of life' (Stenson, 2005: 278). And of course there have been the ever-present consequences of the 'new' racism against new immigrants and refugees.

These sensitive and all to real 'bio-political issues' (defined as relating to the struggle for sovereign control over populations and territories) point to pressing inter- and intra-communal conflicts and suspicions which cannot be adequately understood as the mere stuff of populist fantasies from the mass media, however much the latter may fan the flames of public anxieties and panics. At the same time these same 'bio-political' issues may also generate progressive experiments in local political 'inventiveness' from actors in certain localities. Indeed, reflexive and complex governmental experiments in what may be termed inter-communal 'respect-exchanges' are evident in the local work of some community safety partnerships on the integration and settlement of refugee and asylum seeker groups across the United Kingdom. To cite one example of local 'community integration' experiments regarding 'host' and 'guest' relations in Britain, the Derby community safety partnership in 2004 took a leading role in addressing the threat of inter-communal violence and unrest between the settled and indigenous Pakistani community and the recently arrived Kurdish (male) refugee community in this city. Reacting in part to a headline story in the national tabloid paper, the *Daily Mail* (entitled 'The New Race Time Bomb', 3/1/04) which predicted that Derby would see great violence and unrest as a result of conflicts between young Kurdish and Pakistani men, a 'Dialogue and Capacity-building Project' was formed which resulted in tangible if not easily measurable 'peace-making' achievements. Drawing self-consciously and creatively on the current New Labour Project of 'community cohesion', the work in Derby held the promise of broadening out the 'normal' work of community safety partnerships from that of often short-term crime and disorder reduction interventions to more ambitious 'pan-harm' reduction

(Wiles and Pease, 2000) and to the promotion of public 'goods' associated in this case with dialogic and mutually respectful inter-communal relations. One tangible form taken by this community safety initiative was the facilitation of the dialogue between Kurdish and Pakistani communities around their shared but also very different relationships to Islam in their respective geo-histories. Relatedly, it may be noted that there has also been a growing number of local mediation schemes across Britain linked to tensions and mis-perceptions between 'host' and 'guest' communities which may go some way to fostering Cantle's call for 'routes across diversity' (Home Office, 2001). Such inventive work under the umbrella of community cohesion may help loosen notions of fixed and permanent difference between groups whilst also recognizing that membership of group 'counts' and is not to be dismissed.

Such instances of peace-making work associated with refugee and asylum seeker groups and 'host' communities and pursued by local alliances and authorities are concrete examples of inclusive, preventive initiatives. These are initiatives that continue to operate in an otherwise hostile and visceral national, mass-mediated context of punitiveness and exclusion towards the stranger and outcast. However, they are not adequately explained as 'good' local struggles against a 'bad' national policy strategy that emphasizes repression and exclusion. Rather, the policy directives from the Home Office and other related departments in Britain on asylum, ethnicity, exclusion and community cohesion as well the latest initiative of 'Local Area Agreements' around safety and crime and disorder (see pp. 132–4 above) are themselves complexly constituted and fissured by ambivalent and unpredictable messages. With the arrival in 2005 of annual 'Local Area Agreements' (LAAs) between local authorities and central government based on four national public service agreements on local outcomes, community safety may be being pushed and pulled in several uneasily reconciled directions with potentially important consequences for issues of community cohesion and the 'problem' of the newcomer/stranger (see also Chapter 5 on related developments around the problem of anti-social behaviour). LAA public service agreements (3) and (4) – respectively 'to improve the standard of life for people in the most disadvantaged neighbourhoods and ensure those services are more responsive to neighbourhood needs and improve service delivery' and 'to empower local people to have greater voice and influence over decision making and delivery of services'- are likely to be vehicles for the articulation of competing demands from both 'established' and 'newcomer/outsider' groups in urban localities. And of course such developments also sit alongside the push for more intrusive, 'hands-on' local policing of 'hard-to-reach' communities in the shadow of the threat of and 'war' against terror from Muslim extremists. Deciphering the likely futures of these complexly inter-connected policy issues will represent a major new research challenge for criminology in the United Kingdom and beyond in the first decades of the present century.

European Nightmares and Dreams

In the spirit of developing a comparative criminology sensitive to local geo-histories, let us now examine related developments in some localities in Europe. A growing number of commentators have pointed to the 'dark side' (Crawford, 2002) of the new mobilities and politics of security across Europe. Albrecht (2002), for example, has provided graphic instances of 'pogrom-like events' in recent years by 'host' populations in towns across Europe as far apart as El Ejido in Spain, with mass attacks on illegal Moroccan workers, to the burning of asylum seeker houses in Rostock-Lichtenhangen in Germany. It appears that the articulation of solidarity through, rather than counterpoised to, politically regressive 'criminologies of the other' (Garland, 2001) represents an increasingly central motif in contemporary European politics (Edwards and Hughes, 2005a: 356). There is no doubting the growing salience of immigration for municipal politics across Europe, not least because the impact of migration flows is uneven within national territories. Together with Adam Edwards (Edwards and Hughes, 2005b), I have argued that in some local contexts concerns over inward migration and the attribution of problems of crime, anti-social behaviour and public disorder to immigrants has been a major factor in the rise of authoritarian political movements such as the List Pim Fortuyn (LPF) in Rotterdam (van Swaaaningen, 2005), the British National Party (BNP) in some Northern English towns (Edwards and Hughes, 2002) and the National Front in Marseilles (Body-Gendrot, 2000). The rise of the LPF is perhaps the most striking example to date in Europe of the rise of an anti- (Muslim) immigration and punitive 'turn', not least because it emerged in Holland, a country generally known for its tolerant 'culture of control'. Edwards and myself (2005a,b), drawing selectively on van Swaaningen (2005), have explained the LPF's rise to power as follows. First we noted the basis of the LPF's success lay in its original appeal (and power-base) among the increasingly disaffected white working classes of 'post-Fordist' Rotterdam through its focus on 'live-ability' (*leerbaarheit*) The LPF popularized a narrative of Dutch cultural decline associated in great part with the liberal elite's tolerance for 'alien' communities, especially Muslims from the North and Horn of Africa, who did not share a commitment to traditional Dutch traditions. In the broader national context of Holland this conception of safety as a problem of unregulated migration and 'multi-culturalism' created a broader political climate which rejected the liberal, pragmatic rationalism for which the Dutch culture of control had become renowned. We contended that,

> Whereas previously 'safety' had signified a more social democratic politics of urban renewal, the LPF were successful in capturing this term and re-articulating it to signify a range of external threats from post 9–11 terrorism to street violence and new objects of control, specifically street populations from ethnic minority communities. (Edwards and Hughes, 2005a: 357)

The electoral success of the LPF was short-lived but its impact on Dutch politics may be longer-term and more pervasive (van Swaaningen, 2005).[26]

Whilst noting these worrying political trends, it is also vital to acknowledge that there have also been important differences in the politics of crime, disorder and migration in other localities both noted above in the United Kingdom and elsewhere across Europe, for example, in Nantes in France where a more social democratic interpretation of the 'problem' of crime (as a problem of social inequalities) emerged (de Maillard, 2005). Practices of local 'community governance' regarding the problem of the 'stranger' may also be associated with attempts to 're-define social identities and forms of citizenship' (Selmini, 2005: 318) in more inclusive ways. According to Rosella Selmini's research on *comitati di cittadini* ('citizens' committees') in traditional, urban working class areas in Emilia-Romagna, such mobilizations have certainly been associated with new fears and new images of disorder which were frequently related to the presence and 'threat' of immigrants from North Africa and Eastern Europe who were considered to be in part responsible for the new 'decay' in the city and perceived as being opposed to the values of the former working class. However, Selmini contends that such committees also belonged to the cultural and political field of the Left' and they often privileged the 'discourse of rights and social justice rather than that of defensiveness and victimisation' (Selmini, 2005: 318). In most cases, even during periods of more intense conflicts among citizen committees, immigrant groups and the police and municipal institutions, Selmini contends that such community organizations tended to involve themselves in preventive activities, such as the regeneration of public spaces, mediation of conflicts, revitalization of the neighbourhood through social and cultural initiatives and in which defensive control, surveillance and crime reporting activities remained less important. The lesson from this example from Italy is that local mobilizations around public safety in the context of inter-communal conflicts are not always and necessarily regressive.

On the basis of the foregoing discussion, it is evident that there is local differentiation in the politics of safety, asylum and migration across

Europe. In turn making sense of these differentiated practices in the politics of safety necessitates the examination of how, for example, local political actors interest others in translating, or problematizing, and responding to issues in their preferred terms; enrol supportive coalitions to advance these problematizations; develop the political dynamics of these associations; and relate between formal and informal agents of governance (Stenson, 2005: 276). Neither 'success' nor 'failure' of such translations and coalitions can be guaranteed in advance.

Conclusion

At the beginning of this chapter in the first section an argument was made for the importance of the study of asylum seekers and forced migrants both for criminology as an academic discipline and for the understanding of the politics and practices of community governance of crime and safety and the new politics of security which are central concerns of this book as a whole. In the second section the broad global context of mass forced migration and asylum seeking was discussed. The third section then focussed in depth on the political and policy consequences of the moral panics over asylum seeking and migration, highlighting in particular consequences of the simultaneous 'securitisation' and 'criminalisation' of forced migration across an increasing number of western states. In the fourth section a critical evaluation of the politically dystopian and theoretically totalizing visions of much critical criminological scholarship on migration and the politics of security was undertaken. Arising out of this evaluation, the discussion in this section then proceeded to develop a less pessimistic analysis of the possibilities regarding 'what can be done', normatively and politically, about the problems of belonging and identity as well as safety in an age of diversity when viewed through the lens of forced migration and asylum seeking. In the fifth section the chapter examined the instabilities and volatilities of governing migration and asylum seeking in particular spaces and places, drawing explicitly again on geo-historical explanation of the complex translations of control and safety policy and practice and the volatile adaptations associated with these processes.

Overall this chapter represents a preliminary effort to engage criminologically with the comparative empirical analysis and debate on safety, asylum seeking and migration. It will have achieved its modest goal if it provokes further discussion among criminologists and interested citizens. The discussion in this chapter suggests tentatively that in the community governance of crime and safety, there are translations of the 'problem' of asylum seeking and forced migration which may have a solidary potential when conceived in terms of shared suffering and frailty (Carson, 2004b).

And yet it remains evident that such inclusive translations of community safety are sporadic and fragile in character when compared to the allure of excluding and defensive, 'securitarian populist' (de Maillard, 2005: 336) discourses of security. The aspiration of vibrant, shared public spaces alongside shifting forms of cultural diversity and cohesion in our increasingly globalized and globalizing cities is examined in depth in Chapter 7 which now follows. Finally if one of the lessons of history is that cultures progress through bastardisation, the novelist Kurt Vonnegut's aphorism may be worth remembering: 'We are the sum of the parts we pretend to be. So we must be careful what we pretend to be' (in Younge, 2004).

7

Urban Regeneration, Crime Reduction and Communities of the Future

If we superimpose the newer 'inclusionary' controls onto the more traditional forms of exclusion (notably incarceration) and their counterparts in the city (reservations, sandboxes or whatever), we arrive at the likeliest future of social control. It is a future of decisive and deepening bifurcation: on the soft side there is indefinite inclusion, on the hard side, rigid exclusion.

(Cohen, 1984: 232)

The search for a non-oppressive city which provides opportunity and celebrates diversity takes us on a path towards meritocratic policies in the sphere of justice and transformative policies in the sphere of community ... The solution is to be found not in the resurrection of past stabilities, based on nostalgia and a world that will never return, but on a new citizenship, a reflexive modernity which will tackle the problems of justice and community, of reward and individualism, which dwell at the heart of liberal democracy.

(Young, 1999: 189, 199)

Introduction

This chapter focusses on the third 'new' object of the community governance of crime and safety, namely urban regeneration. This much 'hyped' political and policy project across late modern societies promises the possibility of developing 'sustainable' and 'entrepreneurial' communities but is also linked to a long history of broken promises and failures (Hughes and Mooney, 1998). The present chapter is again necessarily comparative in its orientation, both in terms of an examination of sub-national developments in the United Kingdom (again my primary source of evidence) but also in the exploration of non-UK examples. I will place the current criminological debates on urban regeneration, crime reduction and 'criminogenesis' in the wider context of urban change in our era of neo-liberal globalization and in so doing draw on a number of insights drawn from non-criminological disciplines, perhaps most tellingly from urban geography.

The chapter is structured as follows. In the first section a brief discussion of the images of the city in the social sciences is presented within which the more specific diagnosis of policy developments around urban regeneration or more grandiosely, 'urban renaissance', needs placing. In the second section the chapter focusses on the UK government's current initiatives and thinking around regeneration and community cohesion/social capital as a possible exemplar of broader policy developments across the West. In the third section the burgeoning body of work in critical social science which has highlighted the 'dark side' of urban renewal and its connections with neo-liberal enterpreneurialism and processes of simultaneous securitization and exclusivist 'othering' of seemingly non-productive populations is explored. This largely dystopian body of work is then critically evaluated and contrasted with more critical realist-inclined empirical analyses and detailed ethnographies which point to both contradictory outcomes and spatial struggles in the politics of regeneration in specific geo-historical contexts. In the final and fifth section of the chapter, the possibilities of a more open-ended politics of the city and shared, public spaces is addressed via the concepts of 'geographies of responsibility' and 'power dependence'. The discussion of these contemporary trends in urban 'ordering' provides us with vital insights for understanding the changing contours and processes at work in the late modern field of control and safety more broadly.

Throughout this chapter the recurrent themes in this book are revisited. I argue for a critical realist criminology which combines acuity to the critique of existing practices and outcomes in this case around contemporary strategies of urban regeneration, with a responsibility to attempt to develop progressive, programmatic politics and alternative replacement discourses arising out of theoretical and research-based engagement with these issues. Perhaps more contentiously and in some tension with the work of urban geographers, the question of what constitutes safer and 'transversal' communities in this debate about our urban futures is accorded a key place despite the left's traditional disdain for 'community' as against 'justice' as a possible progressive political mobilizer and normative value. Indeed I argue that a co-joining of justice and community, as hinted at in Young's (1999) observation above, may offer new possibilities for solutions fit for our times despite the worryingly accurate prediction from Cohen (1985) above regarding the probable nature of social control in the contemporary city.

Images of City Life in Social Sciences

In noting that, 'The bulk of the crime and disorder that is the source of so much anxiety in market societies occurs, as a matter of personal experience or more often as a matter of report in public space within cities', Ian Taylor (1999: 91) captures a powerful truth about popular, negative representations of the nexus between crime and disorder and the 'degenerate' city. Nor can such anxiety be easily written off as the stuff of mere media fabrication and a misplaced, paranoiac culture of fear. More generally, however, the city also presents us with a Janus-faced conundrum manifesting both dystopian and utopian tendencies. Variously and simultaneously city life is often understood as being an uncomfortable and confusing mix of the inauthentic and the dynamic, offering allure and fascination alongside fear and loathing. Swyngedouw *et al.* (2003a: 1) capture this ambivalence in stating that

> Cities are brooding places of imagination, creativity, innovation, and the ever new and different. But cities also hide in their underbelly perverse and pervasive processes of physical decay and suffocation, social exclusion and marginalisation, and are rife with all manner of social and political conflict, and often outright despair in the midst of the greatest affluence, abundance, and pleasure.

It is now widely acknowledged in contemporary social theory that cities represent the condensed sites for contemporary global flows and their local bedding down (and arguably the production of the global). They are the spaces where both global propinquity and hybridized connection co-exist with attempts at segregation and the building of walls between the privileged and the poor. Perhaps cities are best understood using a sociologically-infused geographical imagination in which their production is analysed in a context of social relations that stretch beyond the city and by the intersection of social relations within the city (Massey *et al.*, 1999, Allen *et al.*, 1999, Pile *et al.*, 1999). We have then 'worlds within cities' and 'cities in the world' (Massey *et al.*, 1999). In particular, cities are especially important in the partial unbundling of the social with the national, and in expressing the localization of the global. As Saskia Sassen (2005: 460) and others note, cities need to be understood as a bounded space 'where multiple transboundary processes intersect and produce distinct socio-spatial formations' and crucially where the work of globalization 'gets done' and the contradictions of globalization are condensed. For much of the first half of the twentieth century the study of cities was at the heart of sociology and criminology. Sassen (2005: 457) suggests the city is once more emerging as a strategic site for understanding some of the major new trends reconfiguring the social order. We are seeing then a return to the city as a lens for social and criminological theory.

The 'business' of urban regeneration is but the latest manifestation of a long history of political struggles and projects aimed at the re-ordering of the city, particularly in the context of fears over disorder 'from below'

(McLaughlin and Muncie, 2000). In our current times, it is widely argued by social scientists that inequalities between the affluent and the poor, the cosmopolitan and the immobilized, appear to be on the increase and they are being expressed spatially, as for example with the sharp and dramatic divide between 'the urban glamour zone' and 'the urban war zone' of many mega-cities (Sassen, 2005: 464). The attempted purification of urban space is certainly to the fore in much contemporary governance of crime and safety, from the regulation of the 'anti-social' to the dispersal, containment and expulsion of illegal immigrants/asylum seekers (see Chapters 5 and 6). The latest reincarnation of this obsession with orderly, pure, clean and revitalized urban spaces is associated with claims of urban renaissance across many contemporary social formations, locally, nationally and regionally. A large body of contemporary social scientific scholarship has rightly connected much of these city regeneration projects to both a neo-liberal, economic agenda of global competitiveness and footloose entrepreneurialism and a moral communitarian social agenda aimed at remoralizing communities as object, site and agent of governance. Taylor (1999: 97), for example, correctly notes the broad tendency for 'a marketisation of life' as a result of which we are witnessing the intrusion of capital (possession or absence thereof) into the different publics' use of urban space, from beggars' survival strategies to the rise of chic cafes and boutique markets.[27]

Regeneration as Governmental Rhetoric, Project and Policy in the United Kingdom

It is a widely claimed assertion among scholars of regeneration across the west that policy makers and at times practitioners see strategies and experiments in regeneration as an unproblematically good thing and a tangible public good. In turn, urban regeneration is often hailed by political elites, national, local and regional, as an important element in the 'war' against crime and disorder and in promoting the antidote of strong, cohesive communities. This is materially and symbolically expressed in the rebuilding, redevelopment and, at times, demolition, of both city centres and older, 'worn-out' parts of the 'post-Fordist' industrial cities and their hinterlands. There is much hyberbole and posturing from political elites surrounding such regenerative work and its communitarian impetus (Amin, 2005), although it is wise to see these as narratives of intention rather than necessarily indicators of accomplishment. As Hancock *et al.* (unpublished) note, 'In its name, the new 24 hour city has been born, the "social capital" of poor communities ostensibly increased, cultural industries developed and local economies rejuvenated.' Crucially for the concerns of this book, Hancock *et al.,* argue that an integral theme in the emerging discourses around urban regeneration is the connection now routinely made between effective regeneration and crime reduction. Regeneration in other words is also about crime control and community safety and how these can be achieved. Accordingly any overview of developments in the politics of crime and community in the contemporary late modern context cannot ignore the growing importance of these governmental projects.

Both national governments in Europe and the supranational power of the European Union have been (co-) active in devising programmes and providing resources to fund regeneration initiatives across Europe (Swengedouw *et al.,* 2003a and c). Examples in the United Kingdom, date back to the 1980s Safer Cities initiative and relatedly the Single Regeneration Budget (SRB) in which economic growth and prosperity goals associated with an 'enterprise culture' were linked to crime-preventive and safety-promotive projects. Typical contemporary manifestations of such projects are situational measures such as CCTV, physical estate improvements, environmental design alongside youth inclusion schemes and visible patrol presences such as neighbourhood wardens and other members of the extended policing family. Across the periods of Thatcherism and Blairism in the United Kingdom, there is much continuity in the claimed relationship between safer cities and a flourishing economic enterprise and community life.

In the United Kingdom and particularly since New Labour's victory in 1997, a whole raft of initiatives has been formulated and selectively 'rolled out' to address the social exclusion of neighbourhoods experiencing multiple forms of deprivation and in turn promote their regeneration and their sustainability as communities. These have included most importantly the New Deal for Communities, the set of initiatives gathered together in the National Strategy for Neighbourhood Renewal and most recently, the Safer, Stronger Communities Fund. The mode of governance for the local implementation of these initiatives is that of partnerships involving actors (at least rhetorically) across the statutory, private, voluntary and community sectors (see Chapters 2–4). The approach emanating from central government and in particular from its Policy Action Team 17's report *Joining It Up Locally* (DETR, 2000) suggested that earlier regenerative initiatives, dating back to the 1960s, failed for a number of inter-related reasons. These included communities not being adequately involved nor empowered; initial joint strategies not being translated into sustained joined-up working; initiatives being driven by central funding rather than local needs; and central government policies making local joint working difficult (Hancock, 2003: 130).

Among the first regeneration and community-capacity building initiatives funded by the New Labour government was the ten-year New Deal for

Communities Programme set up in 1998/9. Approximately £2 billion has been committed to 39 partnerships, all of which tackle five key themes – poor job prospects, high levels of crime; poor health; educational underachievement; and problems with housing and the physical environment. The programme was designed to close the gap under these themes between the 39 deprived localities and the rest of the country. Another initiative was the Community Empowerment Fund (2001–4) involving the 88 most deprived neighbourhoods and aimed at developing effective community – and voluntary – sector participation in regeneration. In this raft of regeneration programmes the Local Strategic Partnerships (LSPs) in England were to play, and are intended to continue to perform, an ever more important role as catalysts for community involvement and joined up working across different government areas as the single body responsible for the overarching vision and strategy in the area.

More recently the Safer and Stronger Communities Fund and Local Area Agreements (LAAs), initially piloted in 2004 and rolled out across England in 2006 sought to consolidate the lynch-pin role of LSPs in ensuring that joint/multiple strategies are translated into joined up practice across different initiatives, services and in response to local priorities. As Hancock (2003: 130) observes, in formal terms LSPs are forums in which key organizations and interests, including hard-to-reach groups, and voluntary sectors are to be brought together. LSPs have responsibility for developing a community strategy for the renewal of the economic, social and environmental fabric of the locality. Again there is much rhetorical faith in a communitarian-qua-social capital impulse from government in the United Kingdom as noted in Chapters 3 and 4 and articulated in the following government pronouncement:

> Engaging and empowering communities adds value to public policy, helps to build social capital, promotes active citizenship and strengthens community cohesion ... Stronger communities underpin all SSCF outcomes and it is essential that adequate time and resource is committed to support their development. Government Offices will not be satisfied of the success of an Agreement if this has not been ensured. (Office of the Deputy Prime Minister, 2005: 9)

Given the relative novelty of this latest manifestation of the local partnership model of community governance, the 'success' or 'failure' of these formal arrangements cannot be easily assessed. At the same time throughout this book the almost unrelenting scepticism in the critical academy regarding governmental claims for community mobilization, empowerment and responsibilization has been noted. What in fact we often see from academic critics (for example, Amin, 2005) is a 'reading off' of outcomes and effects from public pronouncements and textual exegesis. Whilst it is difficult to disagree with Amin's (2005: 625) conclusion that the 'new literature on community is richly condescending and morally prescriptive', this does not mean that these messages are then embedded and unproblematically rolled out in specific programmes across the country. Nor should this discursive critique rule out the possibility that the 'elision of social and the local' (Amin, 2005: 612) may be subject to 'inventive' translations in certain contexts.[28] To exacerbate matters, evaluations of a rigorous and long-term nature of community involvement and empowerment in crime prevention programmes as rare as reliable sightings of the Loch Ness monster! However, a preliminary evaluation of local efforts to improve community involvement in community safety (Home Office, 2006) concluded that bringing greater efficiency to neighbourhood renewal and partnership working is not currently a priority for many LSPs as most seem to be choosing to work with existing partnerships and groups to make progress in the short-term rather than seeking rationalization. On the positive side, these developments represent, at least at the level of intention and rhetoric, some recognition that tight deadlines and short-term targets are not always appropriate for community-based governmental projects. Note, for example, the DETR commissioned evaluation of City Challenge programmes which accepted that 'the appropriate timescale should be determined by local circumstances, not fixed, and in some cases it may need to be 10–15 years or even longer' (DETR, 1999, in Hancock, 2003: 131). In terms of intention, even a critic such as Hancock acknowledges, with important caveats, that the 'objectives – to improve health, education, housing and the physical environment, and to reduce crime and unemployment, in a joined-up way – are to be commended ... In a number of ways these developments *may* signify that the government has the political will to address the problems of distressed and high-crime neighbourhoods' (Hancock, 2003: 131–2). Hancock, in line with Hope's (1995; 2001) arguments on community crime prevention for high crime areas, goes on to suggest that it is also possible that such developments may go some way to strengthening local community networks and relations, and connect marginal communities to sources of power, influence and resources beyond the locality. But of course many practical problems may thwart these efforts (Hancock, 2003: 132 and see Chapters 3 and 4).

Hancock's recent work has highlighted the contradictions and dilemmas of the assumed relationship made by governments (national, local and supranational) between regeneration and crime reduction alongside the 'unintended' exclusionary consequences of most local regeneration strategies on the often most vulnerable and poor communities. Hancock *et al.* (unpublished) have identified 'a new agenda' for research and debate in this sub-field based on 'critical perspectives on urban regeneration, crime and social control'. Let me summarize this critical agenda. It is argued that the ever growing number of policy documents emerging across the United Kingdom from government departments indicate that policy makers and practitioners regard the connections between 'regeneration', 'crime reduction' and 'social control' in an unproblematic and uncritical fashion. In contrast to this seemingly dominant understanding, Hancock *et al.*, (unpublished: 1) put forward an array of key criminological questions that may be raised about these seemingly unproblematic connections as follows:

- 'Is regeneration unproblematically benevolent or does it produce and reproduce existing criminalizing agendas?
- Is the connection drawn between regeneration and crime prevention necessary or healthy?
- Does regeneration reduce or prevent crime, merely displace crime, or actively increase it?
- Within the broad category of crime, are there particular forms of offending that are more/less likely to be decreased/displaced/increased as a result of regeneration strategies?
- In what ways have regeneration strategies been linked to redefinitions of crime, harm, anti-social behaviour, and so on?
- Can strategies of regeneration themselves be considered criminogenic?'

These penetrative questions provide a crucial starting-point for further future debate on the criminology of urban regeneration, both within the United Kingdom and beyond. In the sections that follow some of these questions are answered by an assessment of the existing body of critical social scientific research and commentary.

The Entrepreneurial City and the Exclusions of Regeneration

It was noted earlier that the life of modern cities has always been one of conditional inclusions and exclusions, socio-geographic segregations as well as shared public places. That said, the nature of such urban processes has never been uniform across time and space. And it is surely incumbent on social scientists, following the likes of the sociologist Richard Sennett (1977, 2003), to comment on both the achievements and failures of shared urban life in our times. There is a particularly powerful contemporary impetus for social scientists to examine the contemporary re-ordering of urban life and its institutional forms, including regeneration, for what it can tell us about dominant processes of social ordering more generally. Indeed many cities appear to be increasingly visible and nationally autonomous players in the competition for both economic and cultural survival if not ascendancy. The following discussion is of necessity selective in its appraisal of this body of critical work. However, I contend that the main case-study chosen (namely that of Roy Coleman and colleagues) reflects accurately the general 'state of play' of critical social science thinking and research on the connections between regeneration and social control.

Mike Raco (2003: 1869) has provided a concise summary of the dominant and widely accepted thesis regarding links between urban regeneration and the new efforts at the securitization and policing of space shared by critical social scientists:

> Urban regeneration programmes in the UK over the past twenty years have increasingly focused on attracting investors, middle-class shoppers and visitors by transforming places and creating new consumption spaces. Ensuring that places are safe and are seen to be safe has taken on greater salience as these flows of income are easily disrupted by changing perceptions of fear and the threat of crime. At the same time, new technologies and policing strategies and tactics have been adopted in a number of regeneration areas which seek to establish control over these new urban spaces. Policing space is increasingly about controlling human actions through design, surveillance technologies and codes of conduct and enforcement. Regeneration agencies and the police now work in partnerships to develop their strategies. At its most extreme, this can lead to the creation of zero-tolerance, or what Smith terms 'revanchist', measures aimed at particular social groups in an effort to sanitise space in the interests of capital accumulation.

Let us examine one illustrative case-study which plots this master pattern of control. Roy Coleman and colleagues' research and neo-Marxist critique of regeneration strategies in Liverpool and Merseyside in the United Kingdom provides a lucid exemplar of critical commentary on the 'dark side' of urban regeneration specifically and of the neo-liberal projects to create competitive 'entrepreneurial cities' across the globe more generally (see Coleman, 2004a and b, Coleman *et al.*, 2002, Coleman, 2005). According to Coleman *et al.*, the recent history of regeneration and of a region-wide safety strategy in Merseyside represents a striking example of how cities are being re-imagined along neo-liberal lines and how the new processes of surveillance and social control are being re-directed and related techniques 're-tooled', to exclude the non-productive/ non-entrepreneurial populations via a coercive multi-agency policy of 'reclaiming the streets' orchestrated by a coalition of the local state and corporate capitalist elites. This work represents a bold thesis on Liverpool as both an entrepreneurial and coercive and excluding city.

According to these authors, the iconic technology of the CCTV and its seemingly Orwellian potential for surveillance is crucial to this process of 'socio-spatial ordering'. As is the case with much critical work on the apparently convergent current and future trends in social control and new cityscapes, Coleman *et al.* draw 'dystopian' inspiration from Davis' (1990) analysis of Los Angeles[29] alongside Neil Smith's (1996) thesis of the 'revanchist' (revengeful) city. According to Coleman (2004b: 2):

> In the last years, not only in the North American context but in Europe too, extending the boundaries of the urban frontier – economically, politically, and culturally – has galvanized powerful urban coalitions in the task of re-taking, both ideologically and materially, city spaces from the visible and symbolic elements of urban degeneration.

We have here a return of the 'convergence thesis' of US modernization theory (Kerr *et al.,* 1973), only this time with a radical twist and premised on what Steinert (2005: 480) has described as Foucault's 'strong functionalism'. The shared fate of late modern societies would appear to be the emulation of the USA again, politically, economically, culturally and technologically, under the combined forces of the revanchist city and the security state.

Focussing on the development of the Safer Merseyside Partnership over the last decade and drawing on a series of interviews with key players and public pronouncements of the partnership, Coleman *et al.* (2002: 92) argue that this partnership is a clear example of an attempt at local hegemonic building of a 'desired urban order' by a coalition of state and corporate capitalist elites. In the pursuit of this sanitized order, the role of CCTV acting as a comprehensive security blanket across the city appears to have been crucial in the aim of overcoming fears over Liverpool's historically 'dangerous' reputation by these local elites. 'This strategy thus has two clear aims: to build a consensus around the ever expanding deployments of coercive and invasive technology in order to mitigate a supposed growing threat to law and order; and to use a strategy of responsibilization to push forward this consensus' (Coleman *et al.,* 2002: 93). They describe the emerging top-down techniques, both coercive (zero-tolerance policing) and situational (CCTV and environmental design), as part of a broader 'network gaze'. The local crime control project is thus 'underpinned by a logic of social and economic regeneration that attempts to forge and disseminate a market-oriented and entrepreneurial inspired notion of the "public interest" ' (Coleman *et al.,* 2002: 97). It is also claimed that the broader regional efforts at regeneration were predicated also on the market ethos of 'trickle down' whereby the sanitization and dynamic entrepreneurialism of Liverpool city centre would create a 'halo effect' for the regional hinterland and satellites.

Coleman (2005: 132) has argued that such developments in Liverpool as the promotion of particular kinds of social space through social control and surveillance practices are clearly indicative of the broader diffusion of a transatlantic orthodoxy on social control whereby the surveillance of city streets is intensifying as part of the changing terrain of urban statecraft. In brief, Coleman suggests that the new 'entrepreneurial urbanism' represents a class-based attempt at reclaiming the streets and which may be discerned across neo-liberal cities of North America and Europe. 'Perform or else' seems to be the underlying message of this new, seemingly dominant, urban ideology. Coleman usefully describes several categories of people who are 'non-performers' and thus subject to coercive exclusion from the sanitized spaces of the city. The reasons for the exclusion of these groups are not difficult to discover: 'The visible "differences" that homeless people, the poor, street traders and youth cultures bring to the city, undermine the hegemonic notions of "public" spatial utility and function. Indeed, for these groups, it is often merely their visibility alone and not their behaviour that is deemed problematic' (Coleman, 2005: 141). As Coleman rightly observes there is a need for critical scholars to reveal their stories and plot the resistances of these non-performing publics.[30] Such important concerns chime with those aired by Johnston and Shearing (2003) in their discussion of zero-tolerance policing in New York and beyond as well as the work of a growing number of commentators in Europe (see, for example, Burney, 2005, van Swaaningen, 2005). Noting that zero-tolerance policing is in effect largely a strategy for cleaning up the streets by moving on risky people and by so doing engendering a situational consciousness and localized culture of control in which risky persons will no longer be tolerated, Johnston and Shearing (2003: 116) contend that the big challenge is 'how to provide occupants of public space (street people) with any opportunity to influence policing in an equivalent way'. According to the body of critical research and commentary on the exclusivizing consequences of urban renewal, the odds on this big challenge winning out seem slight.

To return to Coleman *et al.*'s work, some of claims made about the axial role, symbolically and practically, of CCTV in the social control apparatus in Liverpool are borne out more generally by sociologically-informed researchers looking across the United Kingdom. In particular, Norris and Armstrong's (1997:150) empirical research on the actual operation of CCTV across several sites in Britain clearly showed that certain groups were being targeted disproportionately. Bannister *et al.*'s (1998: 27) work lends further support to the role of CCTV in supporting the *attempted* sanitization of the public sphere – now commercialized as hybrid public/private space – where 'difference is not so much to be celebrated as segregated'. Commenting on this broad body of work, Coleman and Norris (2000: 174) observe that

> CCTV becomes part of the process whereby difference is excluded not by targeting the criminal, but by targeting the 'other': the homeless, the poor, the political activist, who do not contribute to the commercial success of the city. This exclusionary impulse is almost entirely overlooked by those who focus on the crime reduction potential of CCTV.

It is easy and very tempting to be swept along by the righteous condemnation of surveillance 'from above' in all its forms. That said, Tim Newburn (2002b) offers us a timely health warning and corrective against the dystopian inclination within the contemporary criminological literature on 'surveillance' generally and CCTV specifically. He observes that this particular normative stance (dystopianism) almost expunges the possibility that CCTV techniques and the like may have positive consequences for people's safety and as crucially their rights (Newburn, 2002b: 269). Drawing on research on the use of CCTV in a custody suite in a police station in Kilburn, London, Newburn suggests CCTV may often have a dual nature, involving both intrusive social control and an equally intrusive means of ensuring that citizens' rights are respected, provided that public accountability mechanisms are in place.

Much of this important critical work on the connections between regeneration and developments in urban social control, epitomized here by Coleman *et al.*, concerns 'aims' and 'attempts' imputed to be present in the words and actions of local actors and projects. It tells us less about the tangible outcomes of these imputed intentions or their 'success' or 'failure' when put into practice. Despite some limited recognition of contestation, such as noting in passing the possibility of partnership structures creating 'new (if still disconnected) arenas for community-based resistance' (Coleman *et al.*, 2002: 101–2), the central claim in Coleman *et al.*'s work in Liverpool is nonetheless of a further intensification of the neo-liberal hegemony of the decades since the 1980s in which , in homage to the neo-Marxist analyses of Hall *et al.* (1978) and Scraton (1987), corporate and market populism is to the fore, aided and abetted by the 'authoritarian state' and its 'policing of the crisis'. As noted above, this work is also in debt to Cohen's neo-Foucauldian thesis of the 'punitive city' (1985) where there is both a blurring of control and a widening of the nets of regulation. The main contours of what I have previously termed a 'radical totalitarian' thesis (Hughes, 1994; 1998a) may be discerned as the dominant perspective in the current crop of non-governmental, scholarly work in this field.[31] In brief, radical totalitarianism may be broadly defined as work influenced by both neo-Marxist and neo-Foucauldian ideas, generally as 'translated' for criminologists by Stan Cohen (1985) in *Visions of Social Control*. The thesis is generally dystopian, if not Orwellian, in its portrayal of contemporary developments and runs the risk of being theoretically and politically foreclosed in its analysis and critique (see Chapter 8). It is also under the sway of a grand narrative emphasizing international and catastrophic 'convergence' towards both a neo-liberal marketism and political process of securitization. In common with previous debates in earlier chapters of the book (see Chapters 5 and 6) I argue that such a thesis overplays the effectivity of dominant projects and forecloses the analysis of struggle, negotiation and compromise, not just most obviously from 'below' but also from 'across' competing actors and coalitions within governing ensembles. That noted, there is no shortage of support for this master narrative of dystopian change in grand overviews of the field. Heinz Steinert (2005: 470) in his synthetic essay on 'the sociology of deviance and the disciplines of social exclusion', for example, argues that a new politics of exclusion has ushered in a 'new wave of nationalist, race and class discrimination'. There is a similar emphasis on this convergent master narrative in Moulaert, Rodriguez and Swyngedouw (2003)'s work on economic restructuring and social polarization in European cities which have experienced, like Liverpool of late, the development of emblematic development projects. It is of course impossible to deny that cities and 'urban boosterers' in these globalizing times are often engaged in a 'dog eat dog' pursuit of and competition for privileged places in the emergent socio-spatial division of labour. Indeed Swyngedouw *et al.* (2003a: 6) recognize that whilst 'the localization of the global and the globalization of the local become crafted in a place-sensitive manner; yet [they] exhale perplexing, often disturbing, common threads'. In particular, it is argued that the urban revitalization projects which they studied across Europe all tend to refashion the city in an image of a post-Fordist urbanity, 'an urbanity articulated through a spectacularized commodification of urban space; one that redraws the boundaries between public and private, inside and outside, included and excluded' (Swyngedouw *et al.*, 2003b: 9). The same authors note that the dominant tendency across European cities with urban development projects-led regeneration schemes is that they rarely trickle down to deprived communities and there is common trend for a growth- oriented elite configuration to hold local governance under its hegemonic sway (Rodiguez *et al.*, 2003: 43). The present and future looks bleak with European cities becoming characterized as 'islands of wealth in an impoverished environment ... a patchwork of socio-economically highly diversified and more mutually exclusive areas' (Swyngedouw *et al.*, 2003c: 260). Such developments are difficult to ignore. However, I would caution that it is vital to view these processes as '*attempts* to deintensify and regulate the tensions and disorders that inevitably play themselves out in urban spaces' (McLaughlin and Muncie, 2000: 135

emphasis added) and which in turn generate a series of uneasy paradoxes around the building of walls and exclusion zones.

Lessons from Ethnography: Contradictory Outcomes and Spatial Struggles in the Local Politics of Urban Regeneration

Having focused on the important contributions made by 'radical totalitarian' scholarship or so-called 'sociologies of catastrophe' (O'Malley, 2000) on social control and regeneration in the neo-liberal city, this fourth section of the chapter assesses the evidence and arguments currently emerging in this sub-field from contemporary ethnographic studies.

Let me begin with a case study from outside the United Kingdom by examining Nick Blomley's radical research and political interventions in Vancouver, Canada. Blomley's interventions are an exception to the unwritten critical criminological rule of viewing processes of social control and regeneration in broadly blanket and negative ways. Blomley's neo-Marxist starting-point is that gentrification and related dynamics in contemporary cities can be usefully thought of as forms of 'enclosure' of the urban 'commons'. More specifically Nick Blomley and Jeff Sommers' (1999) research and political advocacy in inner city Vancouver offers some vital clues as to how urban space is getting mapped in ways that centre increasingly directly on property as the organizing political rationality in programmes of urban renewal. This work highlights the very specific manner in which property and community are linked in areas undergoing renewal or gentrification. Noting that programmes of renewal often seek to encourage home ownership, given its apparently beneficial effects on economic self-reliance, entrepreneurship and community pride, Blomley and Sommers (1999: 263–4) observe that:

> Gentrification, on this account, is to be encouraged, because it will mean the replacement of a marginal anti-community (non-owning, transitory and problematised) by an active, responsible and improving population of home-owners who will 'improve' a community, both physically and morally, 'stabilise' it through their fixity and presence and serve to represent it given their supposed interest in responsible community activism.

In contrast to this dominant configuration of property and social and political entitlements, the authors point out that there are other translations of claims which may be mobilized in the politics over urban renewal programmes. They specifically highlight the claims made by the activists of the Downtown Eastside in Vancouver – including Blomley and Sommers themselves – who advanced a locally-based claim to community, predicated not on individual entitlements but instead on a collective form of ownership rooted in history and shared struggle (Blomley and Sommers, 1999: 264). 'Community' thus emerged as a key vector of governmental power, for 'good' and 'evil', in this local struggle. Drawing on the insights of O'Malley, Blomley and Sommers contend that resistance should not be simply posited as being an external element and obstacle to governmental programmes, rather we need to think about the ways in which 'government and resistance articulate, mingle and hybridize' (O'Malley, 1996, cited in Blomley and Sommers, 1999: 282). In the case of the struggles in inner city Vancouver, they note that 'mapping' itself is a technology deployed by both 'programmers' and 'community groups' although they also suggest caution in imputing a divide between dominant and resistant maps. Rather Blomley and Sommers (1999: 283) contend that 'the desire is not just to obtain an objective rendering of the reality of changing land markets, but also to be able to turn "expert systems" on their head and to use the authoritative language of the Cartesian map to advance community concerns about the pace of gentrification to outsiders who might otherwise be unpersuaded'. In conclusion, they suggest we need to be very sensitive to the manner in which communities are 'constituted, mobilized, mapped, named and bounded, and alert to the *exclusions and democratizations* that accompany this process' (Blomley and Sommers, 1999: 284, emphasis added). Such sensitivity to both the 'exclusions and democratizations' associated with such struggles marks out this contribution to the radical debate on regeneration from much of the pervasive pessimism of the literature.

To return to comparative examples from the United Kingdom, Evans, Fraser and Taylor's (1996) research on Manchester and Sheffield suggests that much of *real* decline in civility, and growth in *actual* crime and heightened anxiety (in contrast to the radical constructivism of much critical criminological analysis) derives in large part from a 'political antipathy to the exercise of an effective public custodianship of shared public spaces and facilities' (Taylor, 1999: 123). This critical realist work suggests crucially that experiencing the city is both complex and differentiated. Accordingly, 'urban space [needs to be understood] not just as a playful place of pluralistic tribal difference (which can be one way in which the city spaces are experienced) but, with a rather more specific sense of caution or foreboding, as a place in which the symbolic aspects of individual destinies (or market positions) within the post-Fordist markets are played' (Taylor, 1999: 131). 'Our' often unwanted encounters with the 'casualties of life' both reveal the absence of care and custodianship of people and spaces and, according to Evans *et al.*, research (1996) may lead citizens to blame government and local councils rather than the casualties themselves. An instance presumably of popular contestation 'from below' of neo-liberal hegemonic building. In conclusion, Taylor suggests that there is much unevenness in the processes of transformation in different cities and thus very different prognoses may lie in wait for different cities. In particular, it is suggested that the crucial role and positioning of different 'growth coalitions', to borrow Logon and Molotch's concept, needs to be carefully examined (Taylor, 1999: 131).

Simon Hallsworth's (2002) ethnographic study of the 'control effort' in the South London borough of Lambeth (located in the wider context of this area having experienced two decades of urban regeneration) may also be read as a critical realist analysis which unsettles any simple reading of the relationship of governmental intention to practical outcome. Following the work of the left realists and one of their intellectual inspirations, Robert Merton, Hallsworth argues that the high rates of street crime among sections of this borough's most relatively deprived groups are in part explicable as an adaptive strategy to thwarted consumption during a period of selective regeneration which has seen a process of gentrification and the influx of new affluent professional residents. The period of local regeneration resulted in land and property prices rising and in significant parts of the 'indigenous' poor population having to occupy an area characterized by serious pockets of highly deprived and physically denuded estates. This borough also had the highest proportion of unemployed claimants in central London. In turn, Hallsworth (2002: 209) notes that the biggest impact of these tendencies was on the indigenous black population 'which unsurprisingly make up the vast majority of street crime offenders'. Accordingly, this case-study illustrates that regeneration efforts created, however unintentially, a criminogenic environment. In Hallsworth's (2002: 209) own words:

> Let us now draw together the unintended consequences of regeneration policy. First, by making the borough more attractive to professionals and business, while secondly doing little to profoundly impact on the structural conditions of deprivation experienced by local communities, the cumulative and unintended effect has been to accentuate relative deprivation as opposed to reduce it. As a strategy that might be expected to reduce the social conditions that provoke criminal adaptations, the net effect has been to accentuate the very conditions that provoke it. Hell, as they say, is often built out of the best intentions.

Such a conclusion is sadly very common in criminological accounts of local regeneration projects in the poorest areas of the United Kingdom. It clearly confirms the verdict that class-based, and in this case racialized, processes of simultaneous 'gentrification' (for mobile professionals and business groups) and something close to 'ghettoisation' for the least mobile categories of the working and increasingly 'workless' class may be widely occurring. However, in contrast to the somewhat conspiratorial analyses of the processes of exclusion and control offered in much critical commentary, Hallsworth (2002: 211) argues that the edifice of control that emerges in the locality studied is both ineffective and un-concerted. As a consequence, we have 'a world that departs significantly from its theoretical representation'. In particular, Hallsworth (2002: 212) critiques both the official 'liberal conceit of an emerging rational and democratic approach to crime' and 'critical theories who want to see in the emerging configuration of control a system characterized by a progressive widening of what Cohen termed the "social control net" '. Instead he argues that local crime prevention structures in his case-study herald neither a dramatic extension of state power nor a wider dispersal of discipline that might be regarded as specially dangerous or ominous. Hallsworth also conjectures that CCTV may turn out to be 'nothing less than a "white elephant" in the making', with strong evidence that street criminals tend to move on from the CCTV to do their business elsewhere. In contrast to much neo-Marxist and governmentality commentary noted above, Hallsworth's ethnographic encounters with local crime control practitioners suggest that these actors neither view themselves nor act as agents of an oppressive state. Instead the main obstacles to more progressive initiatives on crime reduction and safety lie with the institutional constraints and the 'disjointed, under-funded, labyrinthine edifice' in which they are trapped. Hallsworth (2002: 213) thus concludes that the 'problem is not that of there being too much power, but not enough of the right kind exercised in the right way'.

A similar acuity to the importance of local context and of ethnographic method is evident in Hancock's (2001, 2003) case-study of two Merseyside neighbourhoods in the United Kingdom. Hancock's case-study is important for teasing out the complex and contradictory relationships between specific regeneration initiatives and the levels and harms associated with crime and disorder in Merseyside. In this sense it represents a context- and place-sensitive sociology of community politics eyed through the lens of urban regeneration. It is difficult to dissent from Hancock's (2003: 129) conclusion that 'it is simplistic to assume that urban regeneration will necessarily reduce crime and disorder, particularly in declining and distressed neighbourhoods'. Rather the factors which influence neighbourhood transitions are complex rather than perfunctory. Following Taub *et al.* (1984), Hancock specifies several main drivers of change in urban localities. First, there are ecological facts (employment sources, quality of housing etc.) that shape the social and economic context of areas. Second, there are corporate and institutional decisions which may buttress or abandon neighbourhoods. Third, community organizations may influence levels of neighbourhood satisfaction. And all three interact with each other in complex ways. Nor is the impact of crime direct: for example the impact of high crime may be offset by other 'trade-off' factors associated with the wider context (of economic prosperity and growth and such like). Hancock's (2001) study found evidence of much dissatisfaction with the processes by which regeneration initiatives and priorities often marginalized the local residents. For example, she records local dissatisfaction with the ways in which physical improvements were prioritized over local jobs; outside contractors benefited rather than local small businesses; and short-term remedies were favoured rather than longer term action to address deeply entrenched problems such as unemployment and educational under-achievement (Hancock, 2003: 135). She also highlights the likelihood of tensions among different interests in the public–private partnership arrangements. 'Powerful local-interest groups often dominate regeneration agendas, while other voices are rendered silent, especially where regeneration projects seek to attract inward investment' (Hancock, 2003: 136). At the same time Hancock's research participants did not reject regeneration out of hand; benefits were noted, particularly those associated with environmental improvements. But few residents expected significant numbers of jobs to be created; few regarded the kinds of provisions being developed (arts and leisure industry developments) to be 'for' local people (Hancock, 2003: 137). Hancock's research also alerts us to the distinct probability of selective gentrification in areas undergoing regeneration and differences in rates of victimization from crime in these proximate but divided areas. Finally resentment about unfair allocation of regeneration money is commonplace and at times may lead to major public disorder and acts of internecine, intra-communal violence as in Bradford, Burnley and Oldham in 2001 and the Lozells Road area in Birmingham in 2005 in Britain. To varying degrees mundane and dramatic, regeneration thus appears to be reconfiguring processes of conditional social inclusions and exclusions; even at times, accentuating ideas about cultural domination and subordination, particularly of the more marginal groups, those 'failed consumers' and the 'backward' welfare dependent communities who have been 'left behind'.

Hancock's work is a rare example of a comparative, ethnographic study in this sub-field which draws on the experiences and perceptions of local residents rather than that of the imputed meanings drawn from public texts and pronouncements or at best professional and corporate players' perceptions. Her work illustrates the context-specific contradictions and struggles associated with such governmental projects. The lessons of Hancock's research bear out the continuing pertinence of Tim Hope's (1995: 66) classic essay on community-based crime prevention and its conclusion which rejects the belief that the solution to neighbourhood crime problems can be achieved primarily through the self-help efforts of residents. Rather '[d]isintegrating urban communities may need significant investment in their institutional infrastructure to offset the powerful tendencies of destabilization of poor communities within the urban free-market economy' (Hope, 1995: 78).

Hobbs *et al*'s (2000; 2005) ethnographic research in the North East of England has also highlighted the contradictory outcomes of many efforts to regenerate city centres in the United Kingdom through the manufacturing of a night-time economy (NTE) of clubs, bars and eating outlets. The researchers contend that the market orientation of regeneration agendas now appears to proceed largely unchallenged. 'For municipal politicians and urban entrepreneurs alike, the stress upon market ideology created a fog of city boosterism shrouding the heavy episodic alcohol consumption that lay at the heart of the night-time economy' (Hobbs *et al.*, 2005: 162–3). There remain deep differences between the police (and their concern over the growth of crime and disorder issues) and town planners who see much profit coming from the public, but single generational use of the businesses of pleasure in the liminal NTE (Tierney and Hobbs, 2003). This research confirms that there are clear examples of the growing segregation of city-centre spaces, although it is mostly around the social divisions of generation rather than exclusion of the working-class from the NTE. On the basis of this body of research, Kevin Stenson (2005: 277–8) has graphically concluded that in these settings:

> public safety is coded, principally in terms of the threat of anti-social behaviour, and what are deemed feral forms of post-industrial masculinity. These urban centres have become increasingly age-segregated and violent, creating challenges for community safety partnerships, with limited power to regulate the alcohol retail industry upon which urban economies are highly reliant. This is also associated with burgeoning organised crime networks, linked with an often ambiguous relationship between the pursuit of pleasure and the maintenance of collective order and safety.

Perhaps the lessons of such ethnographic anthropologies of regeneration, immersed in local experiences and contradictions, for criminological scholarship is that 'pure' critique and the painting of an over-deterministic picture is easier when the commentator is not grounded in the complex and uncertain processes, struggles and outcomes in particular places. This body of ethnographic work suggests a less closed set of realities and possibilities. Raco (2003) is surely correct in noting that security issues are deeply politicized and contested in ways that some of the more critical literatures on policing strategies underplay. Drawing on his research on regeneration in Reading, England, Raco (2003: 1879) concludes that:

> The discursive terrains of local security debates have not been a one-way process of promoting and securing the needs of developers and investors (although their requirements have been a crucial element). The local state has played a key role in broadening local agendas and ensuring that a range of perspectives are promoted. What have been excluded, however, are the perspectives of local communities and local groups with local needs being defined and articulated through the representative structures of local authority.

Adam Edwards (2005) correctly observes that a focus on a 'sociology of the mundane' rather than that of the catastrophic and tectonic shifts in ordering and control may enable an opening up to what Rose (1999) refers to as the 'inventiveness' in politics. This in turn is not to air-brush out the state or capital in debates on governance but it is to suggest that such dominant forces will not necessarily have their will done. Unlike much governmentalist literature, we also need to add the critical realist rider that power is asymmetrically distributed and there are likely to be limits to the success of inventiveness in particular places and at particular times.

My own observations of the rolling out of the Safer, Stronger Communities Fund locally in England and Wales and participant observer 'action' research with local practitioners and partnerships in the United Kingdom in the mid-2000s may add some weight to this complex but arguably more realistically drawn picture of the increasingly inter-woven debate on regeneration and safer, stronger communities. It is evident that there is now a whole official institutional architecture of regeneration in the United Kingdom that does not always sit comfortably alongside community safety partnerships (see also Chapters 3 and 4). The likely success or otherwise of Local Strategic Partnerships in England in promoting 'joined-up' solutions and strategies 'sustainable community plans' and 'safe and strong communities' is as yet difficult to discern. Meanwhile insufficient attention has been paid to these complex struggles and their uncertain unfolding in particular contexts. In turn these need to be recognized and built into any critical 'replacement discourse' on regeneration and community development politics. Again, Hancock *et al.* (unpublished: 2) identify a series of key research questions, which may help guide future empirical research into these institutional arrangements. For example, how, and in what ways, can the myriad partnerships assert power and influence in the specific area? What are the different interests ('minority', 'majoritarian' and so on) that are brought to bear in urban regeneration partnerships and crucially how, if at all, are tensions and dilemmas reconciled between them? Whose voices are heard and whose are rendered silent or defined as deviant? Given the background of community involvement, how are community concerns translated? What are the processes involved at different levels and in different places? How do workers, professionals and managers interpret their work and role? It is also vital to ask who and what are the key actors, factors and processes outside the official institutional architecture of regeneration and community safety (including, for example, job opportunities, access to housing, leisure amenities etc.). How and in what ways do official policies and discourses recognize and respond to these? These constitute key questions that require answers from the research community. However, they are also suggestive of more uncertain and open-ended local 'solutions' and 'failures' than implied in much of the existing canon of critical criminological and urban studies analyses. This is not to deny much of the claims made about the direction and nature of urban change and re-ordering but rather to argue that it is neither a smooth machine out of which new products flow smoothly nor an all engulfing/entangling web.

Geographies of Responsibility and the Futures of the 'Urban/Communal'

In this section I begin by examining the new thinking associated with the concepts of 'geographies of responsibility' and what has previously been described as 'geo-histories' of places and contexts. Following this discussion I examine the possible application of the concept of 'power dependence' which Edwards and myself have deployed as part of the 'tool-kit' of critical realist criminology. It is contended that the application of such concepts may help move the public debate on urban regeneration forward in potentially innovative and progressive ways. Put briefly, certain places have particular geo-histories and continuing geographies of power with other places that in turn may generate specific geographies of responsibility. We may look, for instance, to much of Europe and its past imperial/colonial projects: 'we' went to the world as colonisers and now the world as the post-colonial comes to 'us', as exemplified in the discussion on migration and asylum in Chapter 6.

The architect Richard Rogers has correctly observed that 'Active citizenship and vibrant urban life are essential components of a good city and civic identity. To restore these where they are lacking, citizens must be involved in the evolution of their cities. They must feel that public space is in their communal ownership and responsibility.' These sentiments are easily expressed and are of course mightily difficult to realize. We might also at this point examine two quotes at the beginning of the chapter expressed by two of Europe's 'giants' of critical criminology, Stan Cohen and Jock Young. Which prognosis seems closer to our contemporary possibilities in living together in cities? Perhaps rather than choose between the prescient pessimism of Cohen and the guarded optimism of Young, the human geographer Ash Amin (2004) may capture more accurately the urgent significance of city-scapes and urban lives in his claim that cities express 'the most intense manifestations of propinquity and multiple spatial connectivity'. This is so today since they represent 'the forcing ground for challenges that are thrown up when difference is gathered so visibly in one place and a globality of myriad flows and connections is temporarily halted in one place' (Amin, 2004: 43). Let me unravel the implications of what may be termed the new geographies of responsibility and power for understanding where cities may be heading.

In close affinity with the ideas of Amin, Doreen Massey (2004) argues that identity and responsibility (and the potential geographies of both) are neither rooted nor static but are mutually ongoing productions. In articulating a radical politics of identity and responsibility, Massey is suspicious of 'foundational assumptions' although she does recognize that identity is both material and discursive. In turn this would be a geography in which power and responsibility is relational (i.e. constructed in relation to others); it is embodied; and it implies 'extension' (i.e. it is not restricted to the immediate or the very local, Massey, 2004: 6–9). In the context of this age of globalization and the heightened significance of networks and flows which re-fashion but do not deny the politics of place, Massey's work questions the common tendency to see global capitalism and its resources of power as somehow 'up there', 'being everywhere' not least since such notions make political challenge difficult (Massey, 2004: 14). She focuses on the example of an emergent, potentially progressive London identity predicated on 'mixity' rather than coherence derived from common roots. Put bluntly, Massey (2004: 16) contends that a major challenge for contemporary cities is that 'propinquity needs to be negotiated' whilst a politics of 'connectivity' across space may open up global centres of power such as London to other places and relations with elsewhere and even lead to supportive coalitions with alternative globalisations to that of the neo-liberal.

John Allen has also made a significant contribution to this new geographical imagination – in my view a 'sociology on the move' – in his writing on the geographies of power (Allen, 2003, 2004). Allen's work can help re-direct critical criminological research and theorizing on cities and regeneration out of its current dominant mode of analysis predicated on an often foreclosed, totalizing and dystopian convergence thesis. Allen (2004) notes that the undoubted hegemonic power of the United States power bloc and its neo-liberal/neo-conservative credo is often portrayed 'rather unthinkingly as something which radiates out from an identifiable central point, with a reach that appears almost effortless'. Here Allen could be describing much of the critical criminological commentary not just on 'neo-liberal' urban regeneration and the supposed revanchist city but also of related work on securitization and authoritarianism more generally, as discussed in Chapters 5 and 6. In our world of asymmetical global flows and relations of power dependence, it is of course ludicrous to imply that there are not globalizing centres (from New York to Rotterdam in, for example, the field of the 'zero-tolerance' management of the anti-social) but their 'success' is never guaranteed. Instead we need to understand that such centres and their conditions of existence are always constituted by territorially embedded assets and resources – of money, information, people, ideas, symbols, technologies and such like – which of course may be mobilized to great effect, but just as easily misused, abused or simply wasted (Allen, 2004: 24). Exercises of power then are always provisional in nature and we must not rush to take their impact for granted. The talk of 'sites of power', 'hegemonic ensembles', 'securitization networks', 'global surveillance' etc., now so common in 'mainstreamed' critical criminological commentary, should not lead us to the conclusion that power, in this case neo-liberal power, is so pervasive and so all-encompassing in its reach that there is little room for political contestation and manoeuvre. Let us not forget John Clarke's (2004: 105) sanguine caution that whilst neo-liberalism intends to subjugate the world, this is not the same as accomplishing it! In order to articulate an alternative, progressive politics, it is vital to examine the porous and contested spaces associated, in this case, with the governance of cities and their regeneration. Accordingly a radical pluralist agenda is opened up which in turn bears the mark of an interpretive sociology first developed by Max Weber. To quote Allen (2004: 29) again:

> The cross-cutting number of governing relationships as different bodies, partners and organisations mediate the decision-making process, mobilizing resources independently of any central authority, produces a less certain set of spaces open to challenge. It is not that such spaces merely represent 'sites' of power, but rather that those managers, officials and professionals who exercise power in a variety of contexts and settings provide more of a honeycomb for politics where individuals and groups can themselves mobilise to intervene, interrupt or modify the translatable goals of government.

In a related manner, Adam Edwards and myself (Edwards and Hughes 2005a and b) have argued for the centrality of the concept of 'power-dependence' in helping uncover the conditions of existence of different governmental projects and their chances of success or otherwise (ranging from 'pan-European integration/securitisation' to the management of incivilities and control of asylum seeking and such like). We suggest that the ten core propositions of power-dependence theory are as follows:

1. Liberal democratic polities become increasingly differentiated as public administrative systems expand to encompass more competencies and as they respond to pressures for greater intervention in civil society;
2. Through expansion these systems become more complex involving greater functional and institutional specialisation around particular problems of government;
3. This specialisation produces discrete policy networks of intergovernmental relations between actors organized at different territorial levels (sub-national, national, trans-national, supra-national) and in different statutory, commercial and voluntary spheres of governing;
4. These networks accentuate the central paradox of political power: actors who possess the potential to govern are not powerful when they are not actually governing, but neither are they powerful when they seek to govern because they are dependent on others to carry out their commands;
5. As a consequence, would-be sovereign actors are necessarily in a relationship of power-dependence with those, such as 'street-level bureaucrats', through whom they must govern and with whom they must negotiate bargain and enter into exchange relationships;
6. The necessity of bargaining with others generates political competition and the possibility of advancing certain governing projects whilst resisting others;
7. The exchange relationships that produce political competition revolve around certain types of governing resource, such as constitutional-legal, financial, informational, organizational and political resources;
8. These resources are distributed unequally and so relations of power-dependence are asymmetric, privileging certain actors in the institutional structure of governing whilst denying any one actor omnipotence;
9. In any governing project there is, therefore, a *necessary* tension between the wish for authoritative action and dependence on the compliance and actions of others;
10. The substance and outcomes of this tension are, however, a contingent quality of the geo-historical contexts that constitute the struggle

> for authoritative action and, therefore, the differences between governing talk, decisions and action (Edwards and Hughes, 2005a: 351–2).

These propositions alert us to the propensity for governing projects that ignore relations of power-dependence to fail or at least to be limited to talk and decisions. They suggest an approach to the undertanding in this case of urban regeneration (but also more generally across the field of the community governance of crime and safety) that resists inferring action and outcome from the talk and decisions of policy elites. Instead, questions are asked as to how a particular governing project could succeed. What resources would its proponents have to possess? How dependent are these proponents on other resources possessed by other, potentially antipathetic, actors? How do they negotiate this dependence, interest, enrol and mobilize the other actors whose support they need? (adapted Edwards and Hughes, 2005b). In turn, the focus turns to those actors (activists, managers, officials and professionals etc.) who exercise and realize power, unevenly and asymmetrically, in a variety of different contexts and settings. The processes involved will be what Allen (2004: 29) earlier termed a 'honeycomb for politics – where individuals and groups can themselves mobilize to intervene, interrupt or modify the translatable goals of government'.

To return to the insights opened up by the geographers of power and responsibility, there is much conceptual and political mileage in this approach but I would query the juxta-positioning of identity-qua- community being either mutable or rooted. Nor would I accept that the local as community is necessarily politically conservative and restricting (against Amin, 2005). Massey's (2004: 17) assertion that 'all of my arguments work against place as kind of hearth of an unproblematic collectivity' are difficult to disagree with. It is also hard to dissent from the view that we must question the assumption that somehow the local is genuine and the global is the abstract outside or equally that the local always is the product (and victim) of the global. Indeed my argument throughout this book is that communities are surely both rooted *and* mutable. The embedding of actions and their consequences in space produces territories and communities that are often a palimpsest of past rights and wrongs and of the struggles associated with these whose weight continues to influence the lives of subsequent generations. Such geo-histories cannot be wished away. Remembering Sayer's discussion of the specific question of utopias and appeals to community in Chapter 1, the concept of geographies of responsibility alongside that of power dependence can play a key role in mobilizing future research and debate on policy transfer in urban renewal and safety and crime control more generally, alerting us both to the question of what causes policy transfer and to normative questions about the ethics of generalizing strategies of urban renewal irrespective of the particular contexts of regeneration importers (see Edwards and Hughes 2005b).

Conclusion

In the first section of this chapter it was argued that the understanding of the contemporary governmental project on urban regeneration must first be understood as part of a long historical narrative in the social sciences on the shared dreams and nightmares of the city. In the second section the UK government's rhetoric and policy project on neighbourhood regeneration was examined as a possible exemplar of neo-liberal governing more generally across the world. This discussion led us to debate in the third section the relative merits of the critical criminological and critical urban studies literature on the entrepreneurial city and the exclusions of urban renewal. Whilst accepting much of the claims made by this body of work with regard to the exclusions flowing from urban 'boosterism' and 'revanchism', it was contended that the radical totalitarian thesis underpinning much of this literature meant that there are significant absences and gaps in this critical canon. In the fourth section a critical realist perspective was developed which focused on the contradictory outcomes and struggles associated with the politics of regeneration in specific localities. Finally in the fifth section the concepts of 'geographies of responsibility' and 'power dependence' were introduced as a means of opening up new debates on the politics of the city and shared public spaces in late modern times.

In an earlier work (Hughes, 1998a: 138–52), I suggested that three heuristic models of safe city and of crime control futures can be envisaged. The first two models, 'fortress cities of privatism and social exclusion' and 'high trust societies and authoritarian communitarianism' were quite negative and in their different ways represented visions of urban dystopia. The third model, 'towards civic and inclusive safe cities' offered a fragile but more optimistic scenario of urban life and its modes of social ordering. Developments in the first decade of the twenty-first century suggest that the odds are stacked in favour of a merging of the first two scenarios: increasingly militarized control, targeted containment, privatized consumption of the dual city, aided and abetted by a morally stifling and authoritarian neo-conservative communitarianism. That said, the more open and contested politics of inclusive cities of the third scenario is not exhausted, perhaps especially but not uniquely in Europe. Let us hope that the following conclusion by Sassen on the future of political practices in the global city is an accurate diagnosis:

> Today's political practices have to do with the production of 'presence' by those without power and with a politics that claims rights to the city rather than

> protection of property ... Far more so than a peaceful and harmonious suburb, the contested city is where the civic is getting built. After the long historical phase that saw the ascendance of the national state and the scaling of key economic dynamics at the national level, the city is once again today a scale for strategic economic and political dynamics. (Sassen, 2005: 467)

This chapter has self-consciously focused on the urban rather than the rural, the city rather than the small town or village, the global North and West rather than the global South and East. This is not to forget these other presences and future work in criminology must confront these other worlds of the 'glocal' as a matter of urgency. Indeed throughout the discussion in this and the previous two chapters, the so-called outcasts of globalization have had a presence and hopefully some sort of voice. Like community, regeneration is clearly a slippery, contested and capacious signifier. Whilst this signifier has been largely 'colonized' by neo-liberal assumptions of urban regeneration as a market-driven, exclusivizing enterprise, regeneration has not been totally captured by this negative security mentality. Perhaps it is in the spaces opened up by the contradictions and dilemmas of urban regeneration and crime reduction and unearthed by theoretically-informed empirical research that alternative, progressive 'security mentalities' may be articulated. This remains a largely unfulfilled political project that, as I argue in Chapter 8, 'public' criminologists need to prioritize as a matter of urgency.

8

Criminological Futures

Value- the good society- is a messy, murky, highly risky space for political engagement. However, it has never been evacuated by liberals, conservatives, or, for that matter, by progressives either. What has happened, though, in recent decades, has been a reluctance on the part of many on the pluralist left to engage with it fully and openly. Freedom, rights, privacy, equality, democracy, even efficiency – the stuff of modern political discourse- are clearly normative concepts, despite having a successful existence passing as technocratic, obvious and natural.

(Cooper, 2002: 312)

Introduction

Let me begin this final chapter by summarizing the main arguments of each of the preceding chapters and where they have taken us on this journey across what I have described, in short hand, as the new policy field of the community governance of crime and safety in late modern societies. We have also travelled across a normative and political terrain to which Cooper's quotation on 'the good society' at the beginning of this chapter alerts us. Our journey began in Chapter 1 where three inter-related themes which run throughout the book were introduced. These three themes may be best grasped as questions, which the substantive chapters that followed attempted to answer, namely:

- Why the concept of governance matters?
- Why a radical communitarian politics of community matters?
- Why a critical realist perspective on context and comparison matters?

Chapters 2–4 examined in broad terms the new institutional architecture of prevention and safety and the institutional practices associated with this sector. In Chapter 2 the broad conceptual mapping of the field was first outlined based on an exposition of several 'grand narratives' of the preventive turn and the rise of community governance. In this chapter a historical review of the rise of this preventive sector was undertaken, focussed on a national case study of England and Wales in the last three decades and also with reference to comparative developments in local crime control and public safety across Europe. In Chapter 3, the focus shifted away from the institutional overview of Chapter 2 to a detailed empirically-based evaluation of the processes of implementation of crime and disorder reduction and community safety locally. The discussion in this chapter pointed to the analytical importance of understanding local, central and regional governmental relations as relations of 'power dependence'. By the end of the chapter it was hopefully apparent that assessing 'success' and 'what works' is an important and complex question which requires acuity to the political and cultural contexts and geo-histories of places and their key actors *in situ* as well as the assessment of technical measures. In Chapter 4 the discussion drilled down into the occupational and political practices and subcultures of some of the key actors emergent in the field of the community governance of crime and safety. As such this chapter shifted attention to the question of 'who works' and 'how' in community safety and local control. The analysis began with a case study of the knowledge, skills and values, and occupational 'habitus' of the local government community safety practitioner in the United Kingdom. It also explored the influence of practitioner networks and policy coalitions in the political struggles to 'translate' issues of policy and practice in particular directions. In the second section of the chapter the focus shifted to the rapidly pluralizing and possibly fragmenting division of labour around local crime control and community safety 'on the ground' in localities and neighbourhoods. Taken together these chapters do not present either a pessimistic ('nothing works') or an optimistic argument ('what works') with regard to the complex of institutional forms and practices in the preventive sector. Rather the overall conclusion is that there are complex relations of power dependence between different sites and networks of actors, which are irreducible to technical fixes and are indicative of the centrality of values and politics to these processes. Alongside failure, chaos and crisis, the sites of governance in this field also illustrate the embattled possibilities for inventiveness in policy and practice.

In Chapters 5–7 the discussion moved away from what I have previously referred to metaphorically as the focus on the institutional 'plumbing' in Chapters 2–4 to that of the 'waste and recyclable products' of the system – namely the people and places who are objects of control and safety strategies associated with 'new' social problems. In particular each chapter dealt with a heuristically separable 'problem' but which in reality are closely inter-connected and inter-dependent. The three social problems are anti-social behaviour (Chapter 5); asylum seeking and migration

(Chapter 6); and urban regeneration (Chapter 7). These three case studies aimed to provide the reader with comparative, empirical evidence regarding the ways in which the governance of order and of the threats to it are being implemented locally in the late modern control complex. These three chapters also opened up the normative and political challenges made possible by the investigation of these pressing social problems of our times. The three case studies of the management of anti-social behaviour, the control of asylum seeking and migration, and the project of urban regeneration may thus be read as concrete tests for assessing the viability or not of the critical realist perspective in criminology, which this book as a whole has attempted to introduce.

A key claim of this book has been to show how crime control and community safety – which I have inelegantly tied together in the term 'the community governance of crime and safety' – are increasingly inter-connected with both attendant risks and opportunities for inventiveness in politics and policy. This final chapter builds on the cumulative arguments and analyses of the preceding chapters in order to present some claims for a progressive public debate on the 'politics of crime and community' relevant for our present times. In the first substantive section, some of the most pressing criminological challenges associated with the increasingly globalized politics of fear and insecurity in the first decade of the new millennium are outlined in the light of the focus on the community governance of crime and safety throughout most of this book. Following this discussion of the futures of crime control and community safety, the second section of the chapter focusses on the possible futures awaiting criminology. In particular, and building on the discussion of the previous chapters, an argument is made for criminology as social science within which the critical realist perspective may play a productive role. To help in this task I make an argument for a *public criminology*, drawing chiefly on the ideas of and the debate opened up by Michael Burawoy (2004) with regard to 'public sociology' but adapted to the more hybrid field of criminology. This is another way of asking what are the challenges and prospects for contemporary criminology or, more bluntly, what is criminology for?

'Falling Off the Edge'? Futures of Crime and its 'Communitarian' Control

Before the iconic events of '9/11' and the Afghan and Iraq invasions, Eugene McLaughlin, John Muncie and I wrote that we appeared to be 'teetering on the edge' in the global context of a new politics of crime and security (Hughes *et al.*, 2002). Events since then may be more suggestive of our 'falling off the edge' into a catastrophic maelstrom of heightened fears and risks and of deepening draconian, globalizing control and security strategies. As John Urry (2004: 63) argues:

> Through money laundering, the drug trade, urban crime, asylum-seeking, arms trading, people smuggling, slave trading and urban terrorism, the spaces of the wild and the safe are chaotically juxtaposed, time-space is being 'curved' into new complex configurations. September 11 demonstrated this new curvature of space and time.

Crimes appear in new and challenging forms, most obviously associated with the porous criminogenic conditions of a foot-loose neo-liberal globalization but also those generated in the context of new wars and modes of terrorism, both state-sponsored and from dissident groups. Across many contemporary western societies, we also see localized expressions of disorder and lack of respect mundanely epitomized by new and not so new incivilities and more dramatically by gun crimes often linked to battles for local drug markets. However, such developments are not solely the preserve of the poor. Capital and corporate interests also appear to be increasingly characterized by their autonomy from formal political control. And such autonomy has its own criminogenic characteristics and consequences; (Lea, 2001: Castells, 1998). It would appear that societies like the United Kingdom are low trust societies (Cook, 2006). Welcome to the 'neo-liberal jungle'! (Hughes *et al.*, 2002: 321).

Modes of control are similarly on the move, changing their shape and influence. Edwards and Gill (2002), for example, note that in the post-Cold War era, there has been a re-orientation of western security, intelligence and defence agencies towards crime control, often under the banner of a 'high-tech' war against 'transnational organized crime'. Insecurity is now the key ideological trope for explaining the problems of the world and its flipside, security, the solution to them for western policy makers, politicians and increasingly criminologists. Under the banner of 'homeland security', liberty, justice and human rights appear to be on the retreat across the West. There is evidence of an increasing melding of global threats and local fears. The previously privileged position of the (nation-) state and the nation as the primary field of criminological and sociological reference – Beck's 'methodological nationalism' (2005) – is being overshadowed by both trans-national and sub-national configurations (Aas, forthcoming). Note, for example, the global branding of al-Qaida as the 'McDonalds of terrorism' (Murdoch in Aas, forthcoming). For some commentators, this suggests a 'sociology beyond societies' and in which the social is increasingly imagined as 'mobility' (Urry, 2004) although it should be noted that the 'national' (and the nation-state) is not exactly exhausted (Stenson, 2005). We now live in a world of simultaneously differentiated mobilities and enforced immobilities, much removed from 'the escalator notion of geographic and social mobility favoured by the Chicagoans' (Valier, 2003).[32]

I have noted in earlier chapters that there is a strong tendency among both conservative commentators and critical social scientists alike to view present questions of crime and disorder and their control in apocalyptic terms as a radical break with the past (and see Hughes *et al.*, 2002: 320–1). However, there are dangers in accepting the validity of the 'break-model' of change conceptualized in any simple 'before and after' manner. In our present times, we should not downplay counter-flows back to the past. For example, there is a reassertion of the 'pre-modern' moralism in crime control as uncovered by proponents of the 'new punitiveness' (Pratt *et al.*, 2005). Alongside, and in symbiotic relationship to these seemingly catastrophic developments, it is also striking that appeals to the local, the neighbourhood, the communal etc. have never been so strident. Despite community's past and present tarnished reputation, community remains a key figure in imagining the public, along with the consumer and citizen, in the twenty-first century (Hughes, 1998b). Critics of community such as Amin (2005) appear to have a 'top-down' understanding of this unstable signifier, drawn from both government projects and 'sound-bites' as well as from the claims of populist, latter-day pampleteers such as communitarian 'social capitalists' like Putnam and 'ethical moralists' like Etzioni. I have argued in this book that an engagement with 'community cohesion' and related notions is not a secular version of 'supping with the devil'. Communities are not merely the stuff of rhetoric nor are they simply about an off-loading of public responsibility (although they are often acted upon just like this by governing bodies!). A critical engagement with debates on community governance prompts inquiry into such questions as what forms of collective identification, solidarity and attachment can we imagine? Do not the volatile and visceral debates on communities speak simultaneously both to late modern conditions of declining trust in the state and its experts and to the increasing role of local people in the building of, and attempts to maintain, communities as ordered yet fast changing places? Of course the dominant political and moral discourse, such as UK government's 2005–06 communitarian campaign around 'Respect', is often dangerously dichotomous and divisive in its positioning of 'us' (the respectable/respectful) and 'them' (the disrespectable/anti-social). At the very least the arguments in this book suggest that such communitarian posturing cannot avoid opening up opportunities for public debate about what forms of mutual respect, toleration, civics etc. 'fit for our times' may look like, be fashioned and struggled over. This is not a claim to be looking for an 'elsewhere' that is pure but rather a question of identifying sites and forms of struggle over the meaning of the public, the social and the communal. More prosaically it also opens up arguments for the reassertion of the value of a public criminology to which my argument now turns.

Futures of Criminology: Going Public?

In the discussion that follows I begin by questioning three very different arguments for a 'beyond criminology' position in the study of crime and its control. In particular, I critique in brief the claims of the school of critical criminology re-coded as 'zemiology'[33], 'anti-social' crime science, and the 'anti-modern' criminology of the other. These divergent critiques of criminology have a founding assumption in common: that mainstream, *social* or *causative* criminology is intellectually exhausted. The main ambition of this final section of the book is to challenge this assumption of intellectual exhaustion and present a positive and more open-ended agenda for a sociologically- and politically-infused public criminology relevant for our times.

Arguing Against Zemiology

Zemiology's central claim is that mainstream criminology is in the service of the state and is obsessed by a state-defined problem (that of crime) that has no ontological reality, unlike 'social harm' (Hillyard *et al.*, 2004a, b). In turn it is contended that a major raison d'etre of critical criminology is about exposing the social construction of crime[34]. Foucault's typically magisterial and 'radical totalitarian' critique of criminology is taken by zemiologists as proof of criminology's sins, past and present: 'the whole content of criminology – with its "garrulous discourse" and "endless repetitions" – is to be explained with reference to its application by the powerful' (Foucault in Hillyard *et al.*, 2004b: 382). It is suggested that this verdict is seen as especially pertinent given mainstream criminology's 'handmaiden of the state' role in the contemporary context of a 'mass criminalizing state' and neo-liberalism's 'socially destructive trends' (Hillyard *et al.*, 2004b: 386). However, I would argue that few mainstream, social scientific criminologists would now dissent from the claim that state and corporate crimes, as well as the ills brought by an unequal and divided world, are, indeed, key concerns of criminology and are increasingly 'mainstreamed' in the field of study's research, theorizing and teaching, just as domestic violence, crimes of intimates, 'hate crimes' etc. have become so. And of course who would deny the vital role for criminologists to play in the contemporary political context where the human rights movement is on retreat, not least, across western democracies. In turn, it is difficult to dissent from much of the following 'call to arms' from Hillyard *et al* (2004b: 386):

> Being an academic surely means engaging in an inherently critical enterprise – one that requires us to ask awkward questions of power and the existent social order. It is time to face up to the realities of this task and resist the rising tide of commodification and utility corruption that looms before us both inside and outside the walls of educational institutions.

Asking such awkward questions of power is indeed necessary for criminology. However, I have argued throughout this book that equally urgent and pressing is the question of what are the alternative political and moral arrangements which may enable the production of less harmful and criminalizing social formations? On such matters, the reputation of critical criminology-qua-zemiology has been stained by its own silences and tendency for impassioned irrelevance. Furthermore, alongside the study of social harms, social scientists (including criminologists) also need to have theories of social/public goods and of ethical state, corporate and civil actions. I have argued at several points in this book that critical criminological and governmentality accounts alike often offer an image of rule 'so consistent, coherent and integrated, so univocal, that it becomes difficult to prise apart a space for political intervention' (O'Malley *et al.*, 1997: 513). My conclusion regarding this first 'beyond criminology' challenge is that zemiology both sets up a 'strawman' (of 'orthodox/mainstream' criminology) to critique which parodies much of the actually existing, plural forms of contemporary criminological work today and in turn fails to offer a viable critical project for criminology, intellectually or politically.

Arguing Against Crime Science

There is a long tradition of attempts to forge a Science of Crime, associated with positivist thinking and most recently reincarnated as the science and technology of crime reduction. In an earlier discussion of the futures of criminology (Hughes, 1998a: 154–8), I suggested that we might see social/causative criminology increasingly unsettled and threatened by a series of risk management-oriented disciplines. Although this prediction has not been realized in any blanket sense, recent developments associated with a 'what works' paradigm have seen a strong (re-) assertion of a supposedly politics-free, policy-relevant crime science.[35] Nick Tilley

(2005: 760) has defined crime science, in contrast to social scientific criminology, as follows:

> The application of scientific method and the deployment of any scientific disciplines in the interest of crime prevention, crime reduction and crime detection. Crime science is sometimes distinguished from criminology, which has specific associations with the social sciences

One of crime science's most influential proponents is Ken Pease. Pease (2005: 181–2) is confident that little can be done to alter unchanging 'human universals' such as rational self-interest, cupidity and aggression. Instead the future for a practical science of crime reduction lies elsewhere:

> It is unquestionably more profitable to examine the criminal opportunities which a future society will offer, and the ways in which science and technology can reduce or eliminate these, than to look at possible people change, either through socialization or the effects of criminal justice.

Here we have an eloquent expression of an anti-sociological pragmatism allied to the application of positivist science and its technologies for crime reduction. Mike Levi (2005: 20) has noted that it is possible to discern two extremes in the 'broad church' of criminology; at one extreme are those committed to the thesis that criminology is primarily about exposing the social construction of crime, exemplified by zemiology and post-modern criminologies . At the other extreme are those who consider the main purpose of criminology is to reduce crime and that this is a technical process. Crime science would seem to be a prime exemplar of the latter given its mission of acting as a utility-oriented crime science to address users' needs, using the techniques at their disposal (Hope, 2006). It is also part of a global 'what works' advocacy network involving policy entrepreneurs, for example, at the Home Office and Jill Dando Institute in the United Kingdom, National Institute of Justice (NIJ) in USA and the Australian National University's Campbell group offering an 'administrative criminology for the powerful' (Hughes and Stenson, 2006). According to its critics, scientific evaluation research, of which crime science is a belligerent proponent, represents a new orthodoxy in government circles especially in Anglophone societies where it is increasingly contended that experimental methods modelled on natural science can best produce robust evidence to help policy makers address the problem of crime. In some ways crime science does give social criminology a much-needed wake-up call with regard to its public role in informing both policy makers and wider publics on the 'crime problem' and in developing robust methodologies for policy-relevant research. That said, the potential hegemony of crime science may close off other modes of enquiry. As Bottoms observes (2001: 44), '[I]f we place our primary faith in technical solutions, then the mindset can quickly develop whereby any other kind of purported solution is treated as second-rate'. Whatever stance is taken with regard to the emergent 'anti-social' crime science, it is difficult to ignore its contemporary importance in the new governance of crime. The 'what works', crime science paradigm appears to hold out the dubious promise for post-criminological crime scientists to become the practical technicians of order and control.

My main objections to crime science's 'beyond criminology' position may be stated in brief in terms of: its naivety regarding the nature of policy and knowledge transfer; the unwarranted assumption of the international commonality of the conditions and nature of crime; a prioritization of the validity of quasi-experimental methods for the study of complex human processes; ignorance regarding historical change and contingency; and reliance on methodological individualism and psychologically derived rational choice theory (Hughes and Stenson, 2006). Given these flaws in the crime science paradigm policy, 'failure' may reasonably be predicted as has often been the case in attempts to 'oversell' the promise of the academic scientific enterprise to governments (Hammersley, 2004: 441).

Arguing Against Criminology of the Other

The third line of argument against social criminology is made by an 'anti-modern criminology of the other' which is superficially the easiest target for social scientists to critique whilst at the same time being the most influential discourse in the popular imagination on crime and its control. It is increasingly expressed by latter-day 'pamphleteers' and proponents of the new Social Darwinism and socio-biology (see Fuller, 2006).

My objection to this third 'beyond criminology' argument is based on its anti-sociological and pre-given 'natural' assumptions about the human world. It assumes that the social is both simple and epiphenomenal compared to the real stuff of biology, genetics, psychology and related natural 'hard wiring' as well as the unchanging essentials of human nature, including 'evil'. At its most extreme, the 'anti-modern criminologists of the other' understand crime as the 'product of personal and social monstrousness requiring punitive state intervention' (O'Malley: 1999: 181). At the policy level there are indications that we are witnessing the resurrection of forms of 'pre-modern' crime control based on a potent mix of nostalgia, emotion and punitiveness (Pratt *et al.*, 2005). It is clear that such developments associated with this populist criminology of the other sit alongside more obviously 'actuarial' and 'rational' anti-social techniques of control, as epitomized by crime science and situational crime prevention. O'Malley's (1999) explanation for this coexistence is in part a convincing one: namely we have a variety of 'volatile and contradictory' punishments because neo-liberalism is a dominant political rationality which often encompasses both authoritarianism and free market individualism.

These three challenges from both seemingly 'new' and often refurbished 'older' ways of thinking represent a profound unsettling of social or causal criminologies, both mainstream and positivist and critical and interpretive. In facing up to these challenges I argue below for an outward-looking public and social scientific-infused criminology. My argument then is to reject the argument for going 'beyond criminology' and to argue for staying 'within criminology' as a social scientific field of study and labour. Contemporary criminology is far from being hermetically sealed; nor is it alone as a field of study in the social sciences in being both a parasite and force for change on other cognate disciplines. It is a porous, 'rendez-vous' subject (Downes and Rock, 1998) despite claims that is wedded historically to a specific modernist governmental project (Garland, 1994). At the same time this is not to deny that there are important linkages to past (and present) governmental projects and in accepting their effects. However, 'original sin' is hardly an adequate analysis! Remember it may be argued that anthropology was born in the colonial encounter, sociology in the regulation of the contradications of western industrial modernity and so on across the plethora of human and social sciences. There can be no 'innocent' space, no point outside of 'modern', 'capitalist', 'colonial' governmentalies; thus being tainted with the governmental cannot be an adequate reason for abandonment.

Arguing for Public Criminology

> Responding to the growing gap between the sociological ethos and the world we study, the challenge of public sociology is to engage multiple publics in multiple ways. These public sociologies should not be left out in the cold, but brought into the framework of our discipline. In this way we make public sociology a visible and legitimate enterprise, and thereby, invigorate the discipline as a whole. (Burawoy, 2004: 259)

Burawoy's call for a public sociology speaks to some of the most urgent challenges also facing criminology as a social scientific field of study. Indeed, I will unashamedly adapt much of Burawoy's argument to that of the contemporary criminological enterprise in the following still embryonic discussion and call for further debate. To summarize his argument, Burawoy (2004: 266–9) suggests that there are four heuristically distinguishable forms within the sociological division of labour, i.e. policy, public, professional and critical forms. In what follows I adapt this four-fold characterization of the sociological division of labour to the closely related but also distinct organization of contemporary criminology.

'Policy criminology' may be defined as 'instrumental' problem-solving criminology in the service of a goal defined by a client; its raison d'etre is to provide solutions to problems presented to the criminologist. In the main, Burawoy's adapted claim here is largely correct but there is no reason why policy criminology cannot define problems itself. After all, that is often how policy is made. The most famous and influential expression of this mode of criminological labour in recent decades is that of the 'administrative criminology' associated with the Home Office in the United Kingdom and the National Institute of Justice (NIJ) in the USA. Downes and Rock (1998: 376), for example, correctly note that administrative criminology's 'situational control theories, more than any other approach, have helped to fashion the character of late modernity', at least in terms of its preventive crime control processes. However, policy criminology also relates to work carried out for the burgeoning private security sector as well as research and evaluation for local government bodies. Nor is such work necessarily narrowly subservient or conservative in character despite the tendency for such work to be a mode of 'governmental savoir' for the powerful. The left realist victimization surveys in the 1980s in the United Kingdom, for example, may be viewed as a radical social democratic policy criminology (Hughes, 2004c).

In contrast, 'public criminology' is a form of reflexive criminological labour which aims to create a dialogic relation between the criminologist and various publics in which the agenda of each party is brought to the table and in which each adjusts to the other. Major questions remain to be answered of course as to who these diverse publics are and how do we find them. The detailed specification of these publics still requires much further elaboration and they remain somewhat vaguely conceptualized in Burawoy's necessarily broad-brush 'call to arms'.

'Professional criminology' occupies the centre of the criminological division of labour. It struggles to supply 'true' and tested (yet contested) methods, accumulated bodies of knowledge, conceptual frameworks, education and training and such like. It largely represents specialist knowledge concerned with puzzle solving. The previous two types of criminology could not exist without a professional criminology.

Finally 'critical criminology' is the fourth mode of criminological labour. According to Burawoy, the main role of this 'reflexive' form of knowledge is to examine the foundations – both explicit and implicit, normative and descriptive – of research programmes, particularly of professional and policy criminologies. Burawoy argues that professional and critical sociologies are closely inter-related and chiefly address an academic audience. Meanwhile policy and public sociologies are viewed as being tied together in addressing an extra-academic audience. I suggest these distinctions do not work so easily for criminology (nor perhaps for sociology itself, see Calhoun, 2005; Ericson, 2005) in that all four forms of work are inter-related. Critical criminology would certainly claim to critique policy criminology as well as professional criminology. A public criminology in turn would ask questions of the three other types of criminological labour. Note, however, Scott's (2005: 406) defence of Burawoy's four-fold distinction in arguing that the four-fold distinction may be best interpreted as, not fixed sociological (qua-criminological) roles, but as 'specific aspects or moments of the academic career around which people should be able to move with ease'.

According to Burawoy, the original impetus for sociology was based on a search for order in the broken fragments of modernity in the first decades of the twentieth century, seeking to salvage the promise of 'progress'. Although the histories of criminology across the west have always been more closely tied to a statist project and also predicated historically on a pragmatic mix of scientific insights and techniques (Cohen, 1974; Garland, 1994) when compared to modernist sociology, the impetus of much sociologically-infused criminology looks not dissimilar to that of sociology more broadly. Writing with specific regard to American sociology, Burawoy goes on to argue that the subject has become professionalized and technical and in turn increasingly 'inward'-looking (for a critique of 'professional' sociology and criminology in the UK along similar lines, see Wiles, 2002). The challenge that now awaits is described as follows (duly adapted for criminological purposes):

> We have spent a century building professional knowledge, translating common sense into science, so that now, we are more than ready to embark on a systematic back-translation, taking knowledge back to those from whom it came, making public issues out of private troubles, and thus regenerating sociology's [*criminology's*] moral fiber. Herein lies the promise and challenge of public sociology [*public criminology*], the complement and not the negation of professional sociology [*professional criminology*]. (Burawoy, 2004: 261, adapted)

My support for a public criminology has also much affinity with Carrabine *et al.*,'s (2000) more narrowly 'critical' version of the project.[36] It is hard to dissent from their argument that a public criminology 'reflects a shift from narrower concerns with the politics of modernity and the critique of the state, to the incorporation of these within a late-modern project of advocacy on behalf of "the public" against trends of exclusion and injustice, and for human rights and social justice' (Carrabine *et al.,* 2000: 207). Furthermore, among the key features of this public criminology project are that it needs to be transparent, applied in orientation, evidence-based, and committed to empowerment and practical rather than idealistic change, as well as social justice and human rights (Carrabine *et al.,* 2000: 207). In our various roles as policy and public criminologists it is vital then to both work for and through (as well as at times 'against') the state and other governmental agencies at different scales as well as with the forces of civil society, including 'counter-publics' and social movements. Living with ambivalence appears to be a pre-condition of social scientific engagement: the state, non-governmental organizations (NGOs), community, civil society, the market and so on can all be both emancipatory and despotic. Burawoy sees the defence of civil society as sociology's prime public contribution in the present conjuncture. In contrast I suggest that European criminology, and perhaps the social sciences more generally in Europe, is committed both to the defence of the state (as public good) and of a vibrant civil society. And strong states and strong markets may, in Braithwaite's (2005: 348) terms, be important in preventing 'the tyrannies of civil society'. It all depends on circumstance and context. We can agree nonetheless that in times of 'market tyranny and state despotism', criminology as social science shares with public sociology the defence of the interests of humanity (Burawoy, 2004: 287; and see Fuller, 2006).

What are some of the emergent manifestations of this public criminological imagination? I suggest there is a particularly important role for public criminology in the articulation of different 'translations' of conventional and dominant discourses on crime and order. As Paul Wiles (2002: 248) observes, 'without translation into everyday discourse ... criminology can remain only a private activity', that is a 'private interest' rather than a 'public good'. In a similar manner, Edwards and Gill (2002: 246) have called for a re-orientation of the academic community and greater public engagement with debates on security, in their case regarding the problem of transnational organized crime. They argue that there are clear gains to be made through a more intensive dialogue between policy-makers and scholars that steers a middle course between the two extremes of either a theoretical purity which is untainted by the often very messy social realities and the real harmful impact of crime, or a non-reflexive pragmatic approach that reduces deliberation to technical policy 'fixes'. This is not a call for a 'third way' but rather for an engagement with hard things. Further difficult debate is of course necessary regarding to whom 'we' might speak and why 'they' would listen and talk to us (see also Scott, 2005). However, it may be viewed as an embryonic contra-discourse in the face of privatizing/individualizing and increasingly biologistic discourses of 'common-sense' which is not wholly colonized by neo-liberalism and the like. Gramsci's notion of 'good sense' is thus elaborated by intellectuals in dialogue with agents themselves. As Burawoy (2005: 430) puts it, 'Sub-altern groups are subject to dominant ideology but this never totally eclipses their indigenous reason that intellectuals excavate and elaborate – a good sense that springs from their subjugation and transformation of the world'. In non-Marxist terms, this accords with Steve Fuller's ambition that sociology as 'the flagship of the social sciences' recovers its original normative force by means of which its disciplinary practitioners, including social criminologists, see themselves as 'contributing to the constitution of the societies they study, typically by raising subjects' collective self-consciousness' (Fuller, 2006: 1, 7).

Adapting Lauder *et al.*,'s (2004:6) discussion of the contribution of sociology to the policy process, it is possible to discern five sets of theoretical and methodological resources which a social and public criminology is able to marshal and translate to inform policy writ large:

- The ability to link private troubles (from criminality to victimhood) to public issues (such as structural inequalities and social and political exclusions or the anomie of success) through the concepts of agency and power;
- The related role of quantitative studies (and the legacy of 'political arithmetic') in highlighting the consequences of power structures on life chances and risks of criminalisation and victimization (and asking how are the chances of criminalisation and victimization distributed?);
- The role of qualitative empirical research in illuminating the connections between structure and agency in criminality and criminalisation;
- The role of self-reflexivity in linking the identification of power structures to a social democratic politics (asking who gets to be safe or vulnerable?);
- The disciplinary openness of criminology when contrasted, for example, with neo-classical economics and forensic psychology.

There is a long tradition of 'political arithmetic' as one small part of the means of 'holding government to account, especially in the context of increasing social inequalities and the weakening of solidarity' (Lauder *et al.,* 2004). Counting counts despite critical criminology's important impetus to deconstruct and query the power of Jock Young's 'voodoo numbers'. The realist buck stops here: despite the problems of 'fake scientificity', empirical arbitration is crucial in the social sciences. Accordingly we must aim not just to promote systematic scepticism but also systematic rigour with regard to the generation and analysis of new forms of knowledge, both quantitative and qualitative. The power, perhaps obsession, with counting crime is of course marked in public debates on law and order. In their 'policy' or 'administrative' guise, criminologists have been important contributors to the production of quantitative data on crime and its control for government. The importance of the production of such criminological numbers should not be underestimated. The problems associated with the measurement of unemployment, poverty, ill-health etc. are equally difficult and equally problematic, but also equally important. There is an equally vital role for public criminologists as 'expert witnesses' within the broader democratic conversation about policy formation and accountability. Indeed, public criminology has a vital contribution to make in questioning the contemporary governmental desire for generic social researchers-qua-crime scientists which runs the risk of 'producing technologists who are equipped only with investigative skills', resulting in a 'pragmatically driven conceptual empiricism' (Williams in Lauder *et al.,* 2004: 5). It is evident that policy makers and politicians often prefer research that is free of theoretical baggage precisely because it enables them to formulate policies according to their own ideological preferences and political constraints. It is of course also true that the enrolment and mobilization of political support is not played out on a level field. Nonetheless, there is an obligation on academics as public intellectuals to engage in what Callon (1986) has termed 'the sociology of translation', namely 'the process by which coalitions win political arguments and define policy by successfully articulating the identities, interests and appropriate actions of others' (Edwards and Gill, 2002: 250) – and thus endeavour to speak truth to power.

The existence of different publics and social movements may be of crucial importance in helping revitalize stagnant democracies and bringing new issues to public life. It is also important, following Giddens, that people are understood as skilled agents with a capacity to interpret various dominant discourses in myriad, and at times critical ways. There is, however, a limitation to Giddens' conception of public life as a realm of free, open discussion in that it seriously underplays the counter fact that it is also a realm of asymmetrical power struggles (Tucker, 1998: 181). We also need to note that people can be skilled agents without being wholly skilled, wholly knowledgeable or even having time to do all the work: one role for social scientists then may be that of keeping other discourses, codes and decoding skills in circulation. Clarke (2003) has observed that to be 'governmental' – or 'public' – in our research and scholarship necessarily involves us in the agendas of the moment and in their articulation, deployment, defence and legitimation. In saying this the 'governmental' role needs to be counter-balanced by a willingness to discover and voice other publics, and their interests, imaginaries and possibilities that are not conventional or dominant. This represents a vital and vibrant sense of the public interest, allied to a 'more unruly or unsettled conception of the social' (Clarke, 2005) rather than one that over-reads the success of dominant points of view. Publics are not fixed but are in flux and as social scientists we can participate in their creation as well as their transformation. This takes us back to Durkheim and crucial role he argued for professional associations in national political life (Burawoy, 2004: 265) but re-fashioned for our 'glocal' times.

Critical Realism and Social Criminology

Throughout this book and in my collaborations with Adam Edwards (Hughes and Edwards, 2002, 2004, Edwards and Hughes, 2005a), a developing argument has been made for a critical realist criminology that may contribute to a future flourishing of a revitalized and diverse criminological imagination. It is contended that the deconstructionist critique is partial and thus does not represent a sufficient rationale for criminology as social science. Rather new forms of systematic knowledge about crimes, harms and their control and management need to be generated by theoretically-informed empirical research. Furthermore, critical engagement with public and populist debates necessitates political and normative deliberation. Surely Robert Reiner (2000) is correct in calling on criminologists not to forget the social structural causes of crimes (and I would add harms) alongside the discipline's growing fascination with processes of control and security. This focus on control, particularly in the technocratic approach of 'anti-social behaviourists' of the new crime sciences, may in turn reflect the widespread, dominant neo-liberal loss of belief in the possibility of social and economic justice and of non-egoistic cultures.

The tensions between liberty and security are a focus of much criminological work, whether this be critically-, professionally-, publicly- and, to a lesser extent, policy-oriented. Whilst it is true that sociology and, to an even greater extent, criminology have both acted historically as courtiers to the nation-state, the 'big issues' of power, control, oppression, ordering and such like are now centred in much mainstream social criminology rather than the preserve of either the 'critical' or sancrosanct social or political theory. Indeed, according to Bauman (2005b), criminology is increasingly 'teaching' other social sciences about some of the most pressing issues for our times, not least because 'we learn about things when they go wrong'.

Finally it is often asked where are criminologists as public intellectuals? Perhaps a more fruitful line of argument is to test out the possibilities of what the 'public criminologist' may offer broader public conversations on 'crime and disorder' and 'safety and security' rather than the more grandiose and self-important moniker of that of 'public intellectual'. As Burawoy (2004: 294) notes, the public sociologist-qua-criminologist is a specialist variety of public intellectual, limiting public commentary to areas of established expertise rather than expounding on topics of broad interest. It is clear that this project of critical engagement with the plural publics, both already in existence and emergent, will be doomed if we envisage the criminologist as 'hero' informing/transforming the state and its leading politicians. In our role as public criminologists we must look to other publics as well as 'big' government. I hope the arguments and debates opened up in this book suggest that there is much life left in a public, social scientific-driven criminology and not least its potentially progressive role in new imaginaries of communal security, public safety and social justice.

Notes

1. The focus in this book on the 'preventive turn' is not to deny that there is a continuing dominance of penal-punitive logics at work in most late modern crime control complexes which others have prioritized in their work (see, for e.g., Garland, 2001; Pratt *et al.*, 2005).
2. 'Governmental savoir' may be defined as the intellectual insights and substantive data driving, shaping and providing the rationales of governing processes (Stenson and Edwards, 2001).
3. The following critical realist argument on context and comparison first appeared in Edwards and Hughes, 2005b.
4. There has been a global projection of state-sponsored criminology in the USA. At the same time, its proponents may not recognize it as such 'precisely because of their belief in the possibility of identifying law-like generalizations about human conduct that will be universal not "American"' (Edwards and Hughes, 2005a: 358). It is also important to note that certain grand narratives about social control that refer to late modernity, risk and globalization also negate the contextual knowledge in which a critical realist criminology is interested. Weberian ideal-typical comparisons and forms of discourse analysis are employed in the latter which ignore the concrete qualities of crime control and safety in particular places and at specific historical moments (see, for example, Bauman, 2004, Garland, 2001, and Young, 1999).
5. The choice of England and Wales as the primary national case-study throughout this book is justified on several grounds. First, it is the national example with which I am most familiar and knowledgeable. Perhaps more importantly England and Wales is widely regarded in both policy and criminological circles across the world as one of the exemplars of the 'preventive turn' and the promotion of governing through the technique of multi-agency partnership and the apparent devolution of the state's responsibilities for public services to the local level. Finally there is a plethora of information and studies of this developing project when compared with most other countries.
6. For a detailed account of the eventual factors which explain the demise of the Crime Reduction Programme, see Maguire (2004) and the special edition of Criminal Justice (2004) more generally. Chapter 3 below also focusses on the complex politics of counting 'success' in crime reduction associated with this national experiment.
7. Much of the discussion in this section is derived from my collaborative work with Adam Edwards.
8. The routine reliance on a national frame of analysis remains the common approach of comparative criminology, see for example, the regular feature in the European Journal of Criminology on national surveys based largely on overviews of the criminal justice system rather than of cultures of control and safety.
9. There is a potential fifth issue that might have been considered in this empirical evaluation, namely the apparent elective affinity between the habitus of the new preventive/community safety expert and the so-called 'criminologies of everyday life'. The critical evaluation of this claimed connection will be be discussed in Chapter 4.
10. The empirical and conceptual basis for this section of the chapter derives in large part from reviewing the author's own research in, and reflections on the field of community safety and crime and disorder reduction in England and Wales since 1994 (see, for example, Hughes 1998, 2000, 2002a, 2002b, Edwards and Hughes, 2002, Hughes and McLaughlin, 2002, Hughes, 2004b, Hughes and Gilling, 2004,

Gilling and Hughes, forthcoming). See also Crawford, 2001, Edwards, 2002, Hope 2001, 2004, 2005, Maguire, 2004, Stenson, 2005.

11. This is so despite Garland's occasional qualifications to his 'master narrative', such as his recognition of the possibility that elected officials and government ministers at times retreat from the rational, adaptive logic of the preventive strategy due to short-term pressures to be seen to be acting 'tough' and such like (Garland, 2001: 140).
12. The term 'water carrier' was famously employed by the maverick, maestro footballer, Eric Cantona, to describe the solid but unspectacular contribution by the French midfield player and national captain, Didier Deschamps. The term appears an apposite analogy to draw between the work of grand narrators ('maestros') like Michel Foucault, Stanley Cohen and David Garland and those of 'us' engaged in local, *in situ* empirical research into the nooks and cranies of the field of crime control and community governance of safety and security ('water carriers').
13. Since 2002 I have been a co-opted member of the Board of Directors of this practitioner network. This involvement has given me the opportunity to analyse the findings from practitioner surveys and also provided me with much 'insider' knowledge on the work of local, regional and national bodies. The involvement has also involved me directly as an advocate in political debates on where community safety and its practitioners may be heading in the UK. I do not therefore claim to come to this field without political and normative commitments. It also needs to be noted that the comments made here are mine alone and do not necessarily reflect the collective viewpoint of NCSN.
14. It would be an irony of all ironies if my analysis of these debates 'air-brushed out' the different actors and competing coalitions of variously situated actors in central government departments such as the Home Office. To date there has been little empirical research on the Home Office as an institutionally complex and living organism, not least due to the absence of an equivalent policy of 'glasnost' and 'perestroika' in central government. My own observations would suggest, for example, that there were tensions and policy disagreements between the Partnership Support Team and the Anti-Social Behaviour Unit in the Home Office in the mid-2000s over the local management of anti-social behaviour.
15. 'Provocative' and 'ironic', I suggest because of the widely acknowledged and widespread demoralization among local CDRP practitioners, associated *inter alia* with the sense of constant, new, short-notice, 'top-down' demands, 'change fatigue' and concomitant lack of local autonomy and control.
16. 'The criminalization of social policy' thesis points to the tendency for fundamental social policy/public issues, such as poverty, unemployment, educational under-achievement etc., to be marginalized 'except in so far as they are deemed in terms of their criminogenic qualities' (Crawford, 1994: 507).
17. Social inclusion has always been a 'conditional' rather than an unconditional entitlement during both the 'social democratic welfare state' and in the 'post-welfare state' periods (see Hughes and Little, 1999).
18. In media representations of the anti-social in the UK, there is a plethora of drama-documentaries showing the grim realities of 'neighbours from hell', 'children from hell' etc. It is rare to see any 'humanizing' of this latest cast of deviants but note Paul Abbott's 'Shameless' drama series on the Gallagher family on the British TV Channel 4 which is an insightful exception.
19. The 1951 Geneva Convention still provides the international rule that nations should guarantee the right to seek asylum to people 'who owing to a well-founded fear of being persecuted for reasons of race, religion, nationality, membership of particular group or political opinion, is outside the country of his nationality'. An asylum seeker is thus a person seeking refugee status. A migrant is a broader term describing anyone who wishes to move from one nation to another, often for economic reasons. More generally 'asylum' denotes place of refuge, a safe haven in a hostile world. This was of course the original meaning of the term as applied in the nineteenth century to the new lunatic asylums. Of course within decades the lunatic asylum also connoted in the popular vernacular a dreaded place of the deserted, deranged and dangerous. In its contemporary

usage, as 'political asylum' it may again carry the latter connotations for many would-be refugees.

20. There are a few notable exceptions in European criminology such as Crawford, 2002, Albrecht, 2002, Goodey, 2002, Melossi, 2003, Young, 2003b, Valier, 2002, Aas, forthcoming, Welsh and Schuster, 2005.
21. I write 'societies' in inverted commas since it is increasingly evident that sociology, and social scientific criminology more specifically, can no longer easily assume 'society' is the same thing as the 'nation' in these globalizing times (see Beck, 2005, Aas, forthcoming and Chapter 8).
22. In passing it may be argued that this reading 'from' and 'into' official pronouncements on border controls may exaggerate the consensus even in EU elites, never mind when and how such aspirations are enacted and implemented.
23. When we look to Australia, a similar – if not more extreme – national culture of severity is evident. Indeed Australia may be said to occupy the dubious honour of being 'the most unwelcoming country to asylum seekers in the Western world' linked to it having the toughest and most wide-ranging system in the world for the detention of asylum seekers (Gibney, 2004: 167). Furthermore, Gibney (2004) notes that the 2001 elections in Australia were striking for being the site of a new government-led *offensive* politics of asylum which gave massive electoral success to the Liberal Party.
24. See, for example, *The Guardian's* Madeleine Bunting (2004) and Adam Curtis' televisual documentary series, *The Power of Nightmares* broadcast on BBC2 in 2004 whose work suggests, following Bauman, that peddling fear is a lucrative and vote-catching political business, particularly in our fluid and increasingly uncertain world.
25. It is possible that I have misjudged what Bauman's pessimistic narratives are about, both morally and politically. Adam Sutton (personal communication) has argued convincingly that Bauman is not so much making historical predictions as constructing a Weberian ideal type. Accordingly, Bauman may be identifying exclusionary/punitive forces inherent in late-modern global capitalism, exploring their logic and speculating about 'where these forces would take us' if allowed free play. Furthermore, Sutton suggests Bauman's ideal type may also be useful in the context of moral reasoning: offering the reader a sketch of what the world would look and feel like if certain contemporary trends were to prevail and thus to evoke an emotional reaction in the reader. The implicit aim may be to motivate her or him to act in ways that would help avert such a future. This is a powerful defence of Bauman's work with which I have some sympathy. However, as Adam Sutton and myself agree, for the 'trick' of constructing the ideal type to succeed in provoking the possibilities of a positive political and moral response, the exclusionary ideal type does need to be supplemented by the more inclusive ideal type which my later discussion in this chapter suggests is alive and well at various bureaucratic and political sites, in localities and such like. 'Accentuating the positive' alongside the plotting of the negative is not the stuff of utopian idealism but rather of critical realism.
26. In turn, further questions also remain to be answered by locally-nuanced research as to the policy and practice 'outcomes' of this political discourse in the particular sites of public services and varying localities across Holland (Burney, 2005: 146–54; Hughes, 2005).
27. Less often remarked upon in this body of work is the possibility of social democratic and more inclusive programmes of regeneration, both in local initiatives in the UK and perhaps more overtly across Europe (Hughes, 1998a).
28. Kevin Morgan's research at the Regeneration Institute at Cardiff University has explored the tensions between subsidiarity and solidarity in inventive and politically progressive ways. His work critiques the design and delivery of orthodox regeneration policy for its failure to acknowledge or tap local knowledge in the targeted areas. Arising out of this critique, Morgan has developed a 'citizens science' approach to regeneration where local people are directly mobilized to become involved in selecting the indicators and in collecting the data that will ascertain whether a project has enhanced the sense of well-being in a community. When successful this process of learning by doing may help local communities to become self-managing communities in a radical way.

29. As Taylor (1999: 111) notes, we need to be wary of assuming the typicality of US city experiences for European developments, not least given the possibility of suburban fortification and sequestration of homogeneously sealed environments being much more difficult to create in the denser urban settlements of the long established European land mass. For a broader critique of the risks in extrapolating from the LA experience, see Hughes (1998a, chapter 7); Jones and Newburn (1999).
30. I am grateful to Roy Coleman (personal communication) for alerting me to the local struggles now emerging in Merseyside such as the campaign group and magazine, NERVE which seeks to 'promote grass-roots and culture on Merseyside'. This magazine has also supported the New Economics Foundation report, Clone Town Britain, and questioned the cloning implied in much regeneration work in Liverpool with its re-branding as European City of Culture 2008.
31. There are parallels between my critique and O'Malley's (2000) diagnosis of the limitations of grand and dystopian 'sociologies of catastrophe' As Meyer and O'Malley (2005: 201) note, 'Criminology, particularly of the critical sort, is a discipline besotted with catastrophic change'.
32. The Chicagoans referred to here are those social scientists associated with the Chicago School of urban sociology in the early to mid twentieth century.
33. Zemiology is a word developed from the Greek to describe the study of harm. It has not gained widespread support but it indicates the wish of many critical scholars to loosen criminology's ties with the study of crime narrowly defined (see Muncie, 2000). I will employ this word rather than the more inclusive term, critical criminology, not least as I would also contend that much of my own work is located in critical criminological debates although it is of a critical realist complexion. Despite the concerns of my colleague John Muncie, I suggest the words 'critical' and 'realist', when co-joined, do not constitute an oxymoron!
34. The recently forged high profile for a critical 'cultural criminology' (Hayward *et al.*, 2004) departs from the insistent politicized focus of zemiology. Viewed sceptically, cultural criminology may be viewed as a resuscitation of the libertarian sociology of deviance (Hughes, 1994a).
35. Among the key proponents of crime science and 'what works' scientific evaluation, see Ekblom, 1999, Laycock, 2001, Pease, 1997, 2005, Russo, 1997, Sherman *et al.*, 1997, Smith and Tilley, 2005.
36. Carrabine *et al.*'s argument is more narrowly confined to the 'critical' end of criminology in that they do not address how the four sides to criminology which I have adapted from Burawoy may be mutually constitutive of a more rounded and open-ended criminological imagination.

Bibliography

Aas, K. (forthcoming) 'Controlling a world in motion: global flows and the criminology of "methodological nationalism" '.

Albrecht, H. J. (2002) 'Immigration, crime and unsafety', in A. Crawford (ed) *Crime and Insecurity: the governance of safety in Europe*, Cullompton: Willan Publishing.

Allen, J. (2003) *The lost geographies of power*, Malden, MA: Blackwells.

Allen, J. (2004) 'The whereabouts of power: politics, government and space', *Geografiska Annaler*, 86B (1): 19–32.

Allen, J., Massey, D. and Pryke, M. (1999) *Unsettling Cities*, London: Routledge.

Allen, R. (1999) 'Is what works what counts? The role of evidence-based crime reduction in policy and practice', *Safer Society*, 2 (February): 21–3.

Amin, A. (2004) 'Regions unbound', *Geografiska Annaler*, 86B (1): 31–42.

Amin, A. (2005) 'Local community on trial', *Economy and Society*, 34 (4): 612–33.

Ashford, B. and Morgan, R. (2004) 'Criminalizing looked-after children', *Criminal Justice Matters*, 57: 8–9.

Ashworth, A., Garner, J., von Hirsch, A., Morgan, R. and Wasik, M. (1998) 'Neighbouring on the oppressive: the government's Community Safety Orders', *Criminal Justice*, 16 (1): 7–14.

Audit Commission (1999) *Safety in Numbers*, London: Audit Commission.

Balibar, E. (2004) *We, the People of Europe: Reflections on Transnational Citizenship*, Princeton, NJ: Princeton University Press.

Bannister, J., Fyfe, N. and Kearns, A. (1998) 'Close Circuit Television and the City', in C. Norris, J. Moran and G. Armstrong (eds) *Surveilance, Closed Circuit Television and Social Control*, Aldershot: Ashgate.

Barnsley Metropolitan Borough Council. (2005) *One Barnsley: Local Area Agreement 2005–2008*, Barnsley: Barnsley Metropolitan Borough Council.

Bauman, Z. (1991) *Modernity and Ambivalence*. Cambridge: Polity Press.

Bauman, Z. (1997) *Postmodernity and Its Discontents*, Cambridge: Polity Press.

Bauman, Z. (1998) *Globalization: The Human Consequences*, Cambridge: Polity Press.

Bauman, Z. (1999) *In Search of Politics*, Cambridge: Polity Press.

Bauman, Z. (2001) *Community*, Cambridge: Polity Press.

Bauman, Z. (2004) *Wasted Lives: Modernity and its Outcasts*, Cambridge: Polity Press.

Bauman, Z. (2005a) *Europe: An Unfinished Adventure*, Cambridge: Polity Press.

Bauman, Z. (2005b) 'Special panel', *British Society of Criminology* Conference, Leeds, July.

Bayley, D. and Shearing, C. (1996) 'The future of policing', *Law and Society Review*, 30: 3.

Beck, U. (1992) *Risk Society: Towards a New Modernity*, London: Sage.

Beck, U. (2005) 'How not to become a museum piece', *British Journal of Sociology*, 56 (3): 335–44.

Blagg, H., Pearson, G., Smith, D., Sampson, A. and Stubbs, P. (1988) 'Inter-agency coordination: rhetoric and reality', in T. Hope and M. Shaw (eds) *Communities and Crime Reduction*, London: HMSO.

Blomley, N. and Sommers J. (1999) 'Mapping urban space: governmentality and cartographic struggles in inner-city Vancouver', in R. Smandych (ed) *Governable Places*, Aldershot: Dartmouth.

Blunkett, D. (2003) *Civil Renewal: A New Agenda*, London: Home Office.

Body-Gendrot, S. (2000) *The Social Control of Cities*, Oxford: Blackwell.

Bottoms, A. (2001) 'Morality, crime, compliance and public policy', in A. Bottoms *et al.* (eds) *Ideology, Crime and Criminal Justice*, Cullompton: Willan Publications.

Bottoms, A. and Wiles, P. (1996) 'Crime prevention and late modernity', in T. Bennett (ed) *Crime Prevention: The Cropwood Papers*, Cambridge: Cropwood.

Bourdieu, P. (1977) *Outline of a Theory of Practice*, Cambridge: Cambridge University Press.
Bowling, B. and Foster, J. (2002) 'Policing and the Police', in M. Maguire, R. Morgan and R. Reiner (eds) *Oxford Handbook of Criminology*, Oxford: Clarendon Press.
Braithwaite, J. (2000) 'Republican theory and crime control', in S. Karstedt and K.-D. Bussman *The Social Dynamics of Crime, Law and Social Change*. Oxford: Hart Publishing.
Bradley, T. (2005) *Community crime prevention: the New Zealand experience*, Victoria University of Wellington, PhD thesis.
Brown, A. (2003) 'Anti-social behaviour, crime control and social control', *Howard Journal of Criminal Justice*, 43 (2): 203–11.
Braithwaite, J. (2005) 'For public social science', *British Journal of Sociology*, 56 (3): 345–54.
Brubaker, B. (2005) 'The "diaspora" diaspora', *Ethnic and Racial Studies*, 28 (1): 1–19.
Burawoy, M. (2004) 'For Public Sociology', *British Journal of Sociology*, 56 (2): 259–94.
Bunting, M. (2004) 'The age of anxiety', *The Guardian*
Burawoy, M. (2004) 'For public sociology', *British Journal of* Sociology, 56 (2): 251–94.
Burawoy, M. (2005) 'Response: Public sociology: populist fad or path to renewal?' *British Journal of Sociology*, 56 (3): 417–32.
Burney, E. (2004a) 'Talking tough, acting coy: what happened to the anti-social behaviour order?', *Howard Journal*, 41 (5): 469–84.
Burney, E. (2004b) 'Nuisance or crime? The changing uses of anti-social behaviour control', *Criminal Justice Matters*, 57: 4–5.
Burney, E. (2005) *Making people behave: The creation and enforcement of anti-social behaviour*, Cullompton: Willan Publishing.
Byrne, S. and Pease, K. (2003) 'Crime reduction and community safety', in T. Newburn. (ed) *Handbook of Policing*, Cullompton: Willan Publishing.
Calhoun, C. (2005) 'The promise of public sociology', *British Journal of Sociology*, 56 (3): 355–64.
Callon, M. (1986) 'Some elements of a sociology of translation: domestication of the scallops and the fishermen of St. Brieuc Bay', in J. Law (ed) *Power, Action and Belief*, London: RKP.
Campbell, S. (2002) *A Review of Anti-social Behaviour Orders*, London: Home Office Research series.
Carrabine, E., Lee, M. and South, N. (2000) 'Social wrongs and human rights in late modern Britain: Social exclusion, crime control and prospects for a public criminology', *Social Justice*, 27 (2): 193–211.
Carson, W. G. (2003) *Engaging the Community*, Melbourne, Attorney-General's Justice Agenda for Change Conference, 29 October.
Carson, W. G. (2004a) 'Is communalism dead? Reflections on the present and future practice of crime prevention', Part 1, *Australian and New Zealand Journal of Criminology*, 37 (1): 1–21.
Carson, W. G. (2004b) 'Is communalism dead? Reflections on the present and future practice of crime prevention', Part 2, *Australian and New Zealand Journal of Criminology*, 37 (2): 192–210.
Casey, L. (2004) 'Taking a stand', *Criminal Justice Matters*, 57: 6–7.
Castells, M. (1998) *Into the New Millennium*, Oxford: Blackwell.
Castles, S. (2003) 'Towards a sociology of forced migration and social transfromation', *Sociology*, 37 (1): 13–35.
Chakraborti, N. and Garland, J. (eds) (2004) *Rural Racism*, Cullompton: Willan Publishing.
Chan, J. (1997) *Changing Police Culture*, Cambridge: CUP.
Chan, J. (2000) 'Globalization, reflexivity and the practice of criminology', *Australian and New Zealand Journal of Criminology*, 33 (2): 118–35.
Cherney, A. (2003) *'The Dust Never Settles': Crime Prevention Policy and Practice: The Victorian Experience*. Unpublished PhD, University of Melbourne.
Cherney, A. (2004) 'Contingency and politics: The local government community safety officer role', *Criminal Justice*, 4 (2): 115–28.
Clarke, J. (2002) 'Reinventing Community? Governing in contested spaces', paper delivered at *Spacing for Social Work Conference*, Bielefeld, November 14–16.
Clarke, J. (2003) 'Performing for the public: evaluation, evidence and evangelism in social policy'. Paper prepared for *Social Policy Association Conference*, University of Teesside, July 14–16.
Clarke, J. (2004) *Changing welfare, changing states*, London: Sage.

Clarke, J. (2005) 'Fantasies of Order: community as an unstable locus of governing', ESRC Seminar, University of Leicester, 12 December.
Clarke, J., Gewirtz, S., Hughes, G. and Humphrey, J. (2000) 'Guarding the public interest: the rise of audit', in J. Clarke, S. Gewirtz and E. McLaughlin (eds) *New Welfare, New Managerialism*, London: Sage.
Cloke, P. (2004) 'Rurality and racialised others – out of place in the countryside', in N. Chakraborti and J. Garland (eds) *Rural Racism*, Cullompton: Willan Publishing.
Cochrane, A. (1986) 'Community politics and democracy', in D. Held and C. Pollitt (eds) *New forms of democracy*, London: Sage.
Cohen, S. (1974) 'Criminology and the sociology of deviance', in P. Rock and M. McIntosh (eds) *Deviance and Social Control*, London: Tavistock.
Cohen, S. (1985) *Visions of Social Control*, Cambridge: Polity Press.
Cohen, S. (1996) 'Crime and politics: spot the difference', *British Journal of Sociology*, 47: 1–17.
Cohen, S. (1997) 'Intellectual scepticism and political commitment: the case of radical criminology', in P. Walton and J. Young (eds) *The New Criminology Revisited*, Basingstoke: Macmillan.
Cohen, S. (2004) *Folk Devils and Moral Panics, 4th Edition*, Oxford: Blackwells.
Coleman, C. and Norris, C. (2000) *Introducing Criminology*, Cullompton: Willan Publishing.
Coleman, R. (2004a) *Reclaiming the Streets: Surveillance, Social Control and the City*, Cullompton: Willan Publishing.
Coleman, R. (2004b) 'Watching the degenerate: street camera surveillance and urban regeneration', *Local Economy*, 19 (3): 199–211.
Coleman, R. (2005) 'Surveillance in the city: Primary definition and urban spatial order', *Crime, Media and Culture*, 1 (2): 131–48.
Coleman, R., Sim, J. and Whyte, D. (2002) 'Power, politics and partnerships: the state of crime prevention on Merseyside', in G. Hughes and A. Edwards (eds) *op. cit.*
Cook, D. (2006) *Criminal and Social Justice*, London: Sage.
Cooper, D. (2001) 'Against the current', *Feminist Legal Studies*, 9: 119–48.
Cooper, D. (2002) 'Boundary harms: from community protection to a politics of value: the case of the Jewish eruv', in G. Hughes *et al.* (eds) *Crime Prevention and Community Safety: New Directions*, London: Sage.
Cooper, D. (2004) *Challenging Diversity*, Cambridge: Cambridge University Press.
Coutin, S. B. (2005) 'Contesting Criminality', *Theoretical Criminology*, 9 (1): 5–33.
Crawford, A. (1994) 'The partnership approach to community crime prevention: corporatism at the local level', *Social and Legal Studies*, 3: 497–519.
Crawford, A. (1997) *The Local Governance of Crime: Appeals to Community and Partnerships*, Oxford: Clarendon Press.
Crawford, A. (1998) *Crime Prevention and Community Safety: Politics, policies and practices*, Harlow: Longman.
Crawford, A. (2000) 'Justice de Proximité', *Social and Legal Studies*, 9: 29–53.
Crawford, A. (2001) 'Joined-up but fragmented', in R. Matthews and J. Pitts (eds) *Crime, Disorder and Community Safety*, London: Routledge.
Crawford, A. (2002) 'The governance of crime and insecurity in an anxious age: the trans-European and the local', in A. Crawford (ed) *Crime and Insecurity: The Governance of Safety in Europe*, Cullompton: Willan.
Crawford, A. (ed) (2002) *Crime and Insecurity: The Governance of Safety in Europe*. Cullompton: Willan Publishing.
Crawford, A. and Lister, S. (2004) *The Extended Policing Family*, York: Joseph Rowntree Foundation.
Crawford, A. and Newburn, T. (2003) *Youth Offending and Restorative Justice*, Cullompton: Willan Publishing.
Crawford, A. and Matassa, M. (2000) *Community Safety Structures: An International Literature Review*. London: Stationary Office.
Criminal Justice (2004) Special Issue: 'What works in reducing crime? The Home Office Crime Reduction Programme', *Criminal Justice*, 4 (3): 211–325.
Crime Prevention Victoria (2002) *Safer Streets and Homes*, Melbourne: CPU.

Current Issues in Criminal Justice (2002) Special Edition, *Current Issues in Criminal Justice*, 14 (1): 5–87.
Curtin, L. P. (1971) *Apes and Angels: The Irishman in Victorian Caricature*, Washington, DC: Smithsonian Institute Press.
Davies, N. (1997) *Dark Heart: The Shocking Truth of Hidden Britain*, London: Chatty and Windus.
Davis, M. (1990) *City of Quartz*, London: Zed Books.
De Haan. (1992) 'Universalism and relativism in critical criminology', *The Critical Criminologist*, 14 (4): 1–2, 7–8.
De Maillard, J. (2000) 'Les chefs du projet et les recompositions de l'action publique', *Les Annales de la recherché urbaine*, 88: 7–17.
De Maillard, J. (2005) 'The governance of safety in France: Is there anyone in charge?', *Theoretical Criminology*, 9 (3): 325–44.
Domus Project (2005) *Development of model urban safety policies in the European Union: Recommendations*, Modena.
Downes, D. and Rock, P. (1998) *Understanding Deviance*, Oxford: Oxford University Press.
Edwards, A. (2002) 'Learning from diversity: the strategic dilemmas of community-based crime control', in G. Hughes and A. Edwards (eds) *op. cit.*
Edwards, A. (2005) 'The possibilities of community policing in an age of diversity', Paper delivered at the *ESRC Seminar Series 'Community Policing in an Age of Diversity'*, Leicester, 12 December.
Edwards, A. (2006) 'Governance', in E. McLaughlin and J. Muncie. (eds) *Sage Dictionary of Criminology*, London: Sage.
Edwards, A. and Gill, P. (2002) 'The politics of "transnational organised crime": discourse, reflexivity and the narration of "threat" ', *British Journal of Politics and International Relations*, 4 (2): 245–70.
Edwards, A. and Hughes, G. (2002) 'Introduction: the new community governance of crime control', in G. Hughes and A. Edwards (eds) *op. cit.*
Edwards, A. and Hughes, G. (2005a) 'Comparing safety in Europe: a geohistorical approach', *Theoretical Criminology*, 9 (3): 345–63.
Edwards, A. and Hughes, G. (2005b) 'The politics of policy transfer in prevention', Conference paper, *European Society of Criminology Conference*, Cracow, 28–31 August.
Edwards, A. and Hughes, G. (2005c) 'Editorial', *Theoretical Criminology*, 9 (3): 259–63.
Elias, N. and Scotson, J. (1965) *The Established and the Outsiders*, London: Frank Case.
Ekblom, P. (1999) 'Can we make crime prevention adaptive by learning from other evolutionary struggles?', *Studies on Crime and Crime Prevention*, 8: 27–51.
Ericson, R. (2005) 'Publicising sociology', *British Journal of Sociology*, 56 (3): 365–72.
Ericson, R. and Heggarty, K. (1997) *Policing the Risk Society*, Oxford: Clarendon Press.
Esping-Anderson, G. (1990) *The Three Words of Welfare Capitalism*, Cambridge: Polity Press.
Etzioni, A. (1994) *The Spirit of Community: The Reinvention of American Society*, New York: Touchstone Books.
Evans, K. (2004) 'Crime control partnerships: who do we trust?', *Criminal Justice Matters*, 50: 12–13.
Evans, K., Frazer, P. and Taylor, I. (1996) *A Tale of Two Cities: Global Change, Local Feeling and Everyday Life in the North of England*, London: Routledge.
Farrington, D. (2000) 'Explaining and preventing crime: the globalization of knowledge', *Criminology*, 38 (1): 1–24.
Feeley, M. and Simon, J. (1992) 'The new penology', *Criminology*, 30 (4): 452–74.
Feeley, S. and Simon, J. (1994) 'Actuarial justice: the emerging new criminal law', in D. Nelken (ed) *Futures of Criminology*, London: Sage.
Felson, M. (1994) *Crime and Everyday Life*, Thousand Oaks, CA: Pine Forge Press.
Follett, M. (2005) 'Community safety partnerships and elected councillors: part of a "community safety family"?' Paper delivered at the *ESRC Seminar Series 'Community Policing in an Age of Diversity'*, Leicester, 12 December.
Foster, J. (2002) 'People pieces', in G. Hughes. and A. Edwards (eds) *op. cit.*
Foucault, M. (1977) *Discipline and Punish*, Harmondsworth: Penguin Books.
Fuller, S. (2005) 'Lecture', *The Public Uses of Sociology Conference*, Univerity of Liverpool, 8 September.

Fuller, S. (2006) *The New Sociological Imagination*, London: Sage.
Garland, D. (1994) 'Of crimes and criminals: The development of criminology in Britain', in M. Maguire, R. Morgan and R. Reiner (eds) *Oxford Handbook of Criminology*, Oxford: Clarendon Press.
Garland, D. (1996) 'The limits of the sovereign state: strategies of crime control in contemporary society', *British Journal of Criminology*, 36 (1): 445–71.
Garland, D. (2001) *The Culture of Control*, Oxford: Oxford University Press.
Garland, D. and Sparks, R. (2000) 'Criminology, social theory and the challenge of our times', *British Journal of Criminology*, 40: 189–204.
Garton Ash, T. (2004) 'Janus-faced Britain', *The Guardian*, 6 June.
Gelsthorpe, L. and Morris, A. (2002) 'Restorative youth justice: the last vestiges of welfare?', in J. Muncie, G. Hughes and E. McLaughlin (eds) *Youth Justice: Critical Readings*, London: Sage.
Gibney, M. (2004) *The Ethics and Politics of Asylum*, Cambridge: Cambridge University Press.
Giddens, A. (1990) *The Consequences of Modernity*, Cambridge: Polity press.
Giddens, A. (1998) *The Third Way*, Cambridge: Polity Press.
Gilling, D. (1997) *Crime Prevention: Theory, Policy and Politics*, London: UCL Press.
Gilling, D. and Barton, A. (1997) 'Crime prevention and community safety: a new home for social policy', *Critical Social Policy*, 17 (1): 63–83.
Gilling, D. and Barton, A. (2005) 'Dangers lurking in the deep: the transformative potential of the crime audit', *Critical Social Policy*, 5 (2): 163–80.
Gilling, D. and Hughes, G (forthcoming) 'Demythologising "community networked governance" '.
Gilroy, P. (2004) *Postcolonial Melancholia*, New York: Columbia University Press.
Girling, E., Loader, I. and Sparks, R. (2000) *Crime and Social Change in Middle England: Questions of Order in an English Town*, London: Routledge.
Goldblatt, B. and Lewis, P. (1998) 'Reducing offending: an assessment of research evidence on ways on dealing with offending behaviour', *Home Office Research Study 187*, London: Home Office.
Goldson, B. (2002) 'New punitiveness: the politics of child incarceration', in J. Muncie, G. Hughes and E. McLaughlin (eds) *Youth Justice*, London: Sage.
Goodey, J. (2002) 'Whose insecurity? Organized crime, its victims and the EU', in A. Crawford (ed) *Crime and Insecurity: the governance of safety in Europe*, Cullompton: Willan Publishing.
Gormally, B. (2004) 'Community safety in Northern Ireland', *Community Safety Journal*, 4: 2.
Green, P. and Grewcock, M. (2002) 'The war against illegal immigration', *Current Issues in Criminal Justice*, 14 (1): 87–101.
Grewcock, M. (2003) 'Irregular migration, identity and the state – the challenge for criminology', *Current Issues in Criminal Justice*, 15 (2): 114–35.
Hall, S. (1988) *The Hard Road to Renewal*, London: Verso.
Hall, S., Clarke, J., Critcher, C., Jefferson, T. and Roberts, B. (eds) (1978) *Policing the Crisis*, London: Macmillan.
Hallsworth, S. (2002) 'Representations and realities in local crime prevention: some lessons from London and lessons for criminology', in G. Hughes and A. Edwards (eds) *op. cit.*
Hamersley, M. (2004) 'A new political arithmetic to make sociology useful? Comments on a debate', *British Journal of Sociology*, 55 (3): 439–45.
Hancock, L. (2001) *Crime, Disorder and Community*, London: Palgrave.
Hancock, L. (2003) 'Urban regeneration and crime reduction: contradictions and dilemmas', in R. Matthews and J. Young (eds) *The New Politics of Crime and Punishment*, Cullompton: Willan Publishing.
Hancock, L., Tombs, S., Hallsworth, S. and Coleman, R. (unpublished) *Critical Perspectives on Urban Regeneration*.
Hayward, K. *et al.* (2004) *Unleashing Cultural Criminology*, London: Cavendish Publishing.
Hebberecht, P. and Duprez, D. (eds) (2002) *The Prevention and Security Policies in Europe*, Brussels: VUB Brussels University Press.
Hill, J. and Wright, G. (2003) 'Youth, community safety and the paradox of inclusion', *Howard Journal of Criminal Justice*, 42 (3): 282–97.

Hillyard, P., Sim, J., Tombs, S. and Whyte, D. (2004a) 'Leaving a "stain upon the silence": Contemporary criminology and the politics of dissent', *British Journal of Criminology*, 44 (3): 369–90.
Hillyard, P., Pantazis, C., Tombs, S. and Gordon, D. (eds) (2004b) *Beyond Criminology: Taking Crime Seriously*, London: Pluto Press.
Hitchens, P. (2003) *A Brief History of Crime: The Decline of Order, Justice and Liberty in England*, London: Atlantic Books.
Hobbs, D., Lister, S., Hadfield, P., Winlow, S. and Hall, S. (2000) 'Receiving shadows: Governance and liminality in the night-time economy', *British Journal of Sociology*, 51: 701–17.
Hobbs, D., Winlow, S., Hadfield, P. and Lister, S. (2005) 'Violent hypocrisy: Governance and the night-time economy', *European Journal of Criminology*, 2 (2): 161–84.
Hobsbawm, E. (1995) *The Age of Extremes*, London: Abacus.
Home Office (1991) *Safer Communities: The Local Delivery of Crime Prevention Through the Partnership Approach* (Morgan Report), London: Home Office.
Home Office (2001) *Community Cohesion: Report of the Independent Review Chaired by Ted Cantle*, London: Home Office.
Home Office (2002) *Respect and Responsibility*, White Paper, London: Home Office.
Home Office (2004) *Building Communities, Beating Crime*, London: Home Office.
Home Office (2006) *Community Involvement in Community Safety*, London: Home Office.
Hope, T. (1995) 'Community crime prevention', Tonry, M. and Farrington, D. (eds), *Building a Safer Society*, Chicago: Chicago University Press.
Hope, T. (1998) 'Letting social policy off the hook', *Criminal Justice Matters*, No. 37.
Hope, T. (2000) 'Introduction', in T. Hope (ed) *Perspectives on Crime Reduction*, Aldershot: Ashgate.
Hope, T. (ed) (2000) *Perspectives on Crime Reduction*, Aldershot: Ashgate.
Hope, T. (2001) 'Community crime prevention in Britain: a strategic overview', *Criminal Justice*, 1 (4): 421–39.
Hope, T. (2004) 'The new local governance of crime reduction', in M. Emmerich (ed) *Public Services Under New Labour*, London: IPPR.
Hope, T. (2005) 'The new local governance of community safety in England and Wales', *Canadian Journal of Criminology and Criminal Justice*, 47: 369–87.
Hope, T. (2006) 'Book Review: Crime Science', *Theoretical Criminology*, 10 (2): 245–50.
Hough, M. (2005) 'Hands-on or hands-off? Central government's role in managing CDRPs', *'What works in crime reduction'*, Conference, Chester: 23 September.
Hughes, G. (1991) 'Taking crime seriously? A critical analysis of left realism?', *Sociology Review*, 1 (2): 18–23.
Hughes, G. (1994a) 'Talking cop shop', *Policing and Society*, 4: 253–70.
Hughes, G. (1994b) 'Whatever happened to the sociology of deviance?', *Social Science Teacher*, 23 (2): 9–11.
Hughes, G. (1996a) 'Communitarianism and law and order', *Critical Social Policy*, 16 (4): 17–41.
Hughes, G. (1996b) 'Strategies of crime prevention and community safety in contemporary Britain', *Studies on Crime and Crime Prevention*, 5: 221–44.
Hughes, G. (1998a) *Understanding Crime Prevention: Social Control, Risk and Late Modernity*, Buckingham: Open University Press.
Hughes, G. (ed) (1998b) *Imagining Welfare Futures*, London: Routledge.
Hughes, G. (2000a) 'Community safety in the era of the risk society', in S. Ballintyne, K. Pease and V. McLaren (eds) *Secure Foundations: Issues in Crime Prevention, Crime Reduction and Community Safety*, London: IPPR.
Hughes, G. (2000b) 'In the shadow of crime and disorder: the contested politics of community safety', *Crime Prevention and Community Safety*, 2 (4), 47–60.
Hughes, G. (2002a) 'Plotting the rise of community safety: critical reflections on research, theory and politics', in G. Hughes and A. Edwards (eds) *op. cit*.
Hughes, G. (2002b) 'The audit culture and crime and disorder partnerships: exorcising the wicked issue of community safety', *Crime Prevention and Community Safety*, 4 (2): 9–18.
Hughes, G. (2002c) 'Crime and Disorder Reduction Partnerships: the future of community safety?', in Hughes *et al.* (eds) *Crime Prevention and Community Safety: New Directions*.
Hughes, G. (2004a) 'Communities, crime prevention and the politics of articulation: a reply to Kit Carson', *Australian and New Zealand Journal of Criminology*, 37 (3): 431–42.

Hughes, G. (2004b) 'Straddling adaptation and denial: crime and disorder reduction partnerships in England and Wales', *Cambrian Law Review*, 35, 1–22.
Hughes, G. (2004c) 'Il criminologo realistico', in R. Selmini (ed) *La Sicurezza Urbana*, Milano: Il Mulano.
Hughes, G. (2004d) 'The community governance of crime, justice and safety: challenges and lesson-drawing', *British Journal of Community Justice*, 3 (2): 7–20.
Hughes, G. (2005) 'Lost (and found) in translation: comparing safety in Europe', paper delivered at the British Society of Criminology Southern Branch/Mannheim Centre of Criminology, LSE, London: November.
Hughes, G. and Edwards, A. (eds) (2002) *Crime Control and Community: The New Politics of Public Safety,* Cullompton: Willan Publishing.
Hughes, G. and Edwards, A. (2004e) 'Beyond community safety?', *Community Safety Journal, Special Edition*, 4 (1): 1–7.
Hughes, G. and Edwards, A. (2005) 'Crime Prevention in Context', in N. Tilley (ed) *The Handbook of Crime Prevention and Community Safety*, Cullompton: Willan Publishing.
Hughes, G. and Follett, M. (2006) 'Community safety, youth and the "anti-social" ', in B. Goldson and J. Muncie (eds) *Youth Justice: Policy, Practice and Politics*, London: Sage.
Hughes, G. and Gilling, D. (2004) 'Mission impossible: the habitus of community safety manager', *Criminal Justice*, 4 (2): 129–49.
Hughes, G. and Lewis, G. (eds) (1998) *Unsettling Welfare: The Reconstruction of Social Policy*, London: Routledge.
Hughes, G. and Little, A. (1999) 'The contradictions of New Labour's communitarianism', *Imprints*, 2 (2): 37–62.
Hughes, G. and McLaughlin, E. (2002) 'Together we'll crack it: partnership and the governance of crime prevention', in C. Glendinning, D. Powell and K. Rummery (eds) *Partnership, New Labour and Governance of Welfare*, Bristol: Policy Press.
Hughes, G. and Mooney, G. (1998) 'Community', in G. Hughes (ed) *Imagining Welfare Futures*, London: Routledge.
Hughes, G. and Stenson, K. (2006) 'Researching Community Safety: in retrospect and prospect' paper delivered at the European Society of Criminology conference, Tübingen, August 26–28.
Hughes, G., McLaughlin, E. and Muncie, J. (eds) (2002a) *Crime Prevention and Community Safety: New Directions*, London: Sage.
Hughes, G., McLaughlin, E. and Muncie, J. (2002b) 'Teetering on the edge: the futures of crime control and community safety', in G. Hughes *et al.* (eds) *Crime Prevention and Community Safety: New Directions*, London: Sage.
Hughes, G., Pilkington, A. and Leisten, R. (1997) 'Diversion in a culture of severity', *Howard Journal of Criminal Justice*, 37 (1): 16–33.
Hughes, G. (2006) 'The politics of safety and the problem of "the stranger" ', in G. Brannigan and G. Pavlich (eds) *Adventures in the sociologies of law*, London: Glasshouse Press.
Hughes, G. *et al.* (2006) 'Crime control and community safety in Milton Keynes', in W. Stangl and R. van Swaaningen (eds) *Insecurities in European Cities and Strategies of Governance*, Vienna: Jahrbuch fur Rechts- und Kriminalsoziologie.
Hunt, A. (1992) *Explorations in Law and Society*, London: Routledge.
Hunter, C. *et al.* (2001) *Social Landlords' Use of Anti-Social Behaviour Orders*, Sheffield: Sheffield Hallam University.
Huntington, S. (1998) *The Clash of Civilizations*, New York: Simon and Schuster.
Huysmans, J. (1993) 'Migrants as a security problem: dangers of "securitizing" societal issues', in R. Miles and D. Thranhart (eds) *Migration and European Security*, London: Pinter Publishers.
Huysmans, J. (2000) 'The european union and the securitization of migration', *Journal of Common Market Studies*, 38 (5): 751–77.
Innes, M. (2004) 'Signal crimes and signal disorders: notes on deviance as communicative action', *British Journal of Sociology*, 55 (3): 333–55.
Johnson, T. (1972) *Professions and Power*, London: Macmillan.
Johnston, L. and Shearing, C. (2003) *The Governance of Security: Explorations in Policing and Justice,* London: Routledge.
Jones, T. and Newburn, T. (1999) 'Urban change and policing: mass private property reconsidered', *European Journal on Criminal Policy and Research*, 7: 225–44.

Jordan, B. (1996) *A Theory of Poverty and Social Exclusion,* Cambridge: Polity Press.
Jordan, B. (1998) *The New Politics of Welfare*, London: Sage.
Jordan, B. (2004) *Sex, Money and Power: The Transformation of Collective Life,* Cambridge: Polity Press.
Karstedt, S. (2004) 'Durkheim, Tarde and Beyond: the Global Travel of Crime Policies', in T. Newburn and R. Sparks (eds) *Criminal Justice and Political Cultures: National and International Dimensions of Crime Control*, Cullompton: Willan Publishing.
Kelling, G. and Coles, P. (1997) *Fixing Broken Windows: Restoring Order and Reducing Crime in our Communities,* New York: The Free Press.
Kerr, C. *et al.* (1973) *Industrialism and Industrial Man,* Harmondsworth: Penguin.
Krudy, M. and Stewart, G. (2004) 'Real-life ASBOs: trouble-makers or merely troubled?', *Criminal Justice Matters*, 57: 10–11.
Kumar, K. (1978) *Prophecy and Progress*, Harmondsworth: Penguin.
Kundnani, S. A. (2001) 'In a foreign land: the new popular racism', *Race and Class*, 43 (2): 41–61.
Lacey, N. (2003) 'Penal theory and penal practice: a communitarian approach', in S. McConville (ed) *The Use of Punishment*, Cullompton: Willan Publishing.
Lauder, H., Brown, P. and Halsey, A. (2004) 'Sociology and political arithmetic: some principles of a new policy science', *British Journal of Sociology*, 55 (1): 3–34.
Laycock, G. (2001) 'The Future of Crime Science', *Inaugural Lecture*, London: Jill Dando Institute.
Lea, J. (2001) *Crime and Modernity*, London: Sage.
Lea, J. and Young, J. (1984) *What Is to be Done About Law and Order?*, Harmondsworth: Penguin.
Levi, M. (2004) 'Community safety and white collar crime', *Safer Society,* 15: 21–3.
Levi, M. (2005) 'Report' on Cutting Edge Research Methods Workshop, *British Society of Criminology Newsletter*, 57: 20–1.
Lewis, G. and Neal, S. (2005) 'Introduction: Contemporary political contexts, changing terrains and revisited discourses', *Ethnic and Racial Studies*, 28 (3): 423–44.
Little, A. (2002) *The Politics of Community: Theory and Practice*. Edinburgh: Edinburgh University Press.
Loader, I. (2004) 'Policing, securitisation and democratisation in Europe', in T. Newburn and R. Sparks (eds) *Criminal Justice and Political Cultures: National and International Dimensions of Crime Control*, Cullompton: Willan Publishing.
Loader, I. (2005) 'Policing, recognition and belonging', *British Society of Criminology Conference*, Leeds.
Loader, I. and Walker, N. (2001) 'Policing as a public good', *Theoretical Criminology*, 5 (1): 9–35.
Low, S. (2003) *Behind the Gates: Life, Security and the Pursuit of Happiness in Fortress America,* New York: Routledge.
Maguire, M. (2004) 'The crime reduction programme in England and Wales: Reflections on the vision and the reality', *Criminal Justice*, 4 (3): 213–37.
Maguire, M. and John, T. (2006) 'Intelligence-led policing, managerialism and community engagement', *Policing and Society*, 16 (2): 67–85.
Marfleet, P. (2001) 'Europe's Civilising Mission', J. Fink. *et al.* (eds) *Rethinking European Welfare*, London: Sage.
Massey, D. (2004) 'Geographies of responsibility', *Geografiska Annaler*, 86 (1): 5–18.
Massey, D., Allen, J. and Pile, S. (1999) *City Worlds*, London: Routledge.
Matthews, R. (1992) 'Replacing Broken Windows: Crime, incivilities and urban change', in R. Matthews and J. Young (eds) *Issues in Realist Criminology*, London: Sage
Matthews, R. (2003) 'Enforcing respect and reducing responsibility', *Community Safety Journal*, 4 (2): 5–8.
Matthews, R. (2005) 'The myth of the new punitiveness', *Theoretical Criminology*, 9 (2): 175–201.
Mathiesen, T. (1974) *The Politics of Abolition*, Oxford: Martin Robinson.
McAra, L. (2006) 'The strange death of welfarism in post-devolution Scotland', *Youth and the Anti-Social Conference*, Milton Keynes: The Open University, 31 March.
McEvoy, K., Gormally, B. and Mika, H. (2002) 'Conflict, crime control and the "re"-construction of state-community relations in Northern Ireland', in G. Hughes *et al.* (eds) *Crime Prevention and Community Safety: New Directions*.

McLaughlin, E. and Muncie, J. (2000) 'Walled cities: surveillance, regulation and segregation', in Pryke, M. *et al.* (ed) *Unsettling Cities*, London: Routledge.
McLaughlin, E. (1998) 'Probation Work: Social Work or Social Control?', in G. Hughes and G. Lewis (eds) *Unsettling Welfare: The Reconstruction of Social Policy*.
McLaughlin, J., Muncie, J. and Hughes, G. (2001) 'The permanent revolution: New Labour, new public management and the modernisation of criminal justice', *Criminal Justice*, 1 (3): 301–18.
Meyer, J. and O'Malley, P. (2005) 'Missing the preventive turn? Canadian criminal justice', in J. Pratt *et al.* (eds) *The New Punitiveness*, Cullompton: Willan Publishing.
Miller, L. (2001) *The Politics of Crime Prevention*, Aldershot: Ashgate.
Mills, C. Wright. (1959) *The Sociological Imagination*, New York: Oxford University Press.
Monaghan, B. (1997) 'Crime prevention in Scotland', *International Journal of Sociology of Law*, 25: 21–44.
Morgan, R. (2000) 'The politics of criminological research', in R. King and E. Wincup (eds) *Doing Research on Crime and Justice*, Oxford: Oxford University Press.
Morgan, R. (2006) Lecture, Youth and the Anti-Social Conference, Milton Keynes, The Open University, 31 March.
Moulaert, F., Rodriguez, A. and Swyngedouw, E. (eds) *The Globalised City*, Oxford: Oxford University Press.
Muncie, J. (2000) 'Decriminalising criminology', in G. Lewis, S. Gewirtz and J. Clarke (eds) *Rethinking Social Policy*, London: Sage.
Muncie, J. (2004) *Youth and Crime*, London: Sage.
Muncie, J. and Hughes, G. (2002) 'Modes of youth governance: political rationalies, criminalization and resistance', in J. Muncie *et al.* (eds) *Youth Justice: Critical Readings*, London: Sage.
NACRO (2003) 'The community safety needs of asylum seekers', *NACRO Briefing Paper*, London: NACRO.
Nash, M. (2004) 'Probation and Community Sanctions', in J. Muncie and D. Wilson (eds) *Student Handbook of Criminal Justice and Criminology*, London: Cavendish.
National Community Safety Network (2004a) *Barriers to Performance*, Chester: NCSN.
National Community Safety Network (2004b) ' *"A Vision of Paradise" ': The Ideal CDRP in Ideal Conditions*, Chester: NCSN.
National Community Safety Network (2005) *Anti-Social Behaviour: Key Issues and Some Ways Forward*, Chester: NCSN.
Nelken, D. (1994) 'Whom can you trust? The future of comparative criminology', in D. Nelken (ed) *The Futures of Criminology*, London: Sage.
Nelken, D. (ed) (2000) *Contrasting Criminal Justice*, Aldershot: Ashgate.
Nelken, D. (2002) 'Comparing Criminal Justice', in M. Maguire *et al.* (eds) *Oxford Handbook of Criminology*, Oxford: Clarendon Press.
Newburn, T. (2002a) 'The contemporary politics of youth crime prevention', in J. Muncie, G. Hughes and E. McLaughlin (eds) *Youth Justice: Critical Readings*, London: Sage.
Newburn, T. (2002b) 'The introduction of CCTV into a custody suite: some reflections on risk, surveillance and policing', in A. Crawford (ed) *op.cit.*
Newburn, T. and Jones, T. (2002) *Consultation by Crime and Disorder Partnerships*. London: Home Office.
Newburn, T. and Sparks, R. (2004) 'Criminal justice and political cultures', in T. Newburn and R. Sparks (eds) *Criminal Justice and Political Cultures: National and International Dimensions of Crime Control,* Cullompton: Willan Publishing.
Norris, C. and Armstrong, S. (1999) *The Maximum Surveillance Society: The Rise of CCTV*, Oxford: Berg.
O'Malley, P. (1992) 'Risk, power and crime prevention', *Economy and Society*, 21 (3): 252–75.
O'Malley P. (1996) 'Post-social criminologies: some implications of current political trends fro criminological theory and practice', *Current Issues in Criminal Justice*, 8 (1): 26–42.
O'Malley, P. (1997) 'Politics of Crime Prevention', in P. O'Malley and A. Sutton (eds) *Crime Prevention in Australia*, Sydney: Federation Press.
O'Malley, P. (1999) 'Volative and contradictory punishment', *Theoretical Criminology* 3 (2): 175–96.
O'Malley, P. (2000) 'Genealogies of catastrophe? Understanding criminal justice on the brink of the New Millennium', *Australian and New Zealand Journal of Criminology*, 33 (2): 153–67.

O'Malley, P. (2004a) *Risk, Uncertainty and Government*, London: Glasshouse Press.
O'Malley, P. (2004b) 'The Uncertain Promise of Risk', *Australian and New Zealand Journal of Criminology*, 37: 1.
O'Malley, P., Shearing, C. and Weir, L. (1997) 'Governmentality, Criticism, Politics', *Economy and Society*, 26: 501–17.
O'Neill, M. and Spybey, T. (2003) 'Introduction – Global Refugees: The sociology of exile, displacement and belonging', *Sociology*, 31 (1): 7–13.
Office of the Deputy Prime Minister (2005) *Safer, Stronger Communities Fund*, London: ODPM.
Pahl, R. (1995) 'Friendly society', *New Statesman and Society*, 10 March, 20–2.
Parekh, B. (2000) *The Future of Multi-Ethnic Britain*. London: Runnymeade Trust.
Parker. (1997) 'Dividing organisations and multiplying identities', K. Hetherington and R. Munro (eds) *Ideas of Difference*, Oxford: Blackwell.
Parr, S. (2005) *Anti-Social Behaviour and New Labour*, mimeo.
Parr, S. (2006) *Intensive Family Support – A New Front in the Fight Against Anti-Social Behaviour*, mimeo.
Pavlich, G. (2001) 'The Force of Community', in H. Strang and J. Braithwaite (eds) *Restorative Justice and Civil Society*, Cambridge: Cambridge University Press.
Pavlich, G. (2002) 'Deconstructing restoration: the promise of restorative justice', in E. Wietekamp and H. Korner (eds) *Restorative Justice: Theoretical Foundations*, Cullompton: Willan.
Pawson, R. and Tilley, N. (1997) *Realistic Evaluation*, London: Sage.
Pearson, G. (1983) *Hooligan: A History of Respectable Fears*, London: Macmillan.
Pearson, G. *et al.* (1992) 'Crime, Community and Conflict: The Multi-Agency Approves', in D. Downes (ed) *Unravelling Criminal Justice*, London: Macmillan.
Pease, K. (1997) 'Predicting the future: the roles of routine activity and rational choice theory', in G. Newman, R. Clarke and S. Shoban (eds) *Rational Choice Theory and Situational Crime Prevention*, Aldershot: Ashgate.
Pease, K. (2005) 'Science in the service of crime reduction', in N. Tilley (ed) *Handbook of Crime Prevention and Community Safety*, Cullompton: Willan Publishing.
Phillips, C. (2002) 'From voluntary status to statutory states', in G. Hughes *et al.* (eds) *op.cit.*
Phillips, C., Jacobson, J., Considine, M. and Lewis, R. (2000) 'A review of audits and strategies produced by crime and disorder partnerships in 1999', *Briefing Note*, London: Home Office.
Pickering, S. (2001) 'Immigration, detention centres, human rights and criminology in Austalia', *Current Issues in Criminal Justice*, 13 (2): 219–23.
Pickering, S. and Lambert, C. (2002) 'Deterrence: Australia's refugee policy', *Current Issues in Criminal Justice*, 14 (1): 65–86.
Pile, S., Brook, C. and Mooney, G. (1999) *Unruly Cities?*, London: Routledge.
Pollitt, C. (2001) 'Convergence: the useful myth?', *Public Administration*, 79 (4): 933–47.
Power, M. (1997) *The Audit Explosion*, London: Demos.
Pratt, J., Brown, D., Brown, M., Hallsworth, S. and Morrison, W. (eds) (2005) *The New Punitiveness*, Cullompton: Willan Publishing.
Prior, D., Farrow, K. and Parris, A. (2005) 'Beyond ASBOs?', *Local Government Studies*, 32 (1): 3–17.
Raco, M. (2003) 'Remaking place and securitising space', *Urban Studies*, 40 (9): 1869–87.
Rankin, I. (2004) *Fleshmarket Close*, London: Orion.
Rattansi, A. (2004) 'The end of multi-culturalism: New Labour, 'race' and nation', *Society Matters, 6*: 17.
Reiner, R. (2000) 'Crime and control', *Sociology*, 34 (1): 71–94.
Rhodes, R. (1997) *Understanding Governance: Policy Networks, Governance, Reflexivity and Accountability*, Buckingham: Open University Press.
Robinson, V., Anderrson, R. and Musterd, S. (2003) *Spreading the Burden: A Review of Policies to Disperse Asylum Seekers and Refugees*, Bristol: Policy Press.
Rodriguez, A., Swengedouw, E. and Moulaert, F. (2003) 'Urban restructuring, social-political polarisation and new urban politics', in F. Moulaert *et al.* (eds) *The Globalised City*.
Rogers, R. (2005) 'A uniform approach to order maintenance', *Community Safety Journal*, 3 (4): 15–19.
Rose, N. (1999) *Powers of Freedom*, Cambridge: Cambridge University Press.
Russo, G. (1997) 'Criminology in crisis and the social demand for crime prevention', in G. Newman *et al.* (eds) *Rational Choice Theory and Situational Crime Prevention*, Aldershot: Ashgate.

Rustin, M. (2004) 'A practical utopianism', *New Left Review*, 26, 136–47.
Sales, R. (2005) 'Secure borders, safe havens: A contradiction in terms?', *Ethnic and Racial Studies*, 28 (3): 445–62.
Sassen, S. (2002) 'Governance hot-spots: challenges we must confront in the post-September 11 world', *Theory, Culture and Society*, 19 (4): 233–44.
Sassen, S. (2005) 'The City: Its Return as a Lens for Social Theory', in C. Calhoun, C. Rojek and B. Turner (eds) *The Sage Handbook of Sociology*, London: Sage.
Sayer, A. (2000) *Critical Realism and Social Science*, London: Sage.
Schofield, B. (2002) 'Partners in power: governing the self-sustaining community', *Sociology*, 36 (3), 663–83.
Scraton, P. (ed) (1987) *Law, Order and the Authoritarian State*, Milton Keynes: Open University Press.
Scraton, P. (2003) 'Defining power and changing "knowledge": critical analysis as resistance in the UK', in K. Carrington and R. Hogg (eds) *Critical Criminology: Issues, Debates and Challenges*, Cullompton: Willan Publishing.
Selmini, R. (2005) 'Towards Citta sicure? Political action and institutional conflict in contemporary preventive and safety policies in Italy', *Theoretical Criminology*, 9 (3): 307–24.
Scott, J. (2005) 'Who will speak, and who will listen? Comments on Burawoy and public sociology', *British Journal of Sociology*, 56 (3): 405–10.
Sennett, R. (1977) *The Fall of Public Man*, Cambridge: Cambridge University Press.
Sennett, R. (1999) *The Corrosion of Character*, London: W.W. Norton.
Sennett, R. (2003) *Respect: The Formation of Character in an Age of Inequality*, London: Penguin Books.
Shearing, C. (2001) 'Transforming security: a South African experiment', in H. Strang and J. Braithwaite (eds) *Restorative Justice and Civil Society*, Cambridge: Cambridge University Press.
Shearing, C. (2002) Governing Security, Regulating Possibilities, paper delivered at the *British Society of Criminology Conference*, Keele, July.
Sherman, L., Gottfredson, D., McKenzie, D., Eck, J., Reuter, P. and Bushway, S. (1998) *Preventing Crime: What Works, What Doesn't, What's Promising*, Research in Brief, Washington, DC: National Institute of Justice.
Shiner, B. Thom. B and MacGregor, S. (2004) *Exploring Community Responses to Drugs*, York: Joseph Rowntree Foundation.
Sim, J. (2004) 'The victimized state and the mystification of social harm', in P. Hillyard *et al.* (eds) *Beyond Criminology: Taking Crime Seriously*, London: Pluto Press.
Simmel, G. (1950) *The Sociology of Georg Simmel*, Translated and edited by K. H. Wolf, New York: Free Press.
Simon, J. (1997) 'Governing through crime', in L. Friedman and G. Fisher (eds) *The Crime Conundrum*, Boulder, CO: Westview Press.
Skinns, L. (2005) *Cops, Councils and Crime and Disorder*, University of Cambridge: PhD thesis.
Smandych, R. (ed) (1999) *Governable Places*, Aldershot: Ashgate.
Smith, N. (1996) *The New Urban Frontier: Gentrification and Revanchist City*, London: Routledge.
Sparks, R. (2003) 'States of insecurity: punishment, populism and contemporary political culture', in S. McConville (ed) *The Use of Punishment*, Cullompton: Willan Publishing.
Stangl, W. (2004) 'Crime prevention as a new field of the "Europeanisation" of criminal politics: findings from the compaprative research project "Insecurity in European Cities" ', conference paper, *Fifth Annual Conference of the European Society of Criminology*, Cracow, 31 August–3 September.
Stangl, W. and van Swaaningen, R. (eds) (2006), *Insecurities in European Cities and Strategies of Governance*, Jahrbuch für Rechts- und Kriminalsociologie, Vienna.
Steinert, H. (2005) 'Sociology of deviance: The Disciplines of Exclusion', in C. Calhoun *et al.* (eds) *The Sage Handbook of Sociology*, London: Sage.
Stenson, K. (1998) 'Displacing social policy through crime control', in S. Hänninen (ed) *Displacement of Social Policies*, SoPhi: University of Jyväsylä.
Stenson, K. (2000) 'Crime control, social policy and liberalism', in G. Lewis *et al.* (eds) *Rethinking Social Policy*, London: Sage.

Stenson, K. (2002) 'Community Safety in Middle England', in G. Hughes and A. Edwards (eds) *op.cit.*
Stenson, K. (2005) 'Sovereignty, biopolitics and the local management of crime in Britain', *Theoretical Criminology*, 9 (3): 265–89.
Stenson, K. and Edwards, A. (2001) 'Rethinking Crime Control in Advanced Liberal Government', in K. Stenson and R. Sullivan (eds) *Crime, Risk and Justice*, Cullompton: Willan Publishing.
Stenson, K. and Edwards, A. (2004) 'Policy Transfer in Local Crime Control: Beyond Naïve Emulation', in T. Newburn and R. Sparks (eds) *Criminal Justice and Political Cultures: National and International Dimensions of Crime Control*, Cullompton: Willan Publishing.
Stoker, G. (2004) *Local Government and New Labour*, London: Palgrave.
Sutton, A. (2000) 'Crime prevention: a viable alternative to the justice system?', in D. Chappell and P. Wilson (eds) *Crime and the Criminal Justice System: 2000 and Beyond*, Melbourne: Butterworths.
Sutton, A. and Cherney, A. (2003) 'Crime Prevention and Reduction', in A. Goldsmith *et al.* (eds) *Crime and Justice*, Pyrmont, NSW: Thomson Legal.
Sutton, A. and Cherney, A. (2003) 'Crime Prevention: what's it for?', *Australian and New Zealand Society of Criminology Conference*, Sydney.
Sutton, A. (forthcoming) *Understanding Crime Policy: The Honest Criminologist's Guide.*
Swyngedouw, E., Moulaert, F. and Rodriguez, A. (2003a) ' "The world in a grain of sand": Large-Scale Development Projects and Dynamics of "Glocal" Transformation', in F. Moulaert *et al.* (eds) *The Globalised City*, Oxford: Oxford University Press.
Swyngedouw, E., Moulaert, F. and Rodriguez, A. (2003b) 'The contradictions of urbanising globalization', in F. Moulaert *et al.* (eds) *The Globalised City*.
Taub, R. *et al.* (1984) *Paths of Neighbourhood Change*, Chicago: Cambridge University Press.
Taylor, I. (1999) *Crime in Context*, Cambridge: Polity Press.
Taylor, R. (2001) *Breaking Away from Broken Windows*, Boulder, CO: Westview Press.
Taylor, M. (2003) *Public Policy in the Community*, Basingstoke: Palgrave
Theoretical Criminology. (2005) 'Special Issue: The Governance of safety in Europe', *Theoretical Criminology*, 9 (3): 259–345.
Tierney, J. (2001) 'Audits of crime and disorder: some lessons from research', *Crime Prevention and Community Safety*, 3 (2): 7–17.
Tierney, J. and Hobbs, D. (2003) 'Alcohol-related crime and disorder data: guidance for local partnerships', *Home Office On-line Report 08/03*.
Tilley, N. (ed.) (2005) *Handbook of Crime Prevention and Community Safety*, Cullompton: Willan Publishing.
Tucker, K. (1998) *Anthony Giddens and Modern Social Theory*, London: Sage.
Urry, J. (2004) 'Global complexities of September 11', *Theory, Culture and Society*, 19 (4): 57–69.
Valier, C. (2002) 'Punishment, border crossing and the powers of horror', *Theoretical Criminology*, 6 (3): 319–37.
Valier, C. (2003) 'Foreigners, crime and changing mobilities', *British Journal of Criminology*, 43 (1): 1–21.
Van Swaaningen, R. (2002) 'Towards a replacement discourse on community safety: lessons from the Netherlands', in G. Hughes *et al.* (eds) *Crime Prevention and Community Safety: New Directions*, London: Sage.
Van Swaaningen, R. (2005) 'Public safety and the management of fear', *Theoretical Criminology*, 9 (3): 289–307.
Varnfield, K. (2005) 'Vulnerable young people and the misuse of anti-social behaviour orders', *Community Safety Journal*, 4 (3): 33–7.
Wacquant, L. (2001) 'Deadly symbiosis: When ghetto and prison meet and mesh', *Punishment and Society*, 3 (1): 95–134.
Walklate, S. (2004) 'Conceptualising security', *Community Safety Journal*, 4: 4.
Weber, L. (2002) 'The detention of asylum seekers: twenty reasons why criminologists should care', *Current Issues in Criminal Justice*, 14 (1): 9–30.

Weeks, J. (1996) 'The idea of a sexual community', *Soundings*, 2: 71–84.
Welsh, M. and Schuster, C. (2005) 'The detention of asylum seekers in the US, UK, France, Germany and Italy', *Criminal Justice*, 5 (4): 331–55.
Westwood, S. (2002) *Power and the Social*, London: Routledge.
Wiles, P. (2002) 'Criminology in the 21st century: public good or private interest? The Sir John Barry Memorial Lecture', *Australian and New Zealand Journal of Criminology*, 35 (2): 238–52.
Wiles, P. (2004) 'Policy and sociology', *British Journal of Sociology*, 55 (1): 31–4.
Wiles, P. and Pease, K. (2000) 'Crime prevention and community safety: Tweedledum and Tweedledee', in S. Ballintyne *et al.* (eds) *Secure Foundations: Issues in Crime Prevention, Crime Reduction and Community Safety*, London: IPPR.
Williams, R. (1965) *The Long Revolution*, Harmondsworth: Penguin.
Wilson, J. Q. (1974) 'Crime and the criminologists', *Commentary*, 58 (1): 47–53.
Wilson, J. Q. and Kelling, G. (1982) 'Broken windows', *Atlantic Review*, March, 29–36.
Wittfogel, K. (1957) *Oriental Despotism*, New Haven: Yale University Press.
Young, I. (1990) 'The idea of community and the politics of difference', in L. Nicholson (ed) *Feminism/Postmodernism* (pp. 300–23), New York: Routledge.
Young, J. (1991) 'Left Realism and the Priorities of Crime Control', in D. Cowell and K. Stenson (eds) *The politics of crime control*, Sage: London.
Young, J. (1994) 'Incessant Chatter: Recent Paradigms in Criminology', in M. Maguire *et al.* (eds) *Oxford Handbook of Criminology*, Oxford: Clarendon.
Young, J. (1999) *The Exclusive Society: Social Exclusion, Crime and Difference in Late Modernity*, London: Sage.
Young, J. (2003a) 'Searching for a new criminology of everyday life', *British Journal of Criminology*, 43 (1): 228–43.
Young, J. (2003b) 'To these wet and windy shores', *Punishment and Society*, 5 (4): 449–62.
Younge, G. (2004) 'Bitter white whine', *The Guardian*, 26 February.
Yuval-Davies, N., Anthias, F. and Kofman, E. (2005) 'Secure borders and safe haven and the gendered politics of belonging', *Ethnic and Racial Studies*, 28 (3): 513–35.
Zedner, L. (2002) 'The dangers of dystopianism in penal theory', *Oxford Journal of Legal Studies*, 22 (2): 341–66.

Index